Praise for

# THE SHADOW DOC

"[The shadow docket] has been something that lawyers have been talking about for a long time; it's really important for all of us to understand it."

—Rachel Maddow

"Important....Vladeck is a conscientious guide through the legal thickets. With *The Shadow Docket*, Vladeck has taken it upon himself to translate the court's deliberately cryptic orders and legal technicalities into accessible English."

—*New York Times*

"Vladeck offers a fascinating chronicle of the shadow docket's rise....The author's skill as a law professor shines in thorough, clear explanations of how the court has run roughshod over its own jurisprudence in shadow-docket cases involving abortion, religious liberty, and election law....The illumination in *The Shadow Docket* could help bring more principle, accountability, and 'procedural regularity' to the justices' work—and help stop a controversial institution going completely off the rails."

—*Economist*

"Vladeck offers a well-researched indictment of how the Supreme Court has grown to rely on using procedural orders rather than rulings to make new law, escaping scrutiny while delivering major victories to the political right.... *The Shadow Docket* is comprehensive and sensitive to nuance, written for concerned audiences."

—*Guardian*

"As a court observer, Vladeck is a phenomenon.... *The Shadow Docket* is a work of profound respect for a Court he plainly loves....An important book for anyone who wants a deep understanding of the way the post-Trump Court is moving to reshape the law. Vladeck is a clear and engaging writer."

—*Washington Monthly*

"People who care about the Court and what it's doing should read this." — Poppy Harlow

"The most important recent book attempting to answer the burning question, 'How did we get into this mess?'"

—Esquire.com

"Persuasive and timely.... Critics of the current court will find much to ponder in Vladeck's account." —*Kirkus*

"An expert study.... This insightful and accessible account raises an important alarm." —*Publishers Weekly*

"In *The Shadow Docket*, Vladeck tells an urgent story about an arcane aspect of American law that has momentous implications for a host of pressing political issues—and for the institutional legitimacy of the Supreme Court itself. In elegant, accessible prose, Vladeck exposes the degree to which significant battles, from abortion to immigration, are being adjudicated behind closed doors, in unseen, unsigned, unexplained decisions. This is a powerful work of argument and explication, and a call for a return to transparency and accountability in the decision making of our highest court."

—Patrick Radden Keefe, author of *Empire of Pain*

"The Supreme Court's polling numbers and legitimacy have taken a nosedive in recent years, but the cases it hands down are only part of the problem. The stuff that happens in the shadows is equally alarming, and nobody has been better at explaining these shadow matters than Vladeck. Tackling intricate procedural questions, Vladeck makes absolutely plain that—to repurpose an old adage—procedure isn't just the handmaid of justice, it's now her lord and master. We ignore what happens in the shadows at our peril." —Dahlia Lithwick, author of *Lady Justice*

"Vladeck shines a harsh light on a little-understood SCOTUS sleight of hand—the shadow docket. Vladeck describes in clear and convincing language how the highest court in the land has increasingly used obscure procedural orders to shift the legal landscape to the right, at the expense of transparency, precedent, and fundamental rights. It is vital reading."

—Preet Bharara, former US attorney for the Southern District of New York

"Vladeck uses his intimate knowledge of the Supreme Court to show how the conservative justices are manipulating the court's docket to maximize their power and achieve their desired outcomes. *The Shadow Docket* is essential reading for anyone who wants to understand how today's court really works."

—Linda Greenhouse, author of *Justice on the Brink*

"The best thing you can say about a Supreme Court book is that you learned something, and I learned a ton. Vladeck cogently describes the perhaps well-meant but insidious way that the Supreme Court, in liberal as well as conservative times, slowly eroded the legal levers that prevented the Court from engineering its own agenda."

—Nina Totenberg, legal affairs correspondent, NPR

# THE SHADOW DOCKET

## HOW THE SUPREME COURT USES STEALTH RULINGS TO AMASS POWER AND UNDERMINE THE REPUBLIC

**Updated with a New Preface**

STEPHEN VLADECK

BASIC BOOKS
New York

*For Nasser Hussain, who opened the door,*
*and for Karen, Maddie, and Sydney, who keep it open.*

---



Basic Books
Hachette Book Group
1290 Avenue of the Americas, New York, NY 10104
www.basicbooks.com

Printed in the United States of America

Originally published in hardcover and ebook by Basic Books in May 2023
First Trade Paperback Edition: May 2024

Published by Basic Books, an imprint of Hachette Book Group, Inc. The Basic Books name and logo is a registered trademark of the Hachette Book Group.

The Hachette Speakers Bureau provides a wide range of authors for speaking events. To find out more, go to hachettespeakersbureau.com or email HachetteSpeakers@hbgusa.com.

Basic books may be purchased in bulk for business, educational, or promotional use. For information, please contact your local bookseller or Hachette Book Group Special Markets Department at special.markets@hbgusa.com.

The publisher is not responsible for websites (or their content) that are not owned by the publisher.

Print book interior design by Amy Quinn.

Library of Congress Control Number: 2022054586

ISBNs: 9781541602632 (hardcover), 9781541602649 (ebook),
9781541605183 (paperback)

LSC-C

Printing 1, 2024

# CONTENTS

# PREFACE

For generations, public discussion of the US Supreme Court has treated the Court largely as the sum of its written rulings—the dozens of legal disputes that the justices resolve each term through lengthy opinions handed down via a carefully choreographed procedure after months of briefing, oral argument, and internal deliberations. When we talk about the Court, we talk about *Brown* v. *Board of Education* (the 1954 ruling that desegregated public schools). We talk about *Miranda* v. *Arizona* (the 1966 ruling that requires police officers to warn suspects of their rights before interrogating them). We talk about *Roe* v. *Wade* (the 1973 ruling protecting a constitutional right to previability abortions) and *Dobbs* v. *Jackson Women's Health Organization* (the 2022 decision overruling it). And we view the Court through the lens of these decisions—a lens that focuses attention on the ideological divisions reflected in each of those rulings—which justices joined the majority, and which ones dissented. Our assessment of the Supreme Court is, in the main, driven by our sense of whether these rulings are "right" or "wrong."

When most conversations about the Supreme Court start from that premise, they are naturally going to sort participants into camps aligning with their ideological preferences. And since 2010, those debates have increasingly mapped onto our partisan divisions as well: for the first time in American history, the ideological orientation of each of the justices matches the political preferences of the president who appointed them.

The result is not only to skew debate toward the merits and demerits of specific methodological approaches to legal interpretation (such as "originalism," which suggests that the Constitution ought to be interpreted to align with how it was generally understood when it was adopted); it is also to accept, without much in the way of critical reflection, the notion that the current Court is a lightning rod entirely *because* of the bottom lines of its written decisions. Thus, Democrats criticize a Supreme Court with a majority of justices appointed by Republicans for overruling precedents without sufficient justifications and for aggrandizing power from other institutions in our federal system; and Republicans criticize Democrats—who tolerated, if not embraced, parallel behavior when the Court tilted further to the left—for their hypocrisy.

In the process, we've lost the ability to talk about the Supreme Court as an institution. The Court's blockbuster decisions and the ideological wrangling about them tend to consume all available oxygen—distracting us from other stories about the Court, the justices, or both that are just as significant, if not more so. Thus, no one has noticed as the Court's docket has slowly but steadily shrunk—so that the justices today are handing down written rulings in one-third the total number of disputes as a generation ago, and the fewest number of cases overall since the Civil War. No one has noticed that Congress, which for almost two-hundred years regularly exerted leverage over the Court through lots of ways big and small, has spent several decades sitting on the sidelines. And, until a series of reports emerged from ProPublica and other media outlets beginning in April 2022, no one (including the Supreme Court press corps) had noticed that at least some of the justices have long been engaging in personal behavior infected with serious questions of ethical and financial propriety.

What these developments have in common is accountability—or, more precisely, the lack thereof. The Constitution cements the principle of judicial independence as a bulwark against tyrannies of the majority. But it includes measures for preventing tyrannies of unelected judges as well. The challenge is striking the right balance between an independent Court and an unaccountable one. And although Congress historically pulled various levers to try to keep the Court in check, it has, of late, gradually disengaged from such a role—resulting in a Court that does not believe it is, or ought to be, beholden to anyone else. Justice Samuel Alito captured this point quite directly in July 2023, telling the *Wall Street Journal* in an interview that, in his view, "no provision in the Constitution gives [Congress] the authority to regulate the Supreme Court—period." Alito is wrong as a matter of both the plain text of the Constitution (Article III, Section 2 literally gives Congress the power to "make... regulations" of the Court's jurisdiction) and well-settled historical practice, but the fact that this mentality is even in the zeitgeist is a telling reflection of where we are.[1]

I wrote this book to try to illuminate how we got here—and to do so by providing an introduction to how the Court operates that goes well past the handful of headline-generating decisions that draw the lion's share of public attention. In 2015, my friend Will Baude, a University of Chicago law professor, first used the term "shadow docket" as an evocative shorthand for one critical piece of that context—the thousands of rulings that the justices hand down each year *apart* from the written rulings in the five dozen cases on the "merits docket" that still receive multiple rounds of briefing, oral argument, and lengthy, written opinions respecting their disposition. Indeed, one of the things that we've missed in viewing the Court as the sum of those written rulings is that they represent only about 1 percent of the Court's total output in any given year. Baude thought it obvious that we should pay more attention to the other 99 percent; I took him up on the invitation.[2]

As the book explains, most of these other rulings come down as "orders" (which, by tradition, are unsigned and unexplained)* in one of two contexts: orders denying "certiorari" (that is, refusing to exercise the Court's discretion to hear an appeal); and orders granting or denying "emergency relief" (freezing a lower-court ruling or a government policy that lower courts refused to block *while* an appeal works its way to the justices in Washington). As these orders have come to represent a greater percentage of the Court's overall output throughout the twentieth century and into the first decades of the twenty-first, more and more of the justices' work—and more and more strategic and tactical behavior by government actors, lower courts, and the lawyers involved in these cases—has moved into the literal and proverbial shadows. Among lots of other things, the inscrutability of much of the Court's work has simultaneously facilitated both the rise of an elite and technocratic "Supreme Court bar," which privileges those lawyers more attuned to the institution's unwritten norms, and the decline of public understanding of the Court and how it operates. The first of this book's two goals is to trace the development and expansion of the shadow docket—and to demonstrate how, to borrow from the subtitle, the Supreme Court now uses these "stealth rulings" to "amass power." As it turns out, that's not how the Court operated for more than half of its history.

The second part of the subtitle reflects the far more serious charge the book levels at the justices—that their use of these rulings "undermine[s] the Republic." This claim is directed more specifically toward recent events—and the stunning expansion in when and how the Supreme Court has granted "emergency relief" since 2017. After decades in which the Court tended to intervene through unsigned and unexplained orders only a handful of times each year, and, even then, mostly in death

* Orders from the Court (as opposed to a single justice) never identify an author. And even when the Court issues a majority opinion in *support* of an order, the only attribution is "per curiam," meaning "for the Court."

penalty cases, the Court since 2017 has used unsigned and (usually) unexplained orders to block or unblock everything from former president Donald Trump's immigration policies to state COVID mitigation measures to unlawful congressional district maps to Texas's six-week abortion ban—which a 5–4 majority allowed to go into effect ten months *before* overruling *Roe*.[3]

It would be one thing if the Court's unsigned and unexplained orders were just temporary expedients—a way to freeze the underlying dispute to give the justices time to comprehensively review the underlying legal questions. So long as the Court eventually provides a detailed rationale for its prior action, perhaps the justices could be forgiven for not showing their work at the outset. But it has become the norm, rather than the exception, for disputes that begin on the shadow docket to also end there, so that the justices' first (few) words on the matter are also their last. In suits challenging Trump immigration policies, for instance, the Supreme Court handed down more than a dozen unsigned shadow docket rulings. And yet only one of those initiatives (the third iteration of the "travel ban") ever received a full merits review from the justices. The rest of those policies, from limits on asylum eligibility to the building of the border wall, lived or died on the shadow docket. Even when lower courts had issued lengthy decisions striking them down, these polices rose or fell entirely on the basis of unsigned, unexplained Supreme Court orders.[4]

And in the minority of instances in which a case where the Court granted emergency relief *does* return for plenary review, that review often calls into question the Court's earlier intervention—such as in the post-2020 Alabama redistricting cases. There, lower courts had blocked the map Alabama proposed to use for US House districts in the 2022 congressional election, concluding that the Voting Rights Act required Alabama to draw an additional "majority-minority" district. In February 2022, a 5–4 Supreme Court majority issued an unsigned, unexplained order freezing those rulings and allowing

Alabama to use its map—even though, in June 2023, the Court would *agree* with the district courts on the merits that the map was unlawful. Making matters worse, the Court's February 2022 intervention in Alabama led, directly or indirectly, to parallel developments in four other states, where lower courts either issued similar orders only to have them frozen by the justices (as in Louisiana), or declined to require legislatures to redraw their maps *because* they assumed the Supreme Court would do the same to them (as in Georgia, Ohio, and South Carolina). Taken together, an argument could plausibly be made that unsigned, unexplained orders from the Supreme Court handed Republicans five seats—and thus the majority—in the House of Representatives during the 118th Congress.[5]

In deciding so much while saying so little, the justices are not only failing to provide adequate guidance to lower courts and government actors but also, as the Alabama cases exemplify, exacerbating charges of political partisanship. That's because many of these shadow docket decisions have appeared to align more closely with Republican political preferences than with any consistent, neutral approach to the underlying legal issues. Justice Amy Coney Barrett tried to push back against this perception in an April 2022 speech, encouraging her audience to "read the opinion" before deciding if a new and controversial Supreme Court decision was based on coherent (even if not convincing) legal principles. Less than forty-eight hours later, though, Barrett provided the decisive vote in a 5–4 shadow docket order that made it easier for power plants to pollute nearby waterways. Anyone who wanted to take Barrett up on her suggestion, and read that opinion, would have been profoundly disappointed, for there was no opinion to read. All the majority provided was a disposition: "The application for a stay presented to Justice Kagan and by her referred to the Court is granted."[6]

The only opinion accompanying the April pollution case was a strident dissent by Justice Elena Kagan, to whom the case had initially been referred. Tellingly, Kagan's brief but biting opinion was joined not only by Justices Stephen Breyer and Sonia Sotomayor, but also by Chief Justice John Roberts, whose criticisms of the other conservatives' shadow docket shortcuts have become sharper and more frequent, even in cases in which he sympathizes with their bottom line. But it was Kagan's dissent from the Court's order in the Texas abortion case that provides the true epigraph for this book. The first justice to use the term "shadow docket" in an opinion, Kagan complained that the majority's thinly defended refusal to block the Texas law was "emblematic of too much of this Court's shadow-docket decision-making, which every day becomes more unreasoned, inconsistent, and impossible to defend."[7]

All three of those charges are accurate. If anything, the problem runs even deeper. For a Court that has long tied its own legitimacy to its ability to provide principled justifications for its decisions, the rise of the shadow docket has quickly become a prominent symptom of a larger institutional crisis—even more so than the controversial merits decisions of the past few years. And that crisis ought to have alarming implications even for those who believe the Court may be reaching the "right" results in these cases. To understand why, though, we need a fuller understanding of the shadow docket: what it is, where it came from, and how the Court's recent use of it has departed from prior practice without adequate (or, really, any) public justification.

The point is not just that the shadow docket is worth understanding in itself; it is that it's impossible to properly understand almost anything the Supreme Court does today, or how it has come to exercise such a dominant role over so many facets of US public policy, without understanding the shadow docket—or the broader shift of power from the democratically elected branches to the Supreme Court that it reflects. This book aims to develop that understanding by bringing the shadow docket—and how the modern Supreme Court functions more generally—into the light. After all, if we put the current Court into proper context, we might be better situated not only to understand what is truly alarming about the justices' recent behavior, but also how to fix the Supreme Court—and public faith in it—in ways that will help dispel the perception that it is little more than a vehicle for the exercise of partisan political power.

Austin, Texas
January 2024

# INTRODUCTION

# THE SHADOW DOCKET

On the morning of August 2, 1973, from his summer cottage in Goose Prairie, Washington, Justice William O. Douglas set in motion one of the strangest proceedings in the history of the United States Supreme Court. At the urging of lawyers who had flown across the country the day before and driven through the night to reach him, Douglas agreed to convene a hearing by himself the next day at the US Post Office and Courthouse in nearby Yakima. The federal building was 41 miles from Douglas's cabin in the woods and 2,700 miles away from his chambers in Washington, DC, where such arguments would have usually been held. On his own authority, from the middle of nowhere, Douglas had decided to stop an ongoing military operation in Southeast Asia. And he was going to use the Supreme Court's "shadow docket" to do it.[1]

Six weeks earlier, the Supreme Court's nine justices had adjourned for their annual summer recess, from which they weren't due back until late September. As had become his custom, Douglas used the break as an excuse for a respite from the job he had increasingly come to resent. He had spent much of his career preferring the political arena over the courtroom. Indeed, he had come within a whisker of becoming the Democratic nominee for vice president in 1944. But now, a legal dispute had arisen that couldn't wait for the justices to return to the nation's capital in the fall: Could and should the federal courts halt President Richard Nixon's highly controversial, and quite possibly unlawful, bombing of Cambodia? By far the Court's harshest critic on all things related to the war in Southeast Asia, the never-lacking-for-confidence Douglas finally had the perfect opportunity to speak his mind.[2]

The last US troops had left Vietnam four months earlier. But amid mounting pressure from the ongoing Watergate hearings, President Nixon had continued to bomb Communist strongholds in neighboring Cambodia. And although Congress, having long since soured on US operations in that part of the world, had attempted to cut off all funding for the Cambodia operations, Nixon had vetoed its first attempt to do so. Lacking the votes to override Nixon's veto, on June 29 Congress had passed the "Fulbright Compromise," part of a supplemental appropriations bill, which again terminated funding for any military operations "in or over . . . Cambodia." This time, though, in a bid to secure the president's approval, Congress specified that the cutoff would apply only "on or after August 15, 1973."[3]

On July 1, a besieged Nixon had signed the bill into law—and continued the bombing. After all, as government lawyers would claim, by prohibiting the bombing only as of August 15, Congress had arguably authorized it *until* then. Congresswoman Elizabeth Holtzman (D-NY) and a group of active-duty air force officers stationed in Thailand disagreed, quickly filing a lawsuit in federal court against Secretary of Defense James Schlesinger. They argued that even before the August 15 cutoff, the bombing was still unlawful, because it had not been specifically approved by Congress.[4]

The lawsuit, filed in Brooklyn and assigned to Judge Orrin Judd, asked the court to enter an injunction against Schlesinger—an order that would bar the federal government from continuing with the bombing. On July 25, Judd sided with Holtzman and agreed to temporarily halt the government's aerial campaign. His ruling was the first example in American history of a judicial injunction against an ongoing military operation. There hasn't been a second.[5]

But Judge Judd's ruling did not have any immediate impact. Recognizing the novelty and gravity of the situation, Judd explained that his ruling would not take effect for two days. This gave the government time to seek a stay—an emergency order temporarily pausing a lower-court ruling while the injured party appeals. Sure enough, the Justice Department quickly sought such relief, and the Second Circuit (the Manhattan-based federal appeals court) agreed, allowing the bombing to continue while it considered the government's full appeal of Judd's ruling. Undeterred, Holtzman immediately appealed that ruling to the Supreme Court, asking the justices to vacate the Second Circuit's stay. If that happened, the injunction would go into effect and the bombing would have to be halted for however long it took the government's appeal to be resolved.[6]

Even the government agreed that the bombing had to end by August 15, so the clock was ticking. With most of the justices scattered for the summer break, there wouldn't be time for the full Court to meet in person before there would no longer be anything left for them to decide. With only a couple of weeks to go until the deadline, the question before the Court was not whether the bombing was or was not legal; it was more technical: Which should go into effect—the district court's ruling blocking the bombing, or the Second Circuit's stay allowing it to continue?

At least initially, that question went not to Douglas, but to Justice Thurgood Marshall. The legendary civil rights lawyer, whom President Lyndon B. Johnson had appointed as the Court's first Black justice in 1967, was the designated "circuit justice"—the justice who was automatically assigned to oversee procedural requests relating to the Manhattan-based federal appeals court. To that end, on Monday, July 30, Marshall heard several hours of argument in his wood-paneled chambers in Washington, DC. Two days later, he filed a lengthy opinion that openly agonized over the gravity of the question before him, but ultimately refused to upset the applecart. "I would exceed my legal authority," Marshall wrote, "were I, acting alone," to lift the stay. With the justices unable to convene in person, Marshall felt obliged to act not as he might have wished to, but as he thought the full Court would. Begrudgingly, he sided with Nixon, and the bombing continued.[7]

Normally, that would have been the end of the matter. But this wasn't a normal case. Burt Neuborne, who represented the plaintiffs, flew from Washington, DC, to Portland, Oregon, the next day and drove through the night to Goose Prairie. Neuborne's goal was to persuade Marshall's senior colleague, the seventy-four-year-old Douglas, to come down from the mountain and stop the bombing. It was, in Neuborne's words, a "cross-country hail mary."[8]

The choice of Douglas was no accident. Appointed to the Court by Franklin D. Roosevelt in 1939, five months before World War II began in Europe, by 1973 he was the Court's senior associate justice.* Often referred to by his detractors as "Wild Bill," Douglas had long since established his bona fides as the Court's most ardent and doctrinaire civil libertarian and its loudest critic of the Vietnam War. Douglas was critical not only of the war, but of his colleagues on the Supreme Court, who had repeatedly refused to take up cases asking whether Congress had approved of the government's substantial and sustained uses of military force in Southeast Asia.[9]

On the rare occasions in which the Court had explained its refusal to intercede, it had usually identified some technical, procedural roadblock that would not allow the justices to actually resolve the legality of the war, such as whether the plaintiff was a proper party to bring the challenge, or whether it was

* The seniority of the justices is based upon their date of appointment, except that the chief justice is always senior to the associate justices.

appropriate for the courts, rather than the political branches, to decide the question in the first place. Almost every time, Douglas dissented, just as he had most recently, on June 21, 1973 (four days before the Court adjourned), when the justices had thrown out a civil suit against the Ohio National Guard arising from the Kent State massacre, in which the Guard had opened fire during a campus antiwar rally, killing four students and wounding nine others.[10]

Six weeks later, here, at last, was an opportunity for the tired and irascible Douglas to rule on a piece of the war all by himself, without having to persuade any of his eight colleagues to join him. Under the Court's esoteric rules in such cases, Neuborne couldn't have gone directly to Douglas. But once the assigned "circuit justice" for the relevant lower court (Marshall) had refused to act, the rules technically allowed Neuborne to ask any other justice for the same relief. Allowing an application to be brought to an additional justice reflected two distinct concerns—that the circuit justice might simply be unavailable, and that, in a sufficiently dire emergency, it might be better to give an applicant two bites at the apple rather than one. If the Court had been in session, such a request would have been forwarded to the full Court, to prevent the lawyers from trying to pick and choose justices they thought would be more sympathetic to their case. In early August 1973, with the Court adjourned, Neuborne could ask any of Marshall's colleagues for the same relief Marshall had refused.[11]

So it was that, on the morning of Thursday, August 2, Neuborne's colleague Norman Siegel delivered the relevant legal papers to Douglas at his Goose Prairie home. Unshaven and in a bathrobe, Douglas responded that he would need a few hours to look over the briefs. In one especially notorious prior episode, a lawyer who had similarly hand-delivered a request had returned to find Douglas's order rejecting it nailed to a nearby tree. When Siegel returned, though, he got better news: Circuit Justice Douglas would hear oral argument on the matter the next morning in Yakima, so that the federal government could be represented as well. It wasn't the first time that Douglas had commandeered the nearest federal courtroom, but it was certainly the most dramatic.[12]

The unusual spectacle aside, the result of Friday's hearing—at what is now known as the William O. Douglas Federal Building—was a foregone conclusion. While Neuborne flew home to New York, Douglas—using a series of roadside pay phones along his drive back up into the mountains—dictated his ruling and a brief opinion to a clerk back in DC. When the order was formally handed down from the Supreme Court in Washington at 9:30 on Saturday morning, it lifted the Second Circuit's stay of Judge Judd's injunction; the bombing was to be halted. Douglas did not actually rule that the bombing was unlawful. Instead, he wrote that it was a close question, and that the stakes were too high to allow the bombing to continue until and unless the courts conclusively resolved the dispute. In his words, "Denial of the application before me would catapult our airmen as well as Cambodian peasants into the death zone."[13]

Douglas's mandate, which the military appears to have ignored, was in any event short-lived. Rather than accepting Douglas's ruling as the last word, the Justice Department pursued a clever procedural maneuver. Douglas's Saturday-morning order had lifted the stay that had been imposed by the Second Circuit, clearing the way for Judge Judd's injunction halting the bombing to go back into effect. But the Supreme Court, and each of its justices by themselves, had the power, under a series of old statutes, to issue their *own* stays of trial-court rulings—regardless of what the intermediate court of appeals had done. Quickly, then, the federal government returned to Justice Marshall. This time, instead of asking Marshall to leave the Second Circuit's stay in place (as it had five days earlier), it asked him to issue a stay of his own—to freeze Judge Judd's injunction directly.[14]

Just over six hours after Douglas's order was released, Marshall once again sided with the Nixon administration. Not only did he acquiesce in the government's rare procedural move, but he took an unprecedented step to preempt any further maneuvering by Douglas, writing, in his solo opinion, that he had "been in communication with the other Members of the Court," and all seven of them "agree[d] with this action." Because Marshall was ruling in his individual capacity as circuit justice, he didn't need the concurrences of the other justices. Nor could the other justices provide such concurrences, since the Court was not formally in session. But by emphasizing that he had his colleagues' support, Marshall was sending an unequivocal signal to Douglas to desist. For what appears to be the first time in the Court's history, the justices effectively voted by telephone. And they voted for ten more days of bombing.[15]

Douglas filed a vehement dissent. He did not doubt that the full Court had the power to overrule him; it had happened before. In June 1953, the justices had come back to the bench after recessing for the summer to hold a rare "Special Term," entirely to rebuff Douglas's eleventh-hour effort to block the executions of Julius and Ethel Rosenberg, the only two American civilians sentenced to death for espionage during the Cold War. But unlike in 1953, now the justices had not returned to Washington to hold a public hearing and overrule Douglas in person; this time, they rebuked him privately and by telephone.[16]

Formally, Douglas argued that Marshall's second ruling was void, because only the full Court could supersede *his* ruling. Marshall may have consulted with the other justices by telephone, but because the Court wasn't in session, he couldn't claim a quorum; only a Special Term could accomplish that. But Douglas focused just as much on his practical objections to Marshall's Saturday decision. As he explained, by purporting to vote by telephone, the justices had defeated the purpose of having the full Court gather in person to discuss and decide cases collectively at their Conference, a tradition dating back to the early 1800s. "A Conference brings us all together; views are exchanged; briefs are studied; oral argument by counsel for each side is customarily required," Douglas explained. "But even without participation the Court always acts in Conference and therefore responsibly." Moreover, Douglas wrote, it had been his experience that "profound changes are made among the Brethren once their minds are allowed to explore a problem in depth."* Here, in contrast, "there were only a few of the Brethren who saw my opinion before they took contrary action." Such a "Gallup Poll type of inquiry of widely scattered justices is, I think, a subversion of the regime under which I thought we lived."[17]

Whoever had the better arguments in the Cambodia case, no one doubted that it was a black eye for the Court. The public sniping between Marshall and Douglas painted the justices in a less-than-flattering light on a topic about which the country was already deeply divided. Worse, it made a public spectacle out of the bitter internal debate over the Court's nonintervention in Vietnam. For lawyers, it also appeared to provide a road map for how future parties could shop a case around until they found a single justice willing to grant emergency relief, hardly a message that the Court wanted to send, especially so long as the increasingly unpredictable Douglas remained on the bench.

Most troubling of all, though, was the headline on the front page of the *New York Times* on Tuesday, August 7: "Cambodia Town Hit in U.S. Error; 25 to 65 Killed." Less than thirty-six hours after the denouement of the injunction controversy in Washington, an air force raid in Cambodia had mistakenly bombed the town center of Neak Luong. Although initial reports were that 25 people had been killed and dozens more wounded, later tallies placed the death toll at 137—with more than 250 injured, most of whom were civilians. As Douglas

* Until shortly before the confirmation of Justice Sandra Day O'Connor—the Court's first female justice—in 1981, the justices regularly referred to each other individually as "my Brother" and collectively as "the Brethren."

had feared, the Supreme Court had indeed "catapult[ed] . . . Cambodian peasants into the death zone." It was a stunningly immediate real-world consequence of the justices' procedural machinations.[18]

Neither Douglas nor any of his colleagues ever commented publicly on the Neak Luong bombing. The only visible impacts the Cambodia affair had on the Court were a series of subtle but undeniable shifts in the justices' internal procedures. After the Marshall-Douglas contretemps, the justices changed their method of handling applications seeking emergency relief from a second justice after a first had declined to intervene. They now referred such questions to the full Court rather than ruling on them solo, even during the summer recess. The justices also normalized Marshall's Saturday maneuver, informally taking their colleagues' temperatures when they received applications on which the Court might divide, and only resolving by themselves those on which there was a clear consensus. By the end of the 1970s, the Court would quietly discontinue its practice of formally "adjourning" when the justices left for the summer, so that it would be possible to issue decisions from the full Court even when some (or all) of the justices were elsewhere. (Curiously, the Court would not formalize this change in its rules, to a "continuous" term, until 1990.) At least in those respects, the Court appeared to be reacting to the very concerns about its internal processes that Douglas had raised in the Cambodia affair.[19]

But these technical, procedural changes did nothing to address Douglas's substantive concerns about the danger of the full Court deciding weighty matters on an expedited basis without detailed deliberation, multiple rounds of briefing, and oral argument. If anything, these procedural changes, which made it easier for the entire Court to resolve emergency applications *without* detailed briefing and in-person arguments, may have only exacerbated Douglas's objections. After all, although Marshall and Douglas each had the benefit of detailed briefs and in-person arguments to fully flesh out their views on the questions presented in the Cambodia case, the other seven justices had not. Indeed, when they voted by telephone on that Saturday afternoon in August 1973, it's unclear, in an age before fax machines, let alone email, how many of the other justices had laid eyes on the written opinion Douglas had filed that morning, instead of merely having it summarized for them.

Either way, having the full Court act quickly without full briefing and argument had clearly not served the justices well during the Cambodia affair, a lesson they would forget as the practice became more common in subsequent years. Today, *Holtzman* v. *Schlesinger* is considered an obscure footnote (if it is considered at all). But in retrospect, it was an inflection point in the history of how the Supreme Court handles procedural applications. The Court's disposition of the Cambodia affair marked (and helped to precipitate) a shift in the justices' willingness to collectively—rather than individually—decide controversial and widely impactful matters behind closed doors. Properly understood, it was an early portent of a dramatic uptick in equally troubling behind-the-scenes Supreme Court rulings to come. Those rulings would include even less reasoning than the four contradictory opinions filed by Marshall and Douglas over the first four days of August 1973—and, increasingly, they would have even more of an impact.

Most public discourse about the Supreme Court centers around one of two focal points. First, there's perhaps no single moment when the Court is more in the public eye than during the nomination and confirmation processes for new justices—as we saw with Neil Gorsuch in 2017; Brett Kavanaugh in 2018; Amy Coney Barrett in 2020; and Ketanji Brown Jackson in 2022. And second, of course, there are the series of headline-generating decisions that the justices hand down like clockwork each spring. The typical American may not be able to name all, or even any, of the nine current justices, but anyone who even casually engages with the news likely has at least passing familiarity with the routinized machinery of the Court's merits docket—of the justices hearing oral arguments in their ornate headquarters on the corner of First and East Capitol Streets; deliberating for months; and then handing down their decisions come May and June.

Everything about the Court's merits docket is carefully choreographed. The oral argument dates are set months in advance. The arguments themselves are formal, staid affairs complete with authentic quill pens for the advocates, which many keep as mementos. The Court's internal process for drafting and circulating opinions behind the scenes is governed by a series of long-standing norms and deadlines. Even the protocol for handing down decisions follows a decades-old script, where, on preannounced decision days, the justices take the bench at 10:00 a.m. and issue rulings (or, during the COVID pandemic, have them posted to the Court's website) in reverse order of seniority based upon which justice wrote the majority opinion. You might remember where you were when you heard the news about the 2012 decision upholding the Affordable Care Act; the 2015 ruling recognizing a constitutional right to same-sex marriage; or the 2022 ruling overturning the constitutional right to abortions. But even for those who don't, the headlines and talk shows about them would have been impossible to miss. When (or if) most of us think about the work of the Supreme Court, and not just the justices themselves, these rulings are why.[20]

It turns out, though, that the merits docket is only a small sliver of the Supreme Court's overall output. Consider the Court's "October 2020 Term," which ran from Monday, October 5, 2020, through Sunday, October 3, 2021.* Over those 364

* Since 1990, the Supreme Court's annual "term" has run from the first Monday in October of each year to the Sunday before the first Monday of October the next year. The convention both inside and outside the Court

days, the justices handed down 56 signed decisions in argued cases—the typical format for a ruling on the merits docket. During the same period, the Court considered 5,307 petitions asking it to take up appeals from lower courts, as well as 66 applications for emergency relief, like the one over which Justices Marshall and Douglas sparred in the Cambodia affair; of those 66, 24 were granted. Quantitatively, at least, the shadow docket made up almost 99 percent of the Court's actual decisions.[21]

The shadow docket itself isn't new. For as long as there has been a Supreme Court, the Court has issued unsigned procedural orders shaping and structuring how the justices process and ultimately resolve each of the cases before them. If the justices grant a party more time to file a brief, that happens on the shadow docket. If they reallocate how much time parties have to argue, that happens on the shadow docket. If they refuse to take up an appeal, that happens on the shadow docket, too. The effects of individual orders may sometimes have elicited public interest, as when Douglas attempted to stop the bombing of Cambodia. But the shadow docket itself has been part of the Court's work for a long time, and its output has historically been almost entirely uncontroversial. The Supreme Court's shadow docket output may be larger in terms of the sheer number of cases, but, at least traditionally, it has been far less significant than the justices' decisions on the merits docket.

In recent years, things have changed. Since the mid-2010s, there has been a radical shift in how (and how often) the justices use the shadow docket—not just to manage their workload, but to change the law both on the ground and on the books. From immigration to elections, from abortion to the death penalty, from religious liberty to the power of federal administrative agencies, the Supreme Court has, with increasing frequency,

---

is to use these fifty-two-week periods, rather than calendar years, as the relevant temporal divider. Consistent with that approach, this book is current through the end of the Court's October 2021 Term—that is, October 2, 2022.

intervened preemptively, if not prematurely, in some of our country's most fraught political disputes through decisions that are unseen, unsigned, and almost always unexplained. In the process, these rulings have run roughshod over long-settled understandings of both the formal and practical limits on the Court's authority. Because they are unsigned and unexplained, shadow docket orders are supposed to be exceedingly limited in what they can accomplish. And yet, dozens of times each term, we're now seeing shadow docket orders that fly in the face of those understandings.

Consider, in this respect, the justices' February 2022 intervention in a dispute over congressional redistricting in Alabama. Shortly after Alabama adopted new maps for its seven US House seats in response to the 2020 Census, two different federal district courts blocked the maps, concluding that the way the new districts were drawn diluted the voting power of Black Alabamians in violation of the Voting Rights Act of 1965. These rulings were based upon the Supreme Court's own prior interpretations of the Voting Rights Act—specifically, the standard that the justices had articulated for proving such "vote-dilution" claims. The district courts ordered Alabama to redraw the maps, this time with a second "majority-minority" district. Such a map would almost certainly have created a second safe Democratic seat in Alabama's 6–1 Republican-majority House delegation.[22]

Alabama immediately appealed those rulings, arguing that the Supreme Court was likely to, and should, revisit its prior interpretation of the Voting Rights Act. In the ordinary course, if the justices wanted to, they would have taken up the appeal and set it for plenary consideration, including oral argument, sometime in the fall of 2022. While that happened, the district court's rulings, requiring Alabama to redraw its maps, would have remained in effect for the 2022 primary and general elections. But Alabama also asked the justices to short-circuit that entire process. Specifically, Alabama applied for "emergency" relief in the form of a stay that would freeze the effects of both district court rulings, so that the state could continue to use the invalidated maps throughout the 2022 election cycle.

A few minutes after 5:00 p.m. on Monday, February 7, 2022, the Supreme Court acquiesced. By a 5–4 vote, but with no opinion or even cursory explanation on behalf of the majority, the Court issued stays guaranteeing that the challenged maps would remain in place until the justices decided Alabama's appeals, which would not happen before the 2022 elections. (Oral argument would later be scheduled for October 4, 2022.) The February order was as short as it was inscrutable: "The district court's January 24, 2022 preliminary injunctions in No. 2:21–cv–1530 and No. 2:21–cv–1536 are stayed pending further order of the Court."[23]

Chief Justice John Roberts, who had written for a 5–4 majority in a 2013 decision that heavily weakened the Voting Rights Act, wrote a rare dissent in which he criticized the other five Republican-appointed justices for blocking the district courts' rulings. In his words, the lower courts "properly applied existing law in an extensive opinion with no apparent errors for our correction." From his perspective, Alabama *might* persuade the Court to change the meaning of the Voting Rights Act on appeal, but because the law as it stood supported the lower courts' rulings, the state couldn't come close to making the case for a stay while that appeal unfolded. Emergency interventions from the Supreme Court are supposed to be for emergencies. For obvious reasons, lower courts faithfully following the justices' existing precedents had not historically qualified as such.[24]

The more acerbic dissent came, once again, from Justice Kagan. Writing for herself and the other two more liberal members of the Court, Justices Breyer and Sotomayor, Kagan tore into the majority. "Accepting Alabama's contentions," she wrote, "would rewrite decades of this Court's precedent about Section 2 of the VRA," a change that "can properly happen only after full briefing and argument—not based on the scanty review this Court gives matters on its shadow docket." By overriding the district courts, even temporarily, Kagan concluded, "today's decision is one more in a disconcertingly long line of cases in which this Court uses its shadow docket to signal or make changes in the law, without anything approaching full briefing and argument."[25]

The order in the Alabama cases produced immediate effects not just in Alabama, but elsewhere as well. Just ten days after the ruling, for example, a Georgia district court held that it couldn't block Georgia's proposed new district maps, even though they suffered from the exact same legal infirmity as Alabama's. The problem, the district judge wrote, was the Supreme Court's unexplained order in the Alabama cases—and the assumption that the justices would likewise allow Georgia's maps to go back into effect if he blocked them.[26]

A few months later, a Louisiana district court blocked Louisiana's proposed congressional maps as violating the Voting Rights Act, much as the Alabama district court judges had done in that state. Given the Supreme Court's subsequent actions in the Alabama case, the judge in Louisiana wrote a 152-page opinion that carefully explained why it was appropriate to issue an injunction requiring Louisiana to redraw its maps even if it hadn't been appropriate in the Alabama and Georgia cases. The Fifth Circuit, by any measure the most conservative federal appeals court in the country, refused to block the district court's ruling, writing 33 pages of its own leaving the lower-court decision intact. But the Supreme Court once again intervened to put the blocked maps into effect, without providing a single word of explanation for why the voluminous analysis the lower courts had provided—much of which explained why the Alabama case had been different—was wrong. Together, these rulings all but guaranteed that three House seats that would likely have been safe seats for Democratic candidates in the 2022 midterm elections were instead safe seats for Republicans. A subsequent *New York Times* report concluded that the rulings were likely to impact which party controlled as many as seven House seats—if not the House itself.[27]

The justices' interventions in the Alabama and Louisiana cases were emblematic of a much larger pattern. During its October 2019, October 2020, and October 2021 Terms, the Court granted more than sixty applications for emergency relief—staying lower-court decisions like the ones in the Alabama cases; vacating lower-court stays or injunctions; or reaching out to enjoin state executive action directly. Only in the mid-1980s had the shadow docket ever been quite so active—and the overwhelming majority of that activity involved last-minute appeals by death-row inmates seeking to halt their executions.[28]

For the prisoners involved in those 1980s cases, the matter was literally one of life or death. However, the disputes they brought before the Court, and the Court's resolution of them, tended not to have broader legal or practical ramifications. The Court halted a prisoner's execution or allowed it to proceed, but in either case, the result applied to that prisoner alone. In contrast, as the redistricting cases underscore, the Court's recent decisions on requests for emergency relief have regularly produced statewide or nationwide effects. During the Trump administration, for instance, many of the Court's grants of emergency relief had the effect of putting back into place immigration policies affecting millions of noncitizens, including some policies that would eventually be deemed unlawful by every court that actually ruled on their merits.[29]

Likewise, the Supreme Court's January 2022 emergency order blocking the Occupational Safety and Health Administration's COVID vaccination-or-testing mandate for large employers directly affected more than eighty-three million Americans, roughly one-quarter of the country's population. And emergency rulings refusing to intervene have had equally broad impacts, such as the Court's September 2021 ruling allowing Texas's six-week abortion ban, SB8, to go into effect, halting almost all legal abortions in the country's second-largest state. Unsigned and unexplained orders are now routinely used to determine whether state and federal policies affecting all of us, and perhaps even the exercise of our constitutional rights, will or will not be enforced for years to come.[30]

Although the beginning of this trend can be dated to early 2017, it accelerated precipitously after Justice Ruth Bader Ginsburg's death in September 2020 and the confirmation of Justice Amy Coney Barrett to replace her. Justice Barrett's impact was especially visible in the context of emergency orders directly blocking state policies that lower courts refused to freeze pending appeal. These orders, known as "injunctions pending appeal," are supposed to be a particularly rare form of emergency relief, because, by the time the matter reaches the Supreme Court, at least two different lower courts have already refused to provide them—and now the justices are being asked to reach out and directly restrain government actors. During Chief Justice Roberts's first fifteen years on the bench, for instance, the Court issued a total of four such orders. In Justice Barrett's first five *months* on the Supreme Court (from November 2020 to April 2021), the Court issued six of them—three in which we know her vote was decisive, and three more in which it easily could have been. A number of popular and scholarly assessments of the Court's October 2020 Term that focused only on the merits docket wondered if Justice Barrett had really made that much of a difference. On the shadow docket, though, the effects of her confirmation were both immediate and stark.[31]

For generations, law students have been taught that the typical case reaches the Supreme Court only at the end of what is often an arduous process, including detailed (and often lengthy) proceedings before a trial court and an appeal to intermediate courts of review, typically at the *end* of that litigation. Against that backdrop, the Supreme Court's intended (and self-described) role in our system of government is that it goes last. As Justice Robert Jackson put it in 1953, "We are not final because we are infallible, but we are infallible only because we are final." Or, as the justices regularly describe matters today, the Supreme Court is "a court of final review and not first view." Having the last word not only cements the Court's role as the authoritative interpreter of federal law but also gives it a firm foundation on which to rest those interpretations. The rigors of litigation have a way of sharpening the record and crystallizing the legal dispute, ensuring that by the time a case makes its way to the Supreme Court's merits docket, it truly and fairly presents the legal question that the justices have been asked to resolve.[32]

The justices' recent use of the shadow docket is fundamentally inconsistent with this understanding. It inverts ordinary appellate process, having the justices answer complicated (and, in some cases, hypothetical) questions of statutory or constitutional law at the outset of litigation, rather than after the issue has worked its way through the lower courts. And it almost certainly diverts the Court's finite resources away from the merits docket. Indeed, as the shadow docket has grown, the merits docket has shrunk, giving the justices less time and fewer resources with which to conduct plenary review in cases not presenting real or conjured emergencies. The Court issued fifty-three signed decisions in cases argued during its October 2019 Term, which was the lowest total since 1862. And the fifty-six signed decisions handed down during the October 2020 Term were the fewest since 1864. The total increased to only fifty-eight during the October 2021 Term—even though, as recently as the mid-2000s, the annual total of merits decisions averaged in the eighties. It's hard to believe that these developments are unrelated.[33]

The shadow docket also invites behavior by the justices that makes the Court look even more sharply partisan in its shadow docket rulings than in its decisions on the merits docket. It is, by default, easier for a justice to join an unexplained order than to join a lengthy, reasoned opinion, where joining is tantamount to endorsing its reasoning. Moreover, it is much harder to accuse a justice of taking inconsistent positions in a future case if he or she didn't take a position publicly in the prior one. Justice Barrett unintentionally acknowledged this point in an October 2021 concurring opinion, emphasizing that whether the Court intervenes on the shadow docket should turn not only on whether a party has made the requisite showing for emergency relief, but also on "a discretionary judgment about whether the Court should [one day] grant review in the case." No law, rule, or even norm dictates how the justices exercise that discretion. Instead, they are free to vote for or against relief for any reason (or no reason) whatsoever. And unlike in cases resolved on the merits docket, they're free in the shadow docket decisions to keep those reasons—and their votes—to themselves.[34]

In the context of emergency orders, the increased reliance on the shadow docket has produced unusually rigid ideological homogeneity. During the October 2019 Term, only twelve of the Court's fifty-three signed merits decisions divided the justices 5–4, including two with unusual and nonideological lineups. In contrast, there were eleven decisions on the shadow docket in the same time span from which four justices publicly dissented, and perhaps others in which some of the dissents were not public. (One of the other vexing features of the shadow docket is that the justices are under no obligation to publicly disclose how they voted—so that, unless four justices publicly note a dissent, it's always possible that there were "stealth" dissents even from rulings that outwardly appeared to be unanimous.)[35] In nine of the eleven shadow docket cases taking place during the Court's 2019–2020 session from which four justices publicly dissented, the dissenters were the four more liberal justices—Ginsburg, Breyer, Sotomayor, and Kagan. In the other two, those four were joined by the median justice, Chief Justice Roberts, to form a majority, and the dissents came from the four more conservative justices. Never in its history had the shadow docket produced so many, or so many *similar*, 5–4 splits in the same term. In other words, as the Court's shadow docket behavior has increased in both quantity and impact both in absolute terms *and* relative to the merits docket, these rulings have sorted the justices into their usual camps to a far greater and more consistent degree than the merits docket.[36]

When the Court issues unsigned orders with dramatic real-world effects, it's one thing if, at least publicly, the justices appear to be speaking with one voice. It's something else altogether when these orders appear to reflect entirely partisan, or at least ideological, divisions. And the lack of substantive analysis to support most of these decisions does nothing to contradict the perception that the Court is becoming more partisan. It's difficult to dismiss as coincidence that the Court's interventions in immigration cases, for example, generally allowed President Donald Trump's policies to go into effect and generally blocked President Joe Biden's policies. Ditto the Court's willingness to block COVID restrictions from New York and California, but not from Texas. Perhaps there are substantive explanations for why one administration's interpretations of immigration law were more valid than another's, or why one state's emergency public health measures were more dubious than another's—but if the justices have such explanations, they're not providing them.

All the while, this story has flown under the radar. In response to public perception of the Supreme Court as always dividing along ideological lines, numerous media accounts claiming to take stock of the Court's October 2020 Term, for instance, emphasized that only seven of the fifty-six argued cases produced 6–3 ideological splits, with all of the conservatives in the majority and all of the more liberal justices in dissent. As these stories explained, the Court was unanimous far more often than readers might expect, and even when it wasn't, the divisions often produced "strange bedfellows." All of that is factually correct, but it's an assessment of an increasingly distorted subset of the Court's workload. Including the shadow docket, there were twice as many unsigned rulings (fourteen) during the same term from which Justices Breyer, Sotomayor, and Kagan all publicly dissented, and no conservative publicly joined them—bringing the total across all rulings to twenty-one. Accounting for both the number of those rulings and their substance yields a very different—and more ominous—story about the Court. On the shadow docket, the public perception of justices who are regularly divided into their partisan camps looks far more accurate.[37]

Regardless of whether one believes that the justices are acting in good faith, these developments raise increasingly troubling questions about the Supreme Court's legitimacy. The justices themselves have long insisted that "the Court's legitimacy depends on making legally principled decisions under circumstances in which their principled character is sufficiently plausible to be accepted by the Nation." The point is not that we are all supposed to agree with what the Supreme Court is doing, but that we are at least supposed to be convinced that the justices are acting as judges rather than as politicians vindicating a partisan political agenda. That doesn't just mean wearing robes to oral arguments; it means giving parties a meaningful opportunity to be heard and resolving their claims through principled decision-making in which those principles are publicly accessible.[38]

That understanding cannot be reconciled with the shadow docket, on which there's usually no opinion to read. The absence of legal reasoning for public consumption makes it impossible to know why the justices ruled the way that they did, or even how they voted. And it also provides no guidance to the parties or anyone else about how they can or should adjust their behavior to comply with the Court's ruling and avoid further judicial scrutiny. If the Supreme Court issues a merits decision adopting a new rule to govern traffic stops, for instance, the analysis in that decision quickly makes its way into police department training manuals nationwide, and not just in the jurisdiction in which that case arose. But the same can't be said of most shadow docket orders. In those cases, no one can truly know what the new rule is, or how it does or should apply to other cases. The lack of reasoning may not be a problem when the justices are simply managing the Court's docket. The problem arises when there is little to no reasoning in support of orders that produce massive real-world practical—and legal—effects.

While all of this has happened, Congress and the executive branch, which had historically taken an active role in shaping the Supreme Court's docket, have sat on the sidelines. Indeed, Congress hasn't so much as tweaked the Supreme Court's jurisdiction since 1988, making the ensuing decades the longest period without such legislation in the nation's history. The increasing prevalence and public significance of unsigned and unexplained rulings from unelected and democratically unaccountable judges would be problematic enough if the political branches had demanded it. But one of the most remarkable features of the rise of the shadow docket in recent years is that it has been entirely of the Court's own making, reflecting a series of formal rule and informal procedural and doctrinal changes quietly adopted by the Court with no external catalyst. In that respect, the rise of the shadow docket reflects a power grab by a Court that has, for better or worse, been insulated from any kind of legislative response.

The more one understands the shadow docket, the more troubling the Court's behavior appears to be. In a few short years, the moniker has gone from a clever name for an obscure academic subject to an unintentionally apt metaphor that captures both the problem itself and the reason why it has been so difficult for even legal experts to see.

Making matters worse, unlike merits decisions, many orders on the shadow docket can come anytime and from anywhere. Depending upon what form they take, they can even be posted to any one of five different pages on the Supreme Court's own website, a technical but telling hindrance.[39] In July 2020, for example, when the Bureau of Prisons carried out the first two federal executions in seventeen years, it was only able to do so after a pair of 5–4 decisions on the shadow docket, both of which lifted stays of execution that had been granted by lower courts. The first of those rulings came down at 2:10 a.m. Eastern time on Tuesday, July 14; the second was issued two nights later at 2:46 a.m.[40] Not surprisingly, those rulings garnered far less attention than the much-ballyhooed merits decisions the justices had handed down just the previous Monday, including in a pair of cases involving subpoenas for President Trump's financial records. Ditto the Court's companion 5–4 rulings in November 2020 blocking New York's COVID restrictions as applied to houses of religious worship, which were handed down at 11:56 p.m. on the Wednesday night before Thanksgiving. Each of these decisions would have been front-page news if handed down the "usual" way or at the "usual" time. Instead, they were left to be parsed almost entirely on social media.[41]

With truncated briefing, no argument, little or no public explanation, no vote tally to guide the parties before the Court or to inform lawyers and lower courts in future cases, and decisions that often come down in the middle of the night, it's hard to think of a *better* term for the great majority of the Supreme Court's output today than a docket that exists in the literal and metaphorical shadows. But whatever it's called, the upshot is that it is increasingly impossible to tell any story about the work of the Supreme Court that does not include the shadow docket.

That story begins not in 2017, but in the late nineteenth and early twentieth centuries, when the Court began to take control of its caseload through the increasing use of "certiorari," itself a shadow docket practice through which the justices chose for themselves which cases, and which specific legal questions within those cases, to decide. The rise of certiorari transformed not only the Supreme Court's docket, but also its role in our constitutional system—from narrowly resolving every dispute Congress gave it the power to resolve to broadly resolving only those questions that the justices *wanted* to resolve. Indeed, even the Court's denials of certiorari—cryptic, unexplained orders that are not supposed to create legal precedents—can have massive (and intended) practical effects. Almost everything that the modern Supreme Court does is a result of the fundamental shift in its role that certiorari effected, a shift that has naturally led to a wide array of strategic and tactical behaviors, not just from the justices, but from the parties and the lower courts as well.

After certiorari, the most significant subset of shadow docket cases are rulings on applications for emergency relief, including stays and injunctions pending appeal. The shadow docket encompasses far more than these emergency applications, but they are, in many respects, the focal point for recent developments. Indeed, many of the pathologies that have come to define the contemporary shadow docket have their roots in how the justices reacted to a flood of last-minute requests from death-row inmates that began in the early 1980s, a flood for which the justices themselves—through a series of decisions beginning in the mid-1970s—were almost entirely responsible.

Still, those pathologies have worsened significantly in recent years. The Trump administration's remarkably aggressive (and successful) use of the shadow docket would enable the administration to implement numerous controversial policies even after lower courts had blocked them, and even though the Supreme Court itself would never ultimately sanction them. Some of the Supreme Court's expansion of the use of the shadow docket from 2017 to 2021 has been defended, however unconvincingly, as a response to perceived overreaching by lower courts hostile to Trump's presidency. But it was some of the less obvious and less defensible interventions, both during the Trump years and after, in which the justices set disturbing new shadow docket precedents and normalized a pattern of problematic procedural behaviors that have not just survived the end of Trump's presidency, but have increasingly become the norm, rather than the exception.

Those whose politics align with the results reached by the Supreme Court's current conservative majority may see all of these developments as a feature, rather than a bug. And they may dismiss (and have already dismissed) criticisms of the shadow docket as bad faith arguments by progressives unhappy with those results. My goal in this book is to demonstrate that the rise of the shadow docket risks doing serious long-term institutional harm to the Court—and, as such, the country. That harm could be disastrous even, if not especially, for those who cheer the bottom lines the contemporary Court is reaching. Anyone who believes that a legitimate Court is a necessary part of our constitutional system ought to be invested in pushing the justices to act in a manner that enhances, rather than undermines, public perception of the institution's good faith—only the more so for those who celebrate the current Supreme Court majority, a majority that won't matter much if the Court loses its moral authority.

Before we can seek to cure the disease, though, we must first document and understand its causes and symptoms. And that story begins not at the beginning, but rather at an otherwise obscure point in the middle: February 13, 1925, the day President Calvin Coolidge signed into law the Judiciary Act of 1925—tellingly known to posterity as the "Judges' Bill."

# CHAPTER 1

# THE RISE OF CERTIORARI

## HOW THE "LEAST DANGEROUS BRANCH" CAME TO CONTROL ITS AGENDA

All his life, William Howard Taft aspired to one job, and it wasn't the presidency. Above all else, Taft wanted to be chief justice of the United States.*[1]

While serving in President Theodore Roosevelt's administration, Taft had turned down multiple offers of appointment to the Supreme Court, at least in part because they weren't to its middle (and most prestigious) seat. And when the chief justiceship came open during Taft's own presidency in 1910, he deliberately broke with tradition to elevate a currently serving associate justice, Edward Douglass White, to the job, largely because White's advanced age (he was sixty-five upon his second

* When it was created in 1789, the position was formally styled the "Chief Justice of the Supreme Court of the United States." Starting with Chief Justice Melville Fuller's appointment in 1888, though, every successive chief justice has held the title "Chief Justice of the United States," reflecting the chief justice's precedence not just over the Supreme Court, but over the entire federal judiciary.

confirmation) left open the possibility that the fifty-three-year-old Taft could one day succeed him. White is said to have later told friends that he was waiting for another Republican president to be elected so that he could resign in favor of Taft, but Taft's Democratic successor, Woodrow Wilson, would serve two full terms. Before he could resign, though, White died in May 1921, two months into the presidency of Ohio Republican Warren Harding. Taft, who had carefully cultivated his relationship with the new president in anticipation of just such a moment, was soon granted his lifelong wish. On the same day that the Senate received Harding's nomination, Taft was confirmed as chief justice. He was sworn in on July 12, 1921.[2]

During his nine years presiding over the Supreme Court, Taft penned only a handful of significant constitutional rulings, the best known of them in a 1926 case about the president's constitutional authority to fire postmasters without cause. Even lawyers, then, tend to have only a passing familiarity with Taft as anything other than the one person to serve as both president and Supreme Court justice. But as much as anyone else in the Supreme Court's history, it's Taft who is responsible for the Court's contemporary prominence. Perhaps uniquely among his predecessors and successors, Taft understood that the Court's true power comes not from the substance of its rulings, but from its institutional autonomy and independence, both formally and functionally. And he fought for decades to maximize both.[3]

It was President Taft who had publicly proposed in 1912 that the Supreme Court should have its own building, rather than its notoriously cramped quarters in the Capitol's Old Senate Chamber, in which the justices did not even have their own office space. Later, it was Chief Justice Taft who aggressively lobbied Congress to appropriate funds for the building across the street from the Capitol that would become known as the "Marble Palace," and who hired the architect Cass Gilbert to build it. And, less visibly, but far more importantly, it was Chief

Justice Taft who, just as ferociously, cajoled Congress into giving the Supreme Court far more control over which cases it hears by expanding an obscure judicial practice known by the obscure Latin term *certiorari*.[4]

"To be more fully informed" in Latin, a writ of "certiorari" was an unusual but not unheard-of mechanism used by English appellate courts of the same era. Long before the advent of electronic files or even written legal briefs, an appellate court would issue the writ to a lower court to request the trial record for an appeal that had already been filed, so that the judges on appeal could review the full proceedings and evidence leading to the decision under review and thereby "be more fully informed." In other words, it was not itself usually a means of appealing, but a legal process to augment an existing appeal. Taft's view of how certiorari would work in the United States was far less modest than what this practice encompassed. Certiorari, as he understood it, was about the appeals courts' discretion in deciding what to decide. And discretion is what he desperately wanted the Supreme Court to have, especially over its own docket.[5]

To that end, Taft helped to both draft and push through the reforms to the Supreme Court's powers that Congress adopted in 1925, known informally then and now as the "Judges' Bill," and more formally as the Judiciary Act. Framed as technical amendments to the statutes governing which cases the Court heard, the point of the bill was, far more fundamentally, to reconceive and subtly transform the Supreme Court's role in our constitutional system. Taft's vision of the Supreme Court was as a constitutional court that could operate above and apart from the fray of ordinary judicial business, not a supreme court of appeals that sits just to resolve whichever individual disputes litigants bring before it. The Judges' Bill helped him to achieve it. Indeed, as chief justice, Taft not only put those reforms to immediate use, but did so in ways that went far beyond (and in some cases directly contradicted) what he had proposed and promised to Congress.[6]

Neither of Taft's great projects would be completed in his lifetime: the Supreme Court's ornate building on the corner of First and East Capitol Streets would not open until 1935, five years after Taft's death; and Congress would not finish giving the Supreme Court near-total discretion over its docket until 1988. Perhaps that's why, to the extent that he is remembered for anything other than the (apocryphal) claim that he once got stuck in a bathtub, Taft is principally viewed by historians as something of a middling president. But Taft looms large over any history of the Supreme Court as an institution, not just as the most important and able administrator in the Court's history, but as the individual most responsible for expanding and cementing the power that the justices exercise today—which he achieved by expanding and cementing their discretion to *not* exercise it. Although much of the Supreme Court's formal authority has its roots in the US Constitution, it took the Court the better part of 150 years, and the ambition of the twenty-seventh president and tenth chief justice, to truly consolidate it.[7]

~

The Supreme Court of the United States convened for the first time on Monday, February 1, 1790, on the second floor of the Royal Exchange in New York City, then the seat of the federal government. Or, at least, it was *supposed* to have convened. With only three of the six justices in attendance (the total number of seats created by the Judiciary Act of 1789), there was no quorum, and the Court was awkwardly forced to adjourn. The arrival later that day of Associate Justice John Blair from Virginia allowed the nascent tribunal to formally open for business the next morning. But there were no cases on the docket for the justices to hear. After appointing the Court's officers, admitting twenty-six lawyers to its bar, and dispensing with a few other housekeeping matters, the Court adjourned its first "term" eight days later, not to meet again until August, when it conducted a grand total of two days of business. It was an inauspicious debut for the fledgling Court.[8]

When the Constitutional Convention had gathered in Philadelphia three summers earlier, one of the few points of near-universal consensus was the need for a federal Supreme Court, if for no other reason than to peaceably resolve legal disputes between the states over everything from the location of borders to the control of rivers to the regulation of commerce between them. The Articles of Confederation—the increasingly unpopular patchwork agreement under which the original thirteen states first organized into a loosely united country—left just about all legal process, including civil and criminal suits, to the individual states. Disputes between states were shunted into a cumbersome and inefficient process vaguely resembling modern-day arbitration (where parties agree to have their dispute resolved by a private actor whom they have chosen). The only body with the final say over disputes arising under the Articles was the Confederation Congress itself. And that legislature couldn't take any meaningful action without the assent of nine of the thirteen states. It was not exactly an effective system for conflict resolution.[9]

Thus, although the Constitution's drafters divided bitterly over whether there should be federal courts below a Supreme Court (a matter they eventually punted to Congress in the "Madisonian Compromise"), they agreed, unanimously, that "one Supreme Court" was to be an essential feature of the new, far more centralized government the Constitution contemplated. Not only would this new Court resolve interstate disputes, but with the broader regulatory powers granted to the federal government (powers that would be far easier for the new Congress to wield), the Supreme Court could also resolve conflicts if different lower courts interpreted the same federal law differently. In so acting, the Court would be staffed by justices appointed by the president and confirmed by the Senate, who would hold their offices during "good behavior," tenure during which their salary could not be diminished. These mechanisms were, quite overtly, intended to foster and promote the Court's independence from the other, more democratically accountable branches of government. In that respect, the Constitution embodied a sharp and deliberate break from the British model, in which the courts were an arm of the Crown.[10]

As with the debate over whether to create lower federal courts, the Constitution also left it to Congress to decide the scope of the Supreme Court's power to hear appeals, whether from the lower federal courts that Congress might create or the existing state courts, to which most judicial business was to be directed, at least at first. All that the Constitution provided was the outer bounds, listing nine types of cases Congress *could* empower federal courts, including the Supreme Court, to hear. Three of these nine categories of "subject-matter jurisdiction" were defined by the substance of the suit—disputes over federal law (including the new Constitution); maritime disputes (which implicated foreign relations); and cases "affecting" foreign ambassadors (ditto). The rest were based on the identity of the parties, authorizing a (presumably less biased) federal forum for disputes between parties from different states even when the case involved only questions of state law. A contract dispute between a Georgian and a South Carolinian, then, could be brought in a neutral federal court to avoid—or at least mitigate—the risk of home-state bias in the courts of either of those two states. The Constitution's drafters and adopters presumed that most of these cases would still begin in state court, ending up in the Supreme Court only on appeal.[11]

The idea that the Court was, at the same time, a useful innovation and still a relative weakling compared to the other branches of the federal government was driven home in *The Federalist*, essays penned by Alexander Hamilton, John Jay, and James Madison in an attempt to persuade the voters of New York, whose assent was essential, to ratify the Constitution. As Hamilton famously wrote in *Federalist* No. 78, "The judiciary, from the nature of its functions, will always be the least dangerous to the political rights of the Constitution; because it will be least in a capacity to annoy or injure them." Unlike the executive branch and Congress, the Court "has no influence over either the sword or the purse; no direction either of the strength or of the wealth of the society; and can take no active resolution whatever." Instead, "it may truly be said to have neither FORCE nor WILL, but merely judgment; and must ultimately depend upon the aid of the executive arm even for the efficacy of its judgments."[12]

At the beginning, even "judgment" was a stretch for the Supreme Court, at least in part because service as a justice was a truly onerous (if not odious) distinction. Congress in the Judiciary Act of 1789 had created a trial-level federal "district court" in each state, as well as intermediate "circuit" courts in each district, which would act as trial courts in certain matters and hear appeals from the district courts in others. Although Congress authorized the appointment of district judges, in order to staff the circuit courts Congress borrowed from the English model—where the local district judge would sit as part of a three-judge panel alongside two Supreme Court justices, who would literally ride out to each of the districts within their assigned circuit to hear cases for as much as six to nine months out of every year.[13]

"Riding the circuit" may have worked in prerevolutionary England, but it imposed enormous burdens in postrevolutionary America—a country that was already spread out across far more territory than the island nation of England, that was rapidly expanding, and that presented greater obstacles to travel than in England, with a primitive network of what scarcely deserved to be called "roads." The "Eastern" Circuit ran from the northern reaches of present-day Maine to the Battery at the southern end of Manhattan. The "Middle" Circuit extended from New York Bay to the bottom of the Chesapeake and the far side of the Shenandoah Mountains. And the "Southern"

Circuit included the Carolinas, Georgia, and their western reaches, which extended all the way to the Mississippi River.

The burdens on the justices (who initially paid for their travel out of pocket) were so substantial that Jay, the first chief justice, resigned in 1795 to become governor of New York, a move that one New York newspaper described as "a promotion." His South Carolina colleague John Rutledge left in 1792 for the more desirable job of presiding over one of his state's lower courts, having never bothered to attend a single Supreme Court session. And Justice Thomas Johnson from Maryland lasted all of 163 days, still the shortest tenure in the Court's history by a fair margin, before resigning in protest over the travel obligations.[14]

As part of the Federalists' effort to entrench themselves into the judiciary after losing control of both Congress and the executive branch in the election of 1800, the lame-duck Congress (which, under the original Constitution, remained in session until the March 4 following the election) tried to abolish circuit-riding in February 1801. But among a series of measures designed to retaliate against the Federalists and weaken the courts, the newly elected Democratic-Republicans immediately restored it in 1802. Another anti-Court measure required the justice assigned to the Maryland circuit to return to Washington every August from 1802 to 1838 to resolve procedural matters, a progenitor of the shadow docket that Supreme Court scholar Ross Davies has dubbed "the rump Court." Throughout the nineteenth century, Congress's refusal to alleviate the justices' travel burdens, which became only that much more substantial as the nation expanded westward, was one of the central ways in which the legislature continued to exert its influence over the Court.[15]

Circuit-riding was just one of the problems, though. The Court also didn't have much in the way of interesting work, at least in part because Congress hadn't given the federal courts all that much to do. Although federal courts could hear all cases involving the small set of federal crimes, their subject-matter jurisdiction in civil cases was far more limited. Even disputes over the meaning of federal laws usually had to be brought in state courts first. And so-called diversity cases, where the federal courts' power came from the fact that parties hailed from different states, were limited to those in which the amount in controversy was more than $500—the equivalent of roughly $15,000 today. The largest chunk of federal cases were, perhaps unsurprisingly, maritime disputes; the one place where the new federal government was indisputably busy was in regulating oceangoing intercourse and trade with foreign nations.[16]

Tighter still were the limits on the Supreme Court's power to hear appeals. It had no general power to hear appeals in federal criminal cases; and appeals from lower federal courts in civil cases were available only if the amount in controversy was more than $2,000 ($60,000 today). Congress gave the justices a bit more power to review cases from state courts, including no minimum amount-in-controversy requirement, but only if the state court had rejected a claim based upon a federal statute, a federal treaty, or the Constitution. If the state court decision rested on state law, or upheld a federal claim, the justices had no power to step in. Thus, if a case turned on a claimed conflict between a federal statute and a state law, the Supreme Court could take up the appeal if the state courts resolved the dispute in favor of the state law, but not if they resolved it in favor of the federal law—even if the state court's interpretation of federal law was clearly incorrect.[17]

The details of each font of jurisdiction are less important than the broader theme cutting across them: the justices' complete lack of discretion. If the Court had the power to hear an appeal, it was required to do so. The justices could not simply choose to leave a lower-court ruling as the last word, even one with which they all agreed. As Chief Justice John Marshall would explain in an 1821 appeal, "With whatever doubts, with whatever difficulties, a case may be attended, we must decide it if it be brought before us. We have no more right to decline the exercise of jurisdiction which is given than to usurp that which is not given. The one or the other would be treason to the Constitution."[18]

The Court had to hear every appeal over which Congress had given it jurisdiction; there just weren't that many of them. Into the 1840s, the Court resolved only thirty-five to fifty disputes each year. Congress eventually alleviated at least some of the burdens of circuit-riding (reducing the number of times a justice was expected to ride circuit, and giving the local district judge more power to act on his own), but the explosive growth of the country in both population and land area only increased the justices' time away from Washington—even as it also led to the addition of seats to the Court. From six seats under the Judiciary Act of 1789 (two for each of the three circuits), the Court expanded to seven in 1807 (one for each circuit); nine in 1837; and briefly to ten in 1863. The norm was to have each circuit represented by a justice who came from one of its states, but that made only for a warmer welcome on circuit, not for less travel to and from it. To prevent President Andrew Johnson from filling any vacancies, Congress temporarily reduced the Court to seven seats in 1866 before settling on the current total of nine seats in 1869—part of a broader series of post–Civil War court reforms.[19]

That's not to say that the Court was moribund for its first seventy-five years. Especially under the tenures of Marshall (1801–1835) and Chief Justice Roger Brooke Taney (1836–1864), the Supreme Court issued its fair share of landmark rulings for the new nation. *Marbury* v. *Madison*, in 1803, cemented the Court's power of "judicial review," allowing it to strike down federal laws that violated the Constitution. *Martin* v. *Hunter's Lessee*, in 1816, affirmed the Supreme Court's preeminence over state courts on questions of federal law. *McCulloch* v. *Maryland*, three years later, upheld the constitutionality of the National Bank in an opinion that more generally expounded the supremacy of the federal government over the states. And Taney's deeply misguided and inescapably racist attempt to forestall the Civil War in his 1857 ruling in the *Dred Scott* case enshrined not only the inferior legal status of enslaved people, but Congress's powerlessness to abolish slavery. It also helped to raise the profile of one of the decision's harshest public critics—the Republican candidate in the 1858 Illinois Senate race, an obscure former congressman named Abraham Lincoln.[20]

Still, these momentous rulings were few and far between. The pre–Civil War Supreme Court was, at best, a loose analogue to the modern institution, resolving a handful of mostly unimportant cases each year. The justices spent most of their time on the road (Marshall would die in 1835 from injuries he suffered in an earlier stagecoach accident in Virginia). Except for deciding the few cases the Constitution and Congress told it to hear, it was largely ignored, holding its sessions in the dimly lit, musty basement of the unfinished US Capitol. Basically, throughout the antebellum era, the Court lived up to Hamilton's promise that the federal judiciary would be the "least dangerous branch."

The Civil War precipitated at least three fundamental changes in the structure of the American legal system. The biggest shift is the familiar one: in response to the war, Congress proposed, and the states ratified, the Thirteenth, Fourteenth, and Fifteenth Amendments to the Constitution. Among other things, these transformational reforms guaranteed individuals, especially the formerly enslaved, the same constitutional rights in their dealings with state and local governments that they already had with the federal government, and gave Congress the power to enact statutes to enforce those new protections. The constitutional rights themselves and the statutes Congress enacted to enforce them would both quickly become a fertile source of new federal litigation.[21]

The other two shifts are far less well known. Starting while the war still raged, Congress began exercising its power to regulate routine domestic affairs to a far greater extent than ever before. Part of that was because the war provided substantive justifications for these laws grounded in military necessity. But part of it was simply practical: many of the members who had typically blocked passage of such legislation during the antebellum era (that is, southerners) had absented themselves from the proceedings. From chartering the Pacific Railroad to creating a national currency, from establishing the Department of Agriculture to providing incentives for western states to open public universities, even while the war was on Congress inserted the federal government into new domains of American life. (In a remarkable moment of foreshadowing, one North Carolina editor even referred to the broad regulatory authority exercised by Lincoln's government as a "New Deal.") Thus, the Civil War and its aftermath saw a radical expansion in the breadth and depth of federal law unrelated to the new constitutional amendments, which provoked its own uptick in litigation, whether to enforce these new laws or to defend against their enforcement.[22]

In response to both of these developments, Congress radically expanded the jurisdiction of federal courts, and of the Supreme Court in particular. In 1867, for instance, Congress for the first time gave federal courts the power to review criminal convictions by state courts through writs of habeas corpus—a legal tool by which a prisoner could bring a civil suit to challenge the result of a criminal trial. Congress also expanded the grounds by which state court decisions could be appealed to the Supreme Court to include certain claims arising under the new constitutional amendments. In 1871, Congress authorized civil suits by any person who claimed that their federal rights had been violated by those acting "under color of" state law, from sheriffs to state election officials to state university administrators. And in 1875, Congress finally allowed federal courts to hear *any* suit based upon federal law—so long as the amount in controversy was more than $500. As the Supreme Court itself would note a century later, "With this latter enactment, the lower federal courts ceased to be restricted tribunals of fair dealing between citizens of different states and became the primary and powerful reliances for vindicating every right given by the Constitution, the laws, and treaties of the United States." Virtually overnight, these developments led to a sharp uptick in the volume of cases brought to the federal courts each year.[23]

It wasn't just the lower courts that saw a dramatically expanding workload. By 1890, the Supreme Court's docket had three times as many cases on it as it did in 1870, and it still wasn't able to hear all the cases that it was, by law, obligated to eventually decide. With *1,800* pending appeals, some estimates projected that the Court was running more than three years behind in its work. Modest reforms to further tamp down the justices' circuit-riding duties and to increase the amount in controversy required for most appeals to the Supreme Court were simply overwhelmed by the explosion in federal litigation.[24]

Finally, Congress went back to the drawing board. In the Evarts Act (the Judiciary Act of 1891), Congress created nine standalone circuit courts, staffed by standalone circuit judges, to hear appeals from district courts. By empowering circuit court judges to handle almost all of the new courts' business, the law effectively absolved the Supreme Court justices of their remaining circuit-riding responsibilities. But most importantly, the Evarts Act for the first time gave the justices discretion over whether to hear four specific categories of appeals by deciding whether to grant a "writ of certiorari." The four categories included state-law disputes between citizens of different states; suits under the customs and patent laws; federal criminal appeals; and maritime disputes. At the time, these were hardly viewed as the most important cases on the Court's docket, so they were good fodder for the certiorari experiment. In these relatively less important cases, the Supreme Court still had to hear at least some of the appeal if the lower courts wanted them to; the 1891 act also allowed circuit courts to "certify" a particular legal question for the Supreme Court's resolution, rather than an entire dispute, which would require the Court to consider that legal question. Certiorari, then, was only for cases in which the new courts of appeals both decided a matter incorrectly *and* declined to certify the relevant matter for appeal—for cases that the justices believed to be worth their time even though the lower courts did not.[25]

In the first two years after the bill was enacted, the justices granted only two such discretionary appeals, stressing in the first that "this branch of our jurisdiction should be exercised sparingly and with great caution." And in a quiet precedent that would become far more important later on, the Court inaugurated the practice of offering no explanation when it denied certiorari, on the theory that any explanation could be viewed as providing, if not requiring, the exact labor-intensive substantive resolution that the power to deny certiorari was supposed to avoid. Faced with a dispute that just was not important enough to trouble the justices, the Court could allow the circuit court to have the last word without having to issue a ruling that would, in its mere existence, defeat that purpose.[26]

The 1891 act was directed at federal court reforms. But a separate issue soon began to rear its head in state courts. From 1789, with passage of the Judiciary Act of that year, through the end of the nineteenth century, the Supreme Court could only hear appeals from state courts if those courts had ruled *against* claims based on a federal law or the Constitution. If state courts relied on implausible or even preposterous readings of federal law to *grant* relief (holding, for instance, that federal law created a novel right to relief), the Supreme Court was powerless to stop it. Ironically, the Fourteenth Amendment, by giving citizens new constitutional protections against their own states, had exacerbated that problem by giving state courts a new federal hook for striking down state laws.

One especially prominent example came in 1911, when the New York Court of Appeals, the highest court of what was then the nation's largest state, struck down the first workers' compensation statute in the country. According to the state court, the Due Process Clause of the Fourteenth Amendment protected the right of employers to bargain with their employees, including the right to agree *not* to provide compensation for workplace injuries. Because federal rights had been vindicated, the US Supreme Court had no power to disagree. The decision in *Ives* v. *South Buffalo Railway*, and the problem it highlighted, provoked Congress three years later to authorize Supreme Court review of all state court rulings resting on federal law. But mindful of the increasing size of the justices' docket, Congress specified that these new cases could be taken up only via certiorari. Thus, Congress expanded the Court's ability to review state courts, but only when the justices wanted to, which turned out to be quite often. By the time Taft assumed the Court's center seat in the summer of 1921, the workload was ticking back up, approaching pre-1891 levels.[27]

These technical changes to the Supreme Court's jurisdiction meant that the Court was soon reviewing a far broader array of federal (and, increasingly, state) regulations. In addition to the pitched constitutional disputes of the Progressive era, World War I provoked an array of novel legal questions, including First Amendment challenges to prosecutions brought under the ancient Sedition Act and the brand-new Espionage Act. The Eighteenth Amendment, which kicked off Prohibition, and the Volstead Act (or National Prohibition Act), which provided for its enforcement, provoked myriad new questions about Congress's ability to regulate purely private conduct, such as the consumption of alcohol. Even professional sports were on the Court's docket, including the justices' 1922 decision, in *Federal Baseball Club of Baltimore* v. *National League*, that, to this day, uniquely (and incoherently) exempts baseball from federal antitrust law. The country may have reached its geographic limits, but the expansion of the economy and the concomitant uptick in regulation of private activity by state and federal governments meant that judicial dockets across the country only continued to grow. Most of these disputes were still subject to the Court's mandatory review, even after the 1891 reforms, and so its docket, too, kept expanding. When Taft joined the Court, roughly three out of every four cases on its docket was one that the justices had to hear. He set immediately to work to increase the Court's autonomy and independence, by, among other things, decreasing its caseload.[28]

These efforts culminated on February 13, 1925, the day on which, according to Supreme Court scholar Ed Hartnett, "the modern Supreme Court was born." On that day, President Coolidge signed the Judiciary Act of 1925 into law. The new law was already known far more widely as the "Judges' Bill," but a better name might have been "Taft's Bill." In every way that matters, the most important statutory reform in the Supreme Court's history was the result of years of careful public and behind-the-scenes maneuvering by its new chief justice—efforts that were designed to fundamentally transform the Court's institutional role by technically transforming its docket.[29]

Taft had been pushing to expand the Court's discretion to turn away appeals without deciding them since before his presidency. In an influential 1908 article published while he was running for the White House, he had argued that the Supreme Court's function was *not* to resolve individual cases, but rather, to "cover the whole field of law upon the subject involved." In a 1910 speech as president, Taft directly connected the vision of the Supreme Court as a general expositor of legal principles to its ability to exercise discretionary review over most appeals. And after joining the faculty at Yale Law School at the end of his presidency, Taft explicitly urged Congress, in 1916, to do away with the requirement that the justices hear appeals except in cases involving interpretations of the federal Constitution. Once he was on the Court, he began quietly amassing data to demonstrate both the growth of the Court's docket and the deleterious impact it had on the justices' ability to do their jobs.[30]

Taft wasn't alone in his concerns; by the time he joined the Court, at least three other justices were informally considering potential changes to the Court's jurisdiction. But it was Taft who seized the initiative. In December 1921, less than five months after his swearing-in, he wrote to Senator Albert Cummins (R-IA), who was soon to become chairman of the powerful Judiciary Committee, and Solicitor General James Beck outlining the shell of what would become the Judges' Bill. In general, the idea was to capitalize upon the 1891 introduction of certiorari and its modest expansion in 1914. The prior two bills had made their cautious *additions* to the Court's jurisdiction conditioned on the justices' assent. Now, though, Taft wanted Congress to give the Court discretion over whether to hear most of the appeals it was then required to decide—all except those in which a lower court had invalidated a state or federal law on constitutional grounds, or those in which a lower federal court certified a specific legal question (as opposed to an entire appeal) to the justices.[31]

Three months later, Taft publicly testified before Congress on the need for such legislation. And although many contemporaries credited Justice Willis Van Devanter as the lead author of the reforms (Van Devanter foremost among them), that may have partly been because of how hard Taft worked behind the scenes to reinforce such a misimpression. As Taft explained in a letter to a friend in early 1924, he had tried to publicly minimize his own role because "there are a number who object to any activity on my part in matters of legislation," not least because of Taft's widely perceived hostility to the Progressives and his open and consistent support for business interests.[32]

Regardless of who could claim primary authorship of the bill, Taft was its principal salesman, not just in publicly supporting the version drafted by the justices, but in pushing back against competing proposals behind the scenes. The most prominent alternative was one offered by the American Bar Association, which, among other things, would have added seats to the

Court, and had the justices resolve appeals the same way the circuit courts did—in randomly assigned three-judge panels, rather than with every judge hearing every case. Taft also took the lead in responding to the bill's critics, of whom there were more in Congress than he had expected. Although the criticisms ran the gamut, two concerns predominated. First, some argued that giving the Court discretion to pick and choose its cases would deprive most litigants of their right to Supreme Court review, leaving the last word on important questions of federal law to lower courts notwithstanding the Founders' rationale for creating "one Supreme Court." As alarming a prospect as this was in cases coming through the lower federal courts, it was even more troubling for cases coming from state courts, in which a summary denial of review by the Supreme Court would mean that *no* federal court ever heard the matter.[33]

Second, some feared that the justices could easily abuse such discretion. They might refuse to hear not just frivolous appeals (the typical justification for the reform), but meritorious ones as well. If a lower court reached an incorrect legal result that produced a policy outcome the justices preferred, denying certiorari would allow them to avoid the conflict between their legal principles and their politics. More than that, numerous members of Congress openly worried, the justices could use certiorari as an excuse to pay less attention to entire classes of cases than they deserved, including appeals in criminal cases and suits by unpopular plaintiffs; they might reflexively deny review of those disputes without regard to the strength of any individual case. Indeed, the Judges' Bill was working its way through Congress at the height of what's known as the "*Lochner* era"—a period beginning with the Supreme Court's *Lochner* v. *New York* ruling in 1905, in which the justices were especially hostile to a wide array of state and federal economic regulation. (In *Lochner* itself, a 5–4 Court struck down New York's minimum wage and maximum hour laws for bakers on the ground that they interfered with the "liberty of contract.") At least some of Congress's hostility to Taft's proposals stemmed from the specter of giving *that* Court even more power.[34]

In an attempt to assuage those concerns, Taft lobbied many of the relevant players, from the American Bar Association to President Coolidge himself. In these discussions, Taft downplayed the criticisms, criticized the competing proposals, and reiterated the imperative for reform. By all accounts, a passage of Coolidge's first State of the Union Address in December 1923 arguing in favor of increasing the Court's discretion came directly from Taft's hand. And when Coolidge was elected in 1924, at least in part by opposing Progressive Wisconsin governor Bob La Follette's proposals to radically curb the Supreme Court's powers, the moment was at hand for Congress to formally embrace Taft's designs.[35]

To seal the deal, Taft joined three other justices in again publicly appearing before Congress in late 1924 and early 1925 in support of the bill, insisting that the justices would exercise their discretion carefully and prudentially, and that the purpose of the bill was merely to spare the Court from having to waste limited resources unnecessarily. He even pressured Justice Louis Brandeis, the staunchest opponent of the bill inside the Court, into not going public with his objections. With Taft corresponding with key senators and negotiating last-minute amendments, public opposition eventually collapsed. As the seminal contemporaneous study of the affair concluded, senators "deferred to the prestige of the Supreme Court and its Chief Justice, whose energetic espousal largely helped to realize the Court's proposal." The Judges' Bill—and, with it, Chief Justice Taft's particular and distinctly modern version of the Supreme Court's role in the constitutional system more generally—was now law.[36]

The results of Taft's quest to give the Court "absolute and arbitrary discretion" were immediate. As Hartnett has noted, "In 1924, 40% of the cases filed in the Supreme Court were within the Court's obligatory jurisdiction, with 60% of the filings left to the Court's discretion to decide whether to decide. In 1930, the percentage of obligatory filings fell to 15%, with 85% left to the Court's discretion."[37]

Remarkably, especially given the concerns raised during the drafting process, Congress left it to the Court to articulate the criteria that would govern when it would choose (and how many votes it would take) to grant certiorari. To this day, those criteria remain largely unchanged. The Court has two principal grounds for granting review. One involves cases in which two or more federal circuit courts and/or state supreme courts have reached different interpretations of the same federal law. The other involves cases in which a lower court "has decided an important question of federal law that has not been, but should be, settled by this Court, or has decided an important federal question in a way that conflicts with relevant decisions of this Court." The key here is that it's not enough that a lower court incorrectly resolved a factual dispute or reached the wrong answer on a question of federal law.

Thus, absent a division among lower courts, for a Supreme Court to take a case on appeal, it must involve an "important" question of federal (rather than state) law, with the "importance" of the matter left to the subjective determination of the justices, at least four of whom have to vote in favor of taking the case for certiorari to be "granted." But even if all nine justices agree that a case meets these criteria, there is still no formal requirement that the Court grant certiorari. Just as Taft had intended, the Judges' Bill dramatically expanded the Supreme Court's discretion to choose which cases it would and would not decide based upon criteria that the Court itself would both articulate and enforce.[38]

Taft had two more jurisdictional tricks up his sleeve. And he soon played both of them. First, as early as 1928, the justices began using certiorari to choose not only which cases to hear, but which questions to address within those cases. A prominent early illustration of this phenomenon came in that year's ruling in *Olmstead* v. *United States*, a landmark case about whether police could use the nascent technology of wiretaps to listen in on private phone calls without a search warrant. In a 5–4 decision, the Court, through an opinion by Taft, held that they could (it would reverse course in 1967). Because the appeal came from the lower federal courts, not state courts, whether to hear the case at all was a matter left to the justices' discretion under the Judges' Bill. And in granting review, the Court limited its consideration "to the single question whether the use of evidence of private telephone conversations . . . intercepted by means of wire tapping, amounted to a violation of the Fourth and Fifth Amendments."[39]

Three of the four dissenting justices objected that Roy Olmstead's conviction (for a Prohibition violation) could be overturned without deciding that question. Because the federal officers who conducted the wiretap had violated state law by trespassing on the phone company's property, the dissenters' view was that the evidence couldn't be used against Olmstead regardless of whether the wiretap violated the federal Constitution. Olmstead would still have won, so resolving the Fourth Amendment question would not have been necessary. Taft responded that the state law question wasn't properly before the Court. That was true enough, but only because of how the Court had chosen to exercise its newfound discretion.[40]

The understanding that the Court grants review of questions, and not cases, is well enshrined today; by rule, the first page of a cert. petition must list the "Question(s) Presented." But it was brand-new in *Olmstead*. In the English common law judicial practice from which it was borrowed, a "writ of certiorari" issued by a superior court to a lower court brought the entire case with it. In thirty-four years of experience under the 1891 Judiciary Act, which had first authorized certiorari in at least some cases, no justice had ever argued that Congress had departed from that understanding. And, most strikingly, in lobbying for the Judges' Bill, Taft himself had suggested that one reason for expanding certiorari to include cases from lower federal courts was that, unlike in appeals from state courts (in which the justices were limited to reviewing questions of federal law), in cases from lower federal courts, the justices' "power of review extends to the whole case and *every question presented in it*" (emphasis mine). In other words, Taft had defended the expansion of certiorari partly on the grounds that, because any appeal from a lower federal court required the justices to review the whole case, the justices should be able to choose which full appeals to hear. That he so quickly retreated from that position in practice is hard to view as a belated change of heart rather than a deliberate bait and switch.[41]

Taft's motives aside, *Olmstead* established the now settled precedent that, in Hartnett's words, "the Supreme Court does not so much grant certiorari to particular cases, but rather to particular questions." As in *Olmstead*, that can put the Court in the awkward—or, for the more cynical, advantageous—position of resolving major constitutional questions in cases in which those questions don't actually have to be decided. More than that, the Court not only quickly cemented the practice of limiting every grant of certiorari to individual questions (a practice it follows to this day), but would eventually, in a growing number of cases, write its own questions, in lieu of the questions presented by the petitioner, and then "grant" review of them. Rather than taking up an entire case, or even the specific questions framed by the parties, the justices could choose to hear only a question that *they* brought up. Not even Taft was ever quite that bold; the practice would not begin to surface until the 1960s.[42]

What's more, the "limits" on limited grants of certiorari were a one-way ratchet. As *Olmstead* demonstrated, the Court was not required to decide anything other than the questions it agreed to review in a particular case. But it was free to do so if it wanted to. Thus, when Mississippi first asked the Supreme Court to take up *Dobbs* v. *Jackson Women's Health Organization*, the 2022 abortion case, it pointedly did not ask the justices (and the justices did not agree) to revisit *Roe* v. *Wade*; that came later—and, it should be said, only after Justice Barrett had replaced Justice Ginsburg. In other words, limited grants of certiorari do not actually limit the Court to deciding the questions on which certiorari has been granted—unless, as in *Olmstead*, the justices *want* to be so constrained.[43]

Taft's second trick was introducing a newfangled type of discretion for the Court to exercise even over those appeals it still was theoretically required to hear, the most significant body of which involved appeals from state court decisions rejecting federal claims, including most direct appeals in state criminal cases. In 1928 (the same year as *Olmstead*), the Court issued a new rule requiring parties in appeals that the Court had to hear to file a "jurisdictional statement." Such statements were to set forth in detail the basis for the Supreme Court's mandatory appellate review—for instance, the fact that a lower court had struck down a state or federal law on constitutional grounds.

Styled as a housekeeping measure, the rule was universally understood to introduce an additional procedural layer to mandatory appeals, and, with it, at least a modicum of discretion on the Court's part. By adding a formal requirement that the appealing party had to establish the basis for the Court's mandatory appellate jurisdiction, the new rule gave the justices a way to dismiss appeals at their inception, rather than only after full briefing and argument. Thus, if a mandatory appeal presented a dispute that the justices did not want to resolve for whatever reason, they could dodge it by simply issuing a cursory order stating that it failed to present the kind of substantial federal question on which their mandatory jurisdiction depended.

The first full term in which the rule was on the books, the justices used it to dismiss thirty-six putatively mandatory appeals. By 1945, one of the Court's deputy clerks would publicly acknowledge that "jurisdictional statements and petitions for certiorari now stand on practically the same footing." Moreover, like orders exercising the Court's discretion to deny certiorari, orders dismissing appeals because of defects in the jurisdictional statement were unsigned and unexplained beyond a formulaic recitation that the appeal was dismissed "for want of a substantial federal question."[44]

And because a dismissal for want of jurisdiction wasn't subject to review by anyone else, whether a jurisdictional statement actually failed to present a substantial federal question was entirely in the eyes of the justices; sometimes, the Court could (and would) dismiss an appeal that unquestionably posed a substantial federal question, aided by the fact that it didn't have to explain itself. Like the ability to grant certiorari only to specific questions rather than entire cases, this development was, to quote the celebrated federal courts scholar Herbert Wechsler, "lawless"—a judge-made expansion of the Court's discretion that had never been sanctioned by Congress. That said, it is impossible to think that the timing, coming so soon on the heels of the Judges' Bill, was a coincidence. Having explicitly been granted a significant amount of discretion by Congress in 1925, there was little reason for the justices to shy away from implicitly seizing more.[45]

Again, an illustrative case proves the point. On the heels of the Court's pathbreaking 1954 decision in *Brown* v. *Board of Education*, which held that racially segregated public schools violated the Equal Protection Clause of the Fourteenth Amendment, litigants tried to use *Brown* to challenge Virginia's anti-miscegenation statute, which banned all marriages between a white person and a member of any other race. Because *Naim* v. *Naim* (1956) came to the Supreme Court from the Virginia state courts, and because those courts had rejected the plaintiff's federal constitutional claim, the appeal was well within the Court's mandatory appellate jurisdiction even after the Judges' Bill. But in a cryptic, unsigned order, the Court ducked, refusing to decide the appeal because of claimed defects in the record that have generally been described as "absurd" and "fictitious."[46]

The real reason for ducking, as became clear later, was that Justice Felix Frankfurter didn't think the Court had the political wherewithal to take up anti-miscegenation laws so soon after *Brown*. As Justice Tom C. Clark privately put it, "One bombshell at a time is enough." In a case like *Naim*, the growth of discretion allowed the Court to at least superficially save face—and, more importantly, save its capital—for another day. For interracial couples hoping to marry in Virginia, that day would not come until twelve years later, 1967, when the justices unanimously struck down anti-miscegenation laws in *Loving* v. *Virginia*.[47]

History repeated itself five years after *Loving*, when same-sex couples brought suit arguing that the Court's recognition of a constitutional right to marriage in the Virginia case applied to them as well. As in *Naim*, the state courts rejected the argument. As in *Naim*, the plaintiffs in *Baker* v. *Nelson*, decided in Minnesota in 1971, invoked the Court's mandatory appellate jurisdiction in cases in which state courts rejected federal claims. And, as in *Naim*, the justices used their self-invented discretion to sidestep the issue in 1972, holding only that "the appeal is dismissed for want of a substantial federal question." Unlike denials of certiorari, though, these orders *were* treated as precedential by lower courts—not for *why* the plaintiffs lost, but at least for the summary conclusion that the plaintiffs had no claim in the first place. This time, it would take forty-three years—until lower courts forced the Court's hand—for the justices to revisit the issue, in *Obergefell* v. *Hodges*.[48]

The rise of the Court's discretion over its docket coincided with the birth of what's generally viewed as "modern" constitutional law. In a series of cases beginning in 1937, the Supreme Court fundamentally reconceived its role in enforcing the Constitution against state and federal government actors. Part of that reconceptualization included a repudiation of the aggressive judicial protection of economic rights, such as the right of employers to pay whatever wages the market would bear, that had dominated the first decades of the twentieth century—and in which Taft had been an active participant. And part of it saw the Court shift gears toward more protection of the rights of defendants in both federal and state criminal proceedings, as well as toward the prohibition of discrimination against members of "discrete and insular" minority groups, all while generally embracing judicial deference to government action in other spheres.[49]

In his canonical study of the Judges' Bill (and Taft's role in bringing it off), Hartnett tied the rise of the Court's discretion to the rise, not long thereafter, of this modern understanding of US constitutional law, in which the primary purpose of judicial review is to protect individual rights and subordinated minorities while otherwise deferring to democratic processes. A Court with more time on its hands, and with more of an ability to decide which cases to hear and to not hear, is necessarily better situated for pursuing long-term substantive goals than one that is limited to simply reacting to each case as it comes in. Eventually, justices would begin publicly encouraging litigants to bring certain kinds of claims to the Court, presumably because some number of justices wanted the opportunity to decide those issues and were now empowered to do so.[50]

Just as significant, as the *Naim* case illustrated, was the Court's growing power to *not* decide cases. In his influential 1962 book *The Least Dangerous Branch*, constitutional law scholar Alexander Bickel extolled what he dubbed "the passive virtues," that is, the "wide area of choice open to the Court in deciding whether, when, and how much to adjudicate." Bickel's thesis was that by denying certiorari or sidestepping mandatory appeals in cases such as *Naim*, the justices were in fact reinforcing their formal and moral authority in at least two respects. Most directly, the fewer cases the Court decided each term, the more time the justices would have to look carefully through lower-court decisions to find the ones they most desired to review on appeal, and the more time they would have to spend on each case, so that broader (and, perhaps, better-reasoned) constitutional principles could be expounded. As constitutional scholar Gerald Gunther wrote of Bickel, his was an "emphasis on principle as the highest Court duty, but only in a limited sphere of Court actions; the 100% insistence on principle, 20% of the time."[51]

The power to not decide cases also meant that the justices could hand down decisions opening new frontiers in constitutional law without fearing that such rulings would inundate them with follow-on cases. For instance, as the Supreme Court gradually began to apply the Bill of Rights to the states, the power to choose which cases to take up, and which rights to "incorporate" against the states, almost certainly made it easier for the justices to pursue the project than if their first decision applying a constitutional right to the states had immediately required them to decide dozens (if not hundreds) more. And the more disputes that the Court stayed out of, the more it would appear to be acting responsibly and not overstepping its authority vis-à-vis the other branches of the federal government and the states. For Bickel, the rise of certiorari not only gave the justices more power in choosing which cases (and which issues) to decide, but also gave them more power anytime they chose to do nothing.[52]

Bickel framed his thesis as a not-so-subtle warning to the Warren Court (during Chief Justice Earl Warren's tenure, 1953–1969), which he viewed as moving too quickly to embrace civil rights and new constitutional protections for civil rights plaintiffs and criminal defendants. But the mindset he encouraged persisted even as the Court began turning sharply to the right in the 1970s. Perhaps no set of cases better drives the point home than the Court's noninvolvement in Vietnam. Indeed, between 1965 and 1973, the Court found virtually every conceivable way (and, as the Cambodia bombing episode reveals, some previously inconceivable ones) to avoid deciding the merits of fundamental questions about the legal nature or scope of the Vietnam War.

True, the Court heard various disputes related to the war. Some of those, like the Pentagon Papers Case (*New York Times Company* v. *United States* in 1971), *Cohen* v. *California* (also in 1971, in which a protester was prosecuted for nothing more than walking through a courtroom wearing a "Fuck the Draft" jacket), and *United States* v. *O'Brien* (a 1968 case about burning draft cards), made important contributions to our constitutional doctrine. But every time a litigant, including the Commonwealth of Massachusetts, which tried to invoke the Court's original jurisdiction in one exceptional case, sought to contest the legality of the United States' activities in Southeast Asia, or the means by which soldiers were conscripted, the Court ducked, refusing to review lower-court decisions, either through denials of certiorari or dismissals of mandatory appeals.[53]

Many of the Court's decisions not to decide provoked pointed dissents. But those dissents had no visible effect on the Court's majority, which hardened against intervention as the war dragged on. If the only options for the Court in ruling on these cases were to provide legal sanction for the government's military operations in Southeast Asia or to reject them, the only winning move, from the Court's perspective—to borrow from the 1984 movie *War Games*—was "not to play."[54]

By 1971, the idea that the Supreme Court should have the power to pick and choose which cases it heard, and which issues it decided within those cases, had become an article of faith. Perhaps the best evidence of its ubiquity was that it even pervaded that part of the Court's jurisdiction that had *never* been thought to be up to Congress—the justices' increasingly obscure "original" jurisdiction to act as a trial court of first impression, rather than an appeals court, in cases involving states or foreign ambassadors. Thus, in *Ohio* v. *Wyandotte Chemicals Corporation*, the Supreme Court refused to allow Ohio to bring a suit directly in the Supreme Court against out-of-state chemical companies that were allegedly responsible for mercury pollution of Ohio's rivers. Because Ohio was the plaintiff, the case clearly fell within the constitutional grant of original jurisdiction, a grant the Supreme Court had long held that Congress could neither expand nor contract. But as Justice John Marshall Harlan II wrote for the Court, it wasn't that Ohio's suit fell outside of the Court's jurisdiction; it was that it was a suit that the Court simply didn't need to hear: "In our opinion, we may properly exercise such discretion, not simply to shield this Court from noisome, vexatious, or unfamiliar tasks, but also, and we believe principally, as a technique for promoting and furthering the assumptions and value choices that underlie the current role of this Court in the federal system."

Harlan did not identify *whose* "assumptions and value choices" should inform the Court's exercise of its discretion, but the implication was obvious: he meant the Court's. *Wyandotte* thus said out loud what a half-century of practice under the Judges' Bill had implied: that underneath the Court's increasing exercise of discretion were the justices' personal preferences for which cases were—and were not—worth their time. Here, in print, was the manifestation of Taft's vision.[55]

And deciding a suit between a state and private parties that was almost certain to turn on questions of state—rather than federal—law, and that could also have been brought in the lower courts, was, from the Court's point of view, inconsistent with those assumptions and value choices. The *Wyandotte* ruling was yet another step along the same path: the justices retained the power to hear such a suit if ever they wanted to, but whether to do so was, and would be, entirely up to them. With amorphous standards invented by the justices to circumscribe that discretion, rather than black-letter rules legislated by Congress, it could hardly be a surprise that the justices increasingly accused each other of manipulating (or, at least, misapplying) their standards for whether to hear a case to suit whatever their aims happened to be.[56]

To drive home just how far the justices saw their discretion as extending, they would even apply it not long after *Wyandotte* to cases brought by states against *other states*. Unlike *Wyandotte*, which Ohio could have brought in the lower federal courts before appealing an adverse ruling to the Supreme Court, in disputes in which *both* parties are states, the Supreme Court's original jurisdiction is not just original; it is also exclusive of any other court in the country. Thus, when one state sues another, it's the Supreme Court or bust. After *Wyandotte*, it was increasingly "bust." The Court never bothered to explain *why* it had the power to decline to hear those disputes; it summarily dismissed them through orders that were invariably unexplained and unsigned. Perhaps the most famous of these was the December 11, 2020, order tossing Texas's challenge to the 2020 presidential election results in four states President Biden won. Although some were surprised to learn for the first time that the justices didn't have to hear cases like Texas's, that ruling was entirely consistent with the Court's post-*Wyandotte* approach.[57]

Of course, if Congress had a problem with the Court exercising its discretion in this way, it had the unquestioned power to tighten up the rules. Instead, through a series of reforms beginning in the mid-1970s and culminating in the late 1980s, Congress went the other way. In 1925, Taft had defended the expansion of discretion as housekeeping—a means of freeing the Court of the burden of frivolous appeals. Six decades later, everyone understood what it would mean in practice to give the justices near-complete control over their docket. Because of the continued proliferation of federal laws, and of claims based on federal constitutional rights, the Court was being forced, in the words of legendary court of appeals judge Learned Hand, to "ration justice." The only question was whether the rationing should be self-imposed or dictated by statute. By the time the Supreme Court Case Selections Act of 1988 came before Congress, it was well established that the justices interpreted their certiorari power to pick and choose issues within cases, and not just the cases themselves. Thus, unlike in 1925, when it could fairly be said that the Court had pulled a fast one on Congress, the transfer of power here was in broad daylight.[58]

In the 1988 act, Congress all but finished Taft's work. The three-page statute converted all but one of the remaining fonts of the Supreme Court's appellate jurisdiction into discretionary review, a change that had the most immediate effect on appeals from state courts. Only those rare cases that still had to be brought in the first instance before special "three-judge" federal courts, which Congress had limited in 1976 to challenges to the reapportionment of congressional districts and certain campaign finance disputes, were still subject to "mandatory" review. The impact was immediate. Almost overnight, the number of signed opinions handed down by the Court dropped precipitously, from well north of 150 substantive rulings each term to fewer than 90. By the late 1990s, the Court was issuing fewer signed rulings than it had at any time since the 1860s. Chief Justice William Rehnquist had promised Congress, when it was considering the 1988 bill, that eliminating mandatory appeals would allow the Court to grant certiorari in *more* cases. The reality has been decidedly to the contrary.[59]

In its October 2019 Term, for example, the Supreme Court handed down signed rulings in merits cases in only 53 cases (the fewest since the Civil War), representing fewer than 1 percent of the total appeals that it received. Some of that could be chalked up to the COVID pandemic, which, among other things, led the justices to postpone arguments in 10 cases to the October 2020 Term. But there were only 56 signed decisions in that next term, and 58 in the term after that. (The average was in the eighties as late as the 2000s.) Looking at the raw data alone, the effect of Congress's complete transfer of docket control is undeniable.[60]

But the story is not just that the Court is hearing far fewer cases, or that it's picking and choosing which cases to hear, and which issues to hear within them; it's that the demise of the merits docket has significant—and deleterious—downstream effects. For instance, plaintiffs seeking to recover damages from government officers who violate their constitutional rights, and prisoners seeking to attack a state court conviction in federal court, must show that the relevant action they are challenging was in violation of "clearly established" law. The fewer cases the Supreme Court takes up, the fewer opportunities it has to clearly establish new legal principles, and so the more difficult it is for civil plaintiffs and criminal defendants to prevail. (One of the categories in which the docket has shrunk the most involves appeals from state criminal convictions—the best opportunity for criminal defendants to argue that their convictions ran afoul of their constitutional rights. During the October 2021 Term, for instance, the Court heard only two such cases.) More generally, the fewer the cases the Court is deciding, the more the conflicts between lower-court decisions (and the more errors in lower-court rulings) are necessarily being left unaddressed. And all of this is without regard to the rise, at much the same time, of increasingly significant rulings through the kind of emergency orders that have helped to give the "shadow docket" its name.[61]

Lastly, one cannot truly understand the centrality of certiorari without understanding the extent to which it was hardly a foregone conclusion. For 101 years, the Supreme Court operated, if not always efficiently, without it; it operated without much of a certiorari practice for even longer; and it operated with a robust, if increasingly leaky, mandatory appellate docket until 1988. Nor is certiorari the only way to prevent the Court's docket from swelling beyond control. Among lots of other possible reforms, more justices could be added to handle the workload; the Court could hear most cases in three-justice panels, as is the norm in the intermediate federal appeals courts; Congress could add another layer of appeals courts to further reduce the strain on the Supreme Court; and so on. Indeed, Congress has experience adopting many of these measures, among others, to handle burgeoning caseloads in the lower courts; there is no obvious practical or constitutional reason why it couldn't pursue the same with the Supreme Court. Simply put, certiorari was not inevitable and is not set in stone. But it's also not a coincidence that its emergence coincided with the emergence of a powerful Supreme Court. The contemporary Supreme Court would be unrecognizable without certiorari; that doesn't mean it was meant to be or must always be so.[62]

In the rise of certiorari, we see how procedural technicalities and formalities can produce massive substantive results, and how, per Hartnett, "the Supreme Court's power to set its agenda may be more important than what the Court decides on the merits." We see how the Supreme Court decides cases often by not deciding them, and that not every Supreme Court decision features seventy-five-page opinions full of soaring rhetoric and penetrating legal analysis. We see how, through its internal procedures and jurisdictional rules, the Court projects and implements its broader vision of its role in our constitutional system, both in the abstract and in relation to the rest of the federal government and the states. We see how, over time, Congress has increasingly left the Court to its own devices. And we see how norms become entrenched even as their usage expands, so that the practice of not providing explanations or vote counts when denying (or granting) certiorari today feels as if it's been true since the time of Henry IV.

But, most of all, the rise of certiorari shows how more of the Court's most important work has moved increasingly into the shadows. That's not just because the orders granting or denying certiorari are themselves inscrutable, but because the drift toward certiorari, and toward an unconstrained agenda-setting power, was gradually accomplished through a series of technical statutory reforms and subtle internal shifts in the Court's own internal procedures and published jurisprudence. These developments were not formally out of the public's sight, but they might as well have been. One who reads the Supreme Court's rules might understand what the justices say the criteria are for granting certiorari, but out of context, they'd have little understanding of what that means in practice, or how satisfaction of those criteria is to be demonstrated in individual cases. The justices today have the power to control their docket, and thereby choose their (and the Court's) destiny, in ways that the public doesn't understand and that the Court seldom confronts—and, if anything, regularly avoids even acknowledging. Every other aspect of the work of the contemporary Supreme Court is an outgrowth of that fundamental, but hardly innate, principle.

Chief Justice Taft would have approved.

## CHAPTER 2

# SUBSTANCE IN PROCEDURE

### HOW THE COURT DECIDES WITHOUT DECIDING

The conventional wisdom is that the Supreme Court legalized same-sex marriage on June 26, 2015. That's when it handed down its decision in *Obergefell* v. *Hodges*, which held, by a 5–4 vote, that state bans on same-sex marriage violate the Due Process Clause of the Fourteenth Amendment. But the conventional wisdom is, at best, misleading; *Obergefell* legalized same-sex marriage in only thirteen states. By the time of the 2015 ruling, same-sex couples were legally getting married in thirty-seven states (not to mention the District of Columbia and Guam). And the Supreme Court's use of the shadow docket was directly or indirectly responsible for almost half of that total.[1]

Of the thirty-seven states to achieve marriage equality before *Obergefell*, eleven legalized same-sex marriage through the democratic process, whether through laws adopted by their state legislatures or through amendments to state constitutions adopted by their voters.[2] In another eight states, the state supreme courts had read their *state* constitutions to require marriage equality (the Iowa Supreme Court's ruling to that effect led Iowa's voters to promptly unseat three of their justices in the next election, although the prior decision stood).[3] And because the US Supreme Court generally lacks the power to review the meaning of state laws, including state constitutions, those questions are up to the highest court of each state. Thus, starting with a landmark 2003 ruling by the Massachusetts Supreme Judicial Court, nineteen of the thirty-seven pre-*Obergefell* states had legalized same-sex marriage entirely on their own.[4]

The more interesting story, though, is the other eighteen. In each of those states, same-sex marriage became legal thanks to lower federal court rulings striking down marriage bans. A handful of states refused to appeal those rulings, allowing marriage equality by default. But most attempted to persuade the Supreme Court to take up their appeals of the lower-court decisions, and the justices refused. Those refusals then allowed the lower-court rulings to go into effect, clearing the way for same-sex partners to marry in those states, sometimes within hours of the Supreme Court's "denial of certiorari."

Thus, by the time *Obergefell* was decided, the Supreme Court had effectively legalized same-sex marriage in more states than its far-more-visible (and far-more-controversial) ruling in *Obergefell* would, and in almost as many states as had legalized it themselves. At first blush, that fact may seem deeply counterintuitive. How could the Supreme Court have a greater impact by doing nothing than by doing something? The answer takes a bit of explaining, but it is also central to understanding the implications of the rise of certiorari, and how the Supreme Court hands down the overwhelming majority of its decisions today.

As we've already seen, changes to the American legal system after the Civil War led to an explosion in federal litigation. That explosion also caused a sharp spike in appeals, first to intermediate appellate courts and then, in some cases, to the US

Supreme Court. As Congress increasingly gave the Supreme Court more control over its docket by expanding the practice of discretionary appeals through writs of certiorari, the overall number of cases reaching the Supreme Court continued to increase in rough proportion to the growth of lower-court dockets. What changed was how those cases were resolved. At the beginning of the twentieth century, the Supreme Court issued formal, substantive rulings in almost every case on its docket, more than 300 per year. A century later, roughly 99 percent of the appeals reaching the Supreme Court meet with the same cryptic nine-word fate: "The petition for a writ of certiorari is denied." During the Supreme Court's October 2014 Term, for instance, the Court considered 7,038 petitions for certiorari. It granted 71 of them, or 1.01 percent.[5]

As those nine words suggest, and as we've already seen, an order from the Supreme Court denying a petition for certiorari (a "cert. denial") almost always comes with no public explanation; no public indication of how many justices voted one way or the other; and, except in rare cases, no separate published opinions concurring in or dissenting from the Court's refusal to grant review. Sometimes, that's because the case received very little interest from the justices. It may not even have been discussed at the Court's regular Conference before it was turned away. But sometimes, the opposite is true, and certiorari is denied only after a significant amount of internal debate, politicking, and perhaps even horse-trading. The public is almost never exposed to this side of the Court's work, but that's by design. If the entire point of the shift toward a certiorari docket is to streamline the justices' consideration of appeals and free them up to devote more time to the handful of cases warranting their full attention, requiring the justices to explain their rationale for denying certiorari would defeat that purpose.

As a consequence, the justices have long insisted that when the Supreme Court issues an order denying certiorari, that ruling has no "precedential" value, meaning that it cannot be relied upon by future courts as evidence of the justices' views on the merits of the questions presented in the petition, or whether they believed that the lower-court ruling under appeal was correct. Part of that is because these rulings come as summary orders with no reasoning, so there's no precedent to be made. But part of it is because, as Justice Felix Frankfurter explained in an oft-cited 1950 opinion, there are any number of reasons why the Court might refuse to take up a discretionary appeal, many of which have *nothing* to do with whether the lower court got the matter "right." Reinforcing that understanding, individual justices will occasionally append short statements to one-line denials of certiorari stating that the denial of review was not a reflection of the Court's view of the merits. Sometimes, those statements might also signal that, in a different case, the same issue (and maybe even the same litigant) might receive a different reception; otherwise, why would a justice file such an opinion?[6]

But as the same-sex marriage cases illustrate, even if denials of certiorari are not "precedential," there are circumstances in which they can still have enormous practical impact. Sometimes, they send implicit messages both to lower courts and to policymakers about the justices' lack of appetite for particular issues, or their unwillingness to set aside lower-court judgments even on questions they have never considered. In other cases, where the lower-court ruling at issue blocked the enforcement of a state or federal law or policy, a denial of certiorari preserves that status quo; the policy remains blocked even if the reasons why the lower court froze it have not received the Supreme Court's explicit imprimatur. In general, although denials of certiorari therefore cannot be cited as proof of the Supreme Court's views on any particular issue, they regularly produce significant substantive effects by changing the status quo on the ground.

The marriage cases are a perfect illustration of this phenomenon, not because they're an outlier, but because they are an uncommonly visible example of it. Indeed, one can trace a straight line from the Supreme Court's refusal to take up seven specific appeals on a single day in October 2014 (almost nine months before the decision in *Obergefell*) to the legalization of same-sex marriage in eighteen states. But in every case—and not just highly visible ones like the marriage cases—the justices and their law clerks approach whether or not to "grant cert." with a series of strategic considerations in mind and a series of practical questions to answer, and no statute, rule, or even norm dictates their decision on any of the petitions they consider.

In *Deciding to Decide*, his landmark 1991 study based on interviews with the justices and their law clerks on the considerations that go into granting or denying certiorari, political scientist H. W. Perry described certiorari as the Court's "agenda-setting function." But it's more than that. Because of the substantive effects that even denials of certiorari repeatedly produce, the certiorari process does not just set the Supreme Court's agenda; it sets the nation's. Thus, if the story of the rise of certiorari was about how the Supreme Court seized power and docket control from Congress, the story of the marriage cases is about how the justices use that power, and about how all of the relevant actors structure their behavior in response.[7]

~

The Supreme Court always announces in advance when it is next going to hand down merits decisions. And although it never announces in advance which decisions are coming down on any given day, or how many, it does identify which session will be the last of the term. Thus, when the Court announced that Wednesday, June 26, 2013, would be the last day for handing down decisions in cases argued during the term that began in October 2012, the stage was set for the remaining three decisions in argued cases: a federal criminal case of modest broader importance, and a pair of high-profile cases about same-sex marriage.[8]

Shortly after 10:00 a.m., Chief Justice Roberts announced that Justice Anthony Kennedy would deliver the first opinion for the Court—in *United States* v. *Windsor*, a challenge to the constitutionality of the federal Defense of Marriage Act (DOMA). Signed into law by President Bill Clinton shortly before the 1996 presidential election, DOMA defined marriage for purposes of federal law as being "only a legal union between one man and one woman as husband and wife." For legal purposes, the rules governing marriages are (and always have been) up to each state, not the federal government. One of the goals of DOMA was to ensure that, even in states that allowed same-sex marriage, or at least recognized the legality of same-sex marriages performed elsewhere, same-sex married partners would be ineligible for any federal benefits relating to marriage.[9]

When Edith Windsor's legal wife, Thea Spyer, passed away in 2009, DOMA barred Windsor from claiming the federal estate tax exemption for surviving spouses—an exemption that, in her case, would have saved her over $350,000 in taxes. She promptly sued to challenge DOMA's constitutionality and won in the lower courts. The Obama administration begrudgingly appealed, and for a 5–4 majority, Justice Anthony Kennedy sided with Windsor, holding that DOMA deprived same-sex married partners of their right to equal protection of the laws under the Due Process Clause of the Fifth Amendment. Critically, Justice Kennedy's analysis relied heavily on the federal government's lack of justification for discriminating against marriages that a state had chosen to recognize.[10]

Part of Kennedy's reasoning would be repeatedly invoked in future cases:

> The class to which DOMA directs its restrictions and restraints are those persons who are joined in same-sex marriages made lawful by the State. DOMA singles out a class of persons deemed by a State entitled to recognition and protection to enhance their own liberty. It imposes a disability on the class by

> refusing to acknowledge a status the State finds to be dignified and proper. DOMA instructs all federal officials, and indeed all persons with whom same-sex couples interact, including their own children, that their marriage is less worthy than the marriages of others. The federal statute is invalid, for no legitimate purpose overcomes the purpose and effect to disparage and to injure those whom the State, by its marriage laws, sought to protect in personhood and dignity. By seeking to displace this protection and treating those persons as living in marriages less respected than others, the federal statute is in violation of the Fifth Amendment. This opinion and its holding are confined to those lawful marriages.[11]

Windsor and Spyer had been legally married in New York, and Justice Kennedy's opinion for the Court repeatedly relied upon the fact that New York recognized the marriage to explain why Congress's refusal to do so was problematic. As everyone knew, though, the bigger question was whether state bans on same-sex marriage violated the federal Constitution, and Kennedy's opinion said nothing about whether states could prohibit same-sex marriage in the first place. That question was also before the Court in another case, one that had been argued on the day before *Windsor*. A decision in that case was also expected on the morning of June 26. But as only the justices and their clerks knew until a few minutes after the decision in *Windsor* was announced, the Court was about to sidestep that question, albeit on less-than-obvious procedural grounds.[12]

At issue in the second case, *Hollingsworth* v. *Perry*, was California's Proposition 8. After the California Supreme Court had ruled in 2008 that California's same-sex marriage ban violated the California Constitution, California's voters had enacted a ballot initiative amending the California Constitution. The purpose of the amendment was to override that ruling and ensure that only marriages between men and women would be valid under state law. Two same-sex couples who wished to marry sued in San Francisco federal district court to challenge "Prop. 8" on the ground that it violated the US Constitution (which, under the Supremacy Clause, supersedes any state law with which it conflicts, even state constitutional provisions). After California state executive officials who opposed Prop. 8 refused to defend it, the district court allowed the initiative's sponsors to take charge of the defense of the ballot proposition. Judge Vaughn Walker ultimately agreed with the plaintiffs that Prop. 8 was unconstitutional because it denied equal protection to same-sex couples.[13]

The US Court of Appeals for the Ninth Circuit (the federal appeals court that covers California and ten other western states and territories) affirmed that decision, albeit on grounds that were specific to California. The court's decision played up the extent to which California alone granted same-sex couples every possible legal benefit of marriage except the license itself, whereas other states that banned same-sex marriage generally also denied same-sex couples the legal benefits of marriage. This argument was meant to serve two purposes: First, it highlighted the extent to which Prop. 8 was arbitrary; because same-sex couples in California enjoyed virtually every other benefit of marriage besides the license, withholding only the term "marriage" from them could be motivated only by animus. Second, it attempted to mitigate the nationwide significance of (and, thus, the Supreme Court's interest in) the ruling, because the court's logic could not easily be extended to other states that treated same-sex couples unfavorably in more respects. When the Supreme Court nevertheless agreed to review it, the widespread assumption was that the justices were going to weigh in, one way or the other, on whether the federal Constitution allowed states in general to prohibit same-sex marriage.[14]

Instead, the justices punted. Writing for himself and Justices Scalia, Ginsburg, Breyer, and Kagan, Chief Justice Roberts relied upon a procedural technicality. As he explained, Prop. 8's proponents were not entitled to appeal the district court's ruling because they did not have a personal stake in the outcome, and so lacked "standing." Although they were directly responsible for Prop. 8's enactment, once it became part of the California Constitution, their interest in defending it was no different from anyone else's. Thus, their appeal presented only a "generalized grievance"—a dispute the Supreme Court had long held that the Constitution forbids the federal courts from resolving.[15]

By holding that the proponents lacked standing to appeal Judge Walker's ruling invalidating Prop. 8, the Supreme Court effectively held that it lacked the authority to review the district court's decision, as well, or to decide for itself whether Prop. 8 violated the federal Constitution. As legal scholars William Eskridge and Christopher Riano pointed out in their comprehensive survey of the marriage litigation, the standing argument "appealed to justices wanting to push off the merits of marriage equality for a few more years."[16] Justice Kennedy, joined by Justices Thomas, Alito, and Sotomayor (the only time to date that those last three justices have been in dissent together), wrote a technical and tepid dissent focusing on why he thought the intervenors should have been allowed to appeal, but expressing no view on the constitutional question he thought the Court should therefore have reached.[17]

The day before *Perry* and *Windsor* were decided, same-sex marriage was recognized in only nine states. Overnight, California became the tenth by default: the Supreme Court's ruling in *Perry* not only left in place the district court's ruling striking down Prop. 8, but made it impossible for anyone else to challenge it. Same-sex couples began receiving marriage certificates in the nation's biggest state the next day. Six more states would soon follow. In four (Delaware, Minnesota, Rhode Island, and Hawaii), the state legislatures legalized same-sex marriage; in the other two (New Jersey and New Mexico), state courts held that limits on same-sex marriage violated the state constitution, rulings that could not be appealed to the US Supreme Court.[18]

The Supreme Court in *Windsor* had gone out of its way to say nothing about state marriage bans. Indeed, as Chief Justice Roberts pointed out in his dissent, the majority opinion reinforced the states' prerogative to control marriage policy. Nevertheless, Justice Kennedy's reasoning for striking down DOMA quickly became the central legal argument for challengers, who relied on it to bring new federal court lawsuits objecting to state marriage bans. If, as five justices had concluded in *Windsor*, a federal law based on animus against same-sex marriages was unconstitutional, why was the same not true of state laws that banned same-sex marriages outright? Just as the Reconstruction Amendments had been used first to attack discrimination based upon race, and later based upon sex, could they not likewise be used to attack discrimination based upon sexual orientation? *Windsor* suggested that they could, and within weeks, new challenges were filed in virtually every state with a marriage ban still on the books.[19]

Justice Antonin Scalia had also noted these implications of his colleagues' majority ruling in *Windsor*. His blistering (and, to some, homophobic) dissent had specifically decried them. Indeed, proponents of same-sex marriage would even cite his dissent as proof that the holding in *Windsor* demanded that state marriage bans be overturned. And the lower courts generally agreed. The first lower court to apply *Windsor* to a state marriage ban, perhaps surprisingly, was in Utah. On December 20, 2013, Utah district court judge Robert Shelby ruled that Utah's Amendment 3—a 2004 ballot initiative amending the Utah Constitution to define marriage as being only between a man and a woman—violated both the Due Process Clause and the Equal Protection Clause of the federal Constitution's Fourteenth Amendment. The crux of Judge Shelby's lengthy and careful analysis in the case, captioned *Kitchen* v. *Herbert*, was that the same logic that led the Supreme Court in *Windsor* to strike down DOMA applied equally to state efforts to deny same-sex couples the right to marry.[20]

What was especially significant about Judge Shelby's ruling, though, is what happened next: The plaintiffs in *Kitchen* had asked not just that Judge Shelby declare Amendment 3 to be unconstitutional, but that he issue an injunction against its enforcement. Such a court order would prohibit the defendants, including Utah governor Gary Herbert, from refusing to allow same-sex marriages. Injunctions are an especially coercive form of judicial relief, because a person who defies an injunction is subject to being held in contempt of court, and to being punished with fines and perhaps even incarceration until and unless they comply. As a result, judicial injunctions tend to produce immediate effects. Unlike a damages suit, which is meant to provide a remedy for some harm that occurred in the past, an injunction is meant to stop an ongoing harm. It's the difference between preventing your neighbor from continuing to build on your property and requiring the neighbor to pay for knocking over your fence. Damages awards can eventually be enforced by having a court seize financial assets. But injunctions tend to compel more immediate enforcement, because the wrongful conduct is ongoing. In this context, the ongoing wrongful conduct was Utah's refusal to allow same-sex couples to marry. If Judge Shelby issued an injunction, Utah would have to then either allow such marriages or face escalating court-imposed penalties.

Because Judge Shelby ruled for the plaintiffs, he entered the injunction they requested. Utah made clear that it planned to appeal Judge Shelby's ruling to the US Court of Appeals for the Tenth Circuit (which covers federal courts in Utah and four other states). But the state had initially either declined or forgotten to ask Judge Shelby to pause the effect of his ruling by issuing a stay. Usually, a trial judge who issues an injunction is also asked to consider whether the injunction should take immediate effect or instead be frozen while it is challenged on appeal. That analysis turns not only on the merits, on which the trial judge has already weighed in, but on whether, during the time it takes for an appeal to run its course, it makes more sense to allow the lower-court ruling to take effect or to leave it on hold. Without a stay, injunctions like Judge Shelby's must be followed from the moment they take effect. That's why, with reporters and photographers looking on, local officials in Salt Lake City began allowing same-sex partners to get married within hours of Judge Shelby's ruling. For only the second time (and the first since *Windsor*), a federal court had ruled that the federal Constitution protects the right of same-sex couples to marry.[21]

One day after the ruling, Utah belatedly sought a stay. But Judge Shelby denied its request. One of the factors courts must consider in deciding whether to issue a stay pending appeal is whether, without such a freeze, parties will be injured in ways that can't later be remedied, a concept the law calls "irreparable harm." If a ruling requires a party to pay money that can be recouped, it's unlikely to cause irreparable harm. But if a ruling requires a party to take action that can't be undone, like publicly revealing confidential information, that might be a reason to delay enforcement while that party appeals. In Utah, as Judge Shelby wrote on December 23, "there is no harm to the State in allowing same-sex couples to marry." The Tenth Circuit likewise refused Utah's request for a stay. One week later, Utah asked the US Supreme Court for a stay. On January 6, 2014, the justices agreed, in a summary, unsigned order with no public dissents. While Utah appealed the case to the circuit court, Judge Shelby's district court ruling would be put on hold. And yet, over the two weeks that had elapsed, 1,360 same-sex couples had been legally married in Utah. Even if Judge Shelby's ruling was later reversed, those marriages would remain on the books.[22]

After the Supreme Court's stay in the Utah case, the federal litigation challenging bans on same-sex marriage proceeded on two tracks. In some states, district courts entered injunctions blocking state marriage bans based upon the Supreme Court's reasoning in *Windsor*, and then either stayed the ruling themselves or had their ruling stayed by the court of appeals or the Supreme Court. These states, many of which had Republican governors and/or attorneys general, dug in on their efforts to challenge these rulings on appeal, whether on principle, from political expediency, or with some combination of both.[23]

In a handful of other states, mostly run by Democrats, leaders refused to appeal district court rulings blocking marriage bans. Without an appeal, there was no case for a stay. As a result, same-sex marriage became legal in Oregon on May 19, 2014, and in Pennsylvania one day later. With the Illinois legislature legalizing same-sex marriage on July 1, 2014, almost twice as many states (nineteen) had marriage equality by the summer of 2014 as had been true just one year before.[24]

But what would the Supreme Court do with those cases, like Utah's, in which the state was appealing? That question lingered all summer, especially after three federal appeals courts decided the appeals of lower-court rulings striking down state marriage bans—and each agreed with the trial courts that the bans were unconstitutional. Once again, the Utah case was first. The Tenth Circuit affirmed Judge Shelby's ruling on June 25, 2014. On July 28, the Fourth Circuit (covering Maryland, Virginia, West Virginia, North Carolina, and South Carolina) followed suit, affirming a district court ruling invalidating Virginia's ban on same-sex marriage. And on September 4, the Seventh Circuit (covering Wisconsin, Illinois, and Indiana) affirmed an injunction against Wisconsin's marriage ban. Because the Seventh and Tenth Circuits had subsequently rejected two other states' appeals, the Supreme Court was soon confronted with a total of seven petitions for certiorari from five different states, all asking the justices to resolve the marriage question one way or the other. And because states and lower courts had learned their lesson from the chaotic aftermath of the Utah case, no same-sex marriages were being performed in these states pending the outcome in the nation's capital.[25]

The seven petitions were each considered by the Supreme Court on Monday, September 29, 2014, during its "Long Conference," the name given to the justices' first formal meeting after their summer recess, at which they consider all the petitions for certiorari and other nonemergency procedural matters that have accumulated over the summer. One week later, at 9:30 a.m. on the "First Monday" of the October 2014 Term, the Court denied 1,575 petitions for certiorari. Most of the denials were not surprises. But among those rejections were all seven of the marriage cases, denials that "flabbergasted" the legal community. If that weren't surprising enough, no justice publicly noted a dissent from any of the seven orders.[26]

The Supreme Court's denials of certiorari in the marriage cases were dramatic in more ways than one. In the five states whose bans were at issue, the Court's summary orders had immediate effects. Not only did the denials of certiorari leave in place federal court rulings that had struck down marriage bans in each of those states, but the stays that were in place in those cases—court orders that had prevented those rulings from going into effect, including the Supreme Court's January 6 stay in the Utah case—immediately dissipated. By the afternoon of October 6, clerks were issuing marriage licenses to same-sex couples in Oklahoma, Utah, Virginia, and Wisconsin. In Indiana, licenses became available the following morning.[27]

But the impact went far beyond those five states. By denying certiorari, the Court had not just rejected five states' defenses of their own marriage bans; it had refused to disturb the rulings of three different federal appeals courts, which supervised the federal courts not just in those five states, but in six other states with marriage bans on the books. In each of *those* states, the court of appeals' rulings invalidating another state's marriage ban was now precedent that bound each of the federal district courts. As district courts put those appellate rulings into effect in pending suits challenging other states' marriage bans, the Supreme Court's October 6 cert. denials thus led to marriage equality in Colorado (on October 7, 2014); West Virginia (October 9); North Carolina (October 10); Wyoming (October 21); Kansas (November 12); and South Carolina (November 20). In one fell swoop, the Supreme Court's summary, unsigned, and unexplained decisions to stay out of the marriage issue on October 6 had directly legalized same-sex marriage in eleven states.[28]

And the justices soon legalized same-sex marriage in six more states. In what was surely not a coincidence of timing, the day after the Supreme Court's denials of certiorari on October 6, the Ninth Circuit reached the same conclusion as the Fourth, Seventh, and Tenth Circuits in an appeal brought by Idaho, holding that all state marriage bans—and not just California's, which it had already struck down—violated the federal Constitution. Nevada declined to pursue its own appeal further, so same-sex marriage became legal there on October 9, 2014. And when Idaho asked the Supreme Court to stay the Ninth Circuit's decision the following day, the Supreme Court refused, once more through a summary order with no noted dissents.[29]

Alaska and Arizona followed on October 17, and Montana on November 19. Even the deeply conservative Eleventh Circuit (covering Alabama, Georgia, and Florida), which would never rule on the merits of any state marriage bans, refused to pause a Florida district court ruling blocking that state's marriage ban while Florida appealed. When the Supreme Court likewise turned away Florida's attempt to freeze the district court order, it effectively legalized same-sex marriage in the nation's fourth-largest state on January 6, 2015.[30] In total, between the October 6 cert. denials and the subsequent stay denials, the Supreme Court had legalized same-sex marriage in seventeen states in exactly three months through unsigned, unexplained orders. What's more, only Justices Scalia and Thomas registered public dissents from any of the stay orders, suggesting that the rest of the Court was perfectly happy to continue this pattern, perhaps until same-sex marriage was legal nationwide. As Eskridge and Riano noted, "By voting no, the Supreme Court was in effect saying yes."[31]

But one federal appeals court had other ideas. In a lengthy ruling issued on November 6, 2014, the US Court of Appeals for the Sixth Circuit upheld marriage bans in each of its four states—Kentucky, Michigan, Ohio, and Tennessee. In its 2–1 decision, the court of appeals wrote that, despite the writing on the wall, it could not simply assume that the Supreme Court's consistent procedural actions on and after October 6 were meant to have substantive effects:

> Don't *these* denials of certiorari signal that, from the Court's perspective, the right to same-sex marriage is inevitable? Maybe; maybe not. Even if we grant the premise and assume that same-sex marriage will be recognized one day in all fifty States, that does not tell us how—whether through the courts or through democracy. And, if through the courts, that does not tell us why—whether through one theory of constitutional invalidity or another. . . . If a federal court denies the people suffrage over an issue long thought to be within their power, *they deserve an explanation*. We, for our part, cannot find one, as several other judges have concluded as well.[32] (Second emphasis mine.)

In essence, the Sixth Circuit's decision in *DeBoer* v. *Snyder* was both a loud public dissent from the Supreme Court's efforts to quietly legalize same-sex marriage through denials of certiorari and, at the same time, a fatal obstacle to the success of those efforts. The ruling created what's known informally as a "circuit split," and formally as "a decision in conflict with the decision of another United States court of appeals on the same important matter," one of the principal criteria that the Supreme Court's rules identify as justifying a grant of certiorari. Unlike many other legal systems, which separate the distinct functions of resolving disagreements among lower courts and interpreting the Constitution into two different courts, the US system intentionally combines them into what Article III of the Constitution calls "one Supreme Court." The justices are thus responsible not only for issuing authoritative interpretations of the Constitution, but also for resolving disagreements among the courts of appeals on everything from bankruptcy law to the tax code. Even if, as the October 6 denials demonstrated, the justices could sidestep the former in the case of same-sex marriage, they couldn't possibly ignore the latter.[33]

Each of the plaintiffs in *DeBoer* quickly sought review from the Supreme Court. Their petitions presented as compelling a case for certiorari as the justices ever receive: There was now a disagreement among five federal courts of appeals as to an incredibly significant constitutional question affecting millions of Americans. Only the Supreme Court could conclusively break that logjam, and only by issuing a ruling on the merits. So it was that, on January 16, 2015, the justices granted the four petitions challenging the Sixth Circuit's ruling and consolidated them into a single case. By quirk of the order in which the four separate petitions had been filed back in November, the case became known by the caption of the appeal that had been docketed first, the Ohio suit—*Obergefell* v. *Hodges*.[34]

And yet, even *after* agreeing to resolve the marriage question on the merits once and for all, the Supreme Court used an unsigned, unexplained order to legalize gay marriage in one final state. This time, it was Alabama. On January 23, 2015 (one week after the Court agreed to take up the four Sixth Circuit appeals), Alabama district court judge Callie V. S. Granade struck down her state's ban on same-sex marriage. Judge Granade stayed her ruling for fourteen days to allow either the Eleventh Circuit or the Supreme Court to extend the stay if they so desired. But the Eleventh Circuit refused on February 3, and the Supreme Court followed suit on February 9, at which point Alabama became the eighteenth state in which the Supreme Court had effectively legalized same-sex marriage, and the thirty-seventh with marriage equality, as of February 2015.[35]

This time, Justice Thomas, joined by Justice Scalia, did not just publicly note his dissent from the majority's summary, unsigned, and unexplained one-sentence order, but published a dissenting opinion memorializing his objections. In his separate statement, Thomas expressed surprise that the majority was allowing the district court's ruling to go into effect when it had just agreed to take up the same question on the merits in the Sixth Circuit cases. As he wrote, when the Court had refused to freeze lower-court rulings after the October 6 cert. denials, "there was at least an argument that the October decision justified an inference that the Court would be less likely to grant a writ of certiorari to consider subsequent petitions." A stay could be denied in those cases simply on the ground that it was unlikely that the Court would take up the appeal on the merits, which was one of the four traditional criteria for such relief. There isn't much point in pausing a ruling pending an appeal that won't be heard. But, as Thomas explained, thanks to *Obergefell*, "that argument [was] no longer credible": "The Court has now granted a writ of certiorari to review these important issues and will do so by the end of the Term."[36]

On this point, Justice Thomas was clearly correct. What, then, explained the Court's refusal to stay Judge Granade's ruling in the Alabama case while it was preparing to resolve the exact same constitutional question in *Obergefell* that she had just resolved against Alabama? The answer, in retrospect, is obvious: even though the oral argument in *Obergefell* was still well over two months away, the justices knew how they were going to rule. Before the Sixth Circuit decision, it was at least plausible that the Court had just been keeping its head down, and that its nonintervention was simply a delaying tactic, rather than an intimation of how it would eventually rule on the merits, assuming it ever had to. One could perhaps even argue that it still wasn't clear how the Court would rule as late as January 16, when it agreed to review the Sixth Circuit cases on the merits. Perhaps there was a majority to side with the Sixth Circuit in upholding state marriage bans, rather than siding with the four other circuits that had struck them down. After all, if the justices ended up deciding to uphold state marriage bans, the price would only have been akin to what happened in Utah—allowing a few thousand same-sex marriages to be performed in the interim, which at least some of the justices might have deemed worth it in exchange for trying to stay out of the matter altogether.

But the fact that the Court allowed same-sex marriages to go forward in Alabama even after formally agreeing to decide the issue in *Obergefell* was as clear a signal as the justices could possibly have sent about which way the wind was blowing. If they were planning to uphold bans like Alabama's, it would make little sense to allow same-sex marriages to proceed there for no more than five months before halting them. If same-sex marriage was soon to become the law of the land, on the other hand, why make couples wait any longer? By doing nothing, it turns out that the Supreme Court had already done quite a lot.

There's one more footnote to the Supreme Court's efforts to legalize same-sex marriage in eighteen states prior to *Obergefell*, but it's an important one. As with any Supreme Court case decided through a signed majority opinion, we know the vote count in *Obergefell*: it was the same 5–4 split as in *Windsor*, with Justice Kennedy joining the four justices appointed by Democratic presidents—Justices Ginsburg, Breyer, Sotomayor, and Kagan—in the majority; and Chief Justice Roberts, joined by Justices Scalia, Thomas, and Alito, in dissent. From 2010 (when Justice Kagan replaced Justice John Paul Stevens) to 2018 (when Justice Kavanaugh replaced Justice Kennedy), this was described as the "liberal" split on the Court, whereas 5–4 rulings in which Justice Kennedy joined the other Republican appointees were described as the "conservative" split. Most cases that divided the justices along ideological lines produced one of those two lineups.

That there were four dissenters when the Supreme Court finally resolved the marriage issue in *Obergefell* is a revealing part of this narrative, because it takes only four votes to grant certiorari. Thus, if the same four justices who dissented in *Obergefell*—and voted to uphold state bans on same-sex marriage—had wanted the Court to review the earlier circuit court rulings that had struck down such bans, they could have forced the issue, by voting to grant any (or all) of the seven petitions that had been denied on October 6, 2014. In other words, as legal journalist Chris Geidner has pointed out, at least one of the justices who dissented from the Supreme Court's decision to recognize a federal constitutional right to same-sex marriage in *Obergefell* had nevertheless voted to deny certiorari in each of the seven petitions the Court denied on October 6. At least one of the *Obergefell* dissenters was thus willing to allow the Court to legalize same-sex marriage through unsigned and unexplained orders; he just refused to sign on when the time came to issue an opinion on the merits. We can be fairly sure, because of their dissents from several of the stay denials, that it wasn't either Justice Thomas or Justice Scalia. That leaves Chief Justice Roberts and Justice Alito. And for reasons Geidner persuasively recounts, it was almost certainly Roberts.[37]

Why would Chief Justice Roberts have voted to deny certiorari in the October 6 cases? Doing so left intact lower-court rulings to which, as his subsequent dissenting opinion in *Obergefell* made clear, he strongly objected. More than that, it had the effect of immediately legalizing same-sex marriage in almost a dozen states, and eventually in eighteen of them. We can only speculate, of course, but Eskridge and Riano suggested that it was a "defensive denial," in which a justice votes not to review a lower-court decision of which they disapprove because they fear that a majority of their colleagues agrees with it. Better to have a bad ruling be the law in part of the country than in all of it. Or, at the very least, better to have the law be made through non-precedential orders than through precedential opinions. And better still to take a chance that such a majority may weaken over time. As Eskridge and Riano wrote, "If you were 95 percent certain that you would lose in October 2014, but there was even just a 20 percent chance things would change decisively by April 2015, then your best strategy would be to avoid taking the cases in October." After all, events (and, as we've seen in recent years, the Court's composition) can change much faster than expected. There are plenty of incentives (and, as importantly, very few costs) for voting to put off a merits decision to a future term if you're sure of a defeat during the present one.[38]

In that respect, among others, the marriage cases provide one last, important, albeit heavily tinted window into how the Supreme Court operates behind the scenes: the high and low politics of the certiorari process, and the strategic behavior by *all* parties—the justices, their law clerks, the lawyers, and even the lower courts—that the process involves, both the behaviors the process shapes and the behaviors that shape the process.

Very little about the certiorari process is formalized in any statute or rule. Even the most foundational "rule of four," that it takes only four "yes" votes for the Court to grant certiorari, can't be found in the Constitution, in any federal statute, or even in the Supreme Court's own rules. And although the Supreme Court's rules articulate loose criteria for when a particular petition will be "worthy" of certiorari, those criteria are subjective, nonbinding, and non-exhaustive. As H. W. Perry succinctly put it in his groundbreaking study of the justices' approach to certiorari, the provision in the Supreme Court's rules that sets forth when certiorari will be appropriate, Rule 10, "is really not much help."[39]

Under the Court's current rules, a party that loses in a state supreme court or federal court of appeals has at least 90 days from the last ruling to file a petition for a writ of certiorari. That brief is supposed to make the case for why the Court's intervention is justified, and not necessarily why the lower-court ruling was wrong. (With the Court's permission, the deadline can be extended to 150 days.) Once the other side has either responded or waived its right to respond, the petitions are formally distributed to the justices, but are distributed in reality to their clerks. Most of the justices participate in the "cert. pool," in which one law clerk, typically a recent law school graduate in one justice's chambers, writes a brief memo with a recommendation circulated to the entire Court as to whether the justices should grant the petition or deny it. At that point, the petition is formally placed on the calendar for "discussion" at one of the justices' upcoming formal gatherings—the "Conference." In practice, though, at least one justice must specifically request that a petition be discussed for the matter to be verbally addressed when the justices meet in person. For a time, all capital cases were automatically discussed at Conference, but that no longer appears to be the case. Only specifically flagged petitions (well under 20 percent of the total, by most estimates) go onto the "discuss list." At Conference, the justices go around the table, in seniority order, expressing their vote on the petition and, in a handful of cases, briefly offering reasons for their position.[40]

Every other petition scheduled for that Conference goes on the "dead list," never to be discussed by the Court before it is summarily denied. We can't know how much time the justices or their clerks spend on petitions on the dead list. But every attempt at an estimate has concluded that, contra Chief Justice Taft's assurances in the lead-up to the Judges' Bill, it's minimal, at best. And jumping through all of these hoops is what parties must do just to get the Court to take up a case; an altogether different—and more intensive—process kicks in on the "merits" docket.[41]

For obvious reasons, the enormous discretion baked into the certiorari process begets at least the appearance of strategic behavior by the justices. Among other things, justices who want a petition granted but are not sure they have the votes have ways to defer consideration. One common approach is to request the record from the lower courts to buy time to persuade colleagues to join them. Petitions will thus sometimes be "rescheduled" or "relisted" as the wheels turn inside One First Street. Justices will vote to "join three," meaning that, although they are not a standalone vote to grant certiorari, they will provide a fourth vote if there are three others. Justices will time grants of certiorari to allow cases to be heard during the current term or to push them back to the next term. Some have even wondered if the justices may occasionally horse-trade, voting to grant or deny a petition in exchange for a colleague's promise to do the same in another case.[42]

And, perhaps most significantly, as in the marriage cases, justices will engage in defensive denials, in which those who believe a petition meets the criteria, and/or that the decision under review was erroneous, nevertheless vote against granting certiorari solely out of concern that a merits decision from the Supreme Court would be "worse." Especially as the Court has become more polarized along partisan political lines, the widespread consensus is that defensive denials have become far more common than in the past. In politically charged cases from 2006 to 2018, neither the more conservative justices nor the more liberal ones could always be sure about Justice Kennedy's views, for example, even though, in most of those cases, his vote would be necessary to form a majority on the merits. And after Justice Kennedy's retirement, and the solidification of a more sharply conservative majority, there was understandable suspicion that the four more liberal justices were likewise holding their fire, refusing to push the Court to take up lower-court rulings with which they vehemently disagreed, but which they also worried the conservative justices would affirm. Once Justice Barrett replaced Justice Ginsburg in 2020, the liberals could no longer force a case onto the Court's docket by themselves even if they wanted to.[43]

This strategic behavior by the justices naturally leads other relevant actors to follow suit. Take lower courts, for instance. As the Sixth Circuit's decision in the same-sex marriage cases suggests, lower courts will sometimes willfully create circuit splits, knowing that, by creating a division of authority, they dramatically increase the likelihood of the issue being resolved by the Supreme Court. Lower-court judges who disagree with a ruling their colleagues have made will often write especially colorful dissenting opinions to help draw attention to the majority opinion, and to arm the party that lost with material for their cert. petition. And even appellate judges who were not on the original three-judge panel that decided a case in a federal court of appeals can send signals to the Supreme Court to accept a petition, by asking their colleagues to rehear the three-judge panel's decision "en banc," that is, before every active judge on the court of appeals, and by publishing a dissenting opinion if and when those colleagues refuse. These attention-seeking missives, which were not even permitted by the Federal Rules of Appellate Procedure for a time, and which were strongly disfavored as late as the 1960s (because they necessarily reflected a judge who had not participated in a case criticizing those colleagues who did), have become so common that they've been given their own nickname: they're not "dissents," they are "dissentals." And they are understood, for better or worse, as transparent attempts to increase the likelihood that the Supreme Court will grant certiorari.[44]

Just as lower courts routinely engage in strategic behavior to increase the chances that the Supreme Court will agree to hear a specific case or to resolve a broader legal issue, they also engage in strategic behavior to try to decrease the odds of Supreme Court review. Judges worried about their decisions being reversed by the Supreme Court have been known to try to "cert.-proof" their analyses by writing decisions that rest on independent grounds, so that even if the Supreme Court wants to reverse on one ground, that wouldn't actually change the result. Likewise, lower courts often try to find narrow ways to rule to minimize the likelihood that the justices would want to take up that particular case. Recall that, in the Prop. 8 case, the Ninth Circuit had tried to rest its invalidation of California's same-sex marriage ban on grounds unique to the Golden State. The California-specific reasoning was a transparent effort to minimize the justices' interest in the decision. It didn't succeed.

At her confirmation hearing to the Supreme Court in 2009, Justice Sotomayor came under at least some criticism for what was portrayed as a similar move while she was a judge on the Second Circuit. In a high-profile appeal about whether the New Haven Fire Department could throw out a civil-service test because it didn't produce enough high scores from minority applicants, Sotomayor joined a short, "unpublished" memorandum decision siding with the fire department that critics claimed was crafted to avoid the Court's attention. Like the Prop. 8 case, that gambit, if a gambit it was, didn't work; the Supreme Court subsequently agreed to review that decision and reversed it.[45] Unlike lower federal courts, state courts can also avoid review by the US Supreme Court if their rulings rest on state law, even if the state law at issue is a technical, procedural rule that was only invoked at the last minute.[46]

Savvy advocates and parties that regularly appear before the Court play similar games. Cert. petitions are timed precisely at a time in the Court's term when the justices may need cases to fill out their calendar, which usually comes in late December, to increase their chances of being considered, leading to lots of filings in August and September. Well-regarded members of the Supreme Court bar hired to represent a party that won their case below have even been known to ghostwrite briefs in opposition to certiorari rather than signing them, in order to obscure the involvement of a lawyer whose skill and reputation might otherwise be a factor that the clerks and justices weigh in favor of granting review. If a former solicitor general is representing a party that prevailed below, the justices might see that as a sign that the case truly is important, even if the brief argues against granting certiorari at least in part by suggesting otherwise. Obscuring the lawyer's involvement mitigates that concern. This is especially an issue when there are numerous cases presenting the same question, and the Court is considering which of the cases to pick. Of course, the federal government, by far the most frequent litigant before the Supreme Court, can't hide its involvement when it is defending against a petition. But it nevertheless will often try to signal its views of the relative strengths (or weaknesses) of a petition by simply waiving its right to file a response. In those cases, the petition will automatically be dead-listed unless at least one justice calls for a response. And even once a response is filed, the petition will still only be discussed at Conference if a justice separately requests it.[47]

And parties have increasingly tried to line up predictable or unpredictable coalitions of *amici curiae*—"friends of the Court" who will file their own briefs explaining why that case, in particular, merits the Court's time. Many of the same *amici* will then file briefs on the merits if the justices grant the petition, either to advance a particular substantive viewpoint or to signal to the justices their broader interest in the underlying dispute. When the US Chamber of Commerce files an *amicus* brief in support of certiorari, for example, that's usually seen as an effort by the business community to signal its interest in the justices' intervention as much as it is to signal their support for a particular legal position.[48]

The justices themselves will often also ask the federal government to file an *amicus* brief in cases in which it is not already a party, to share with the Court the executive branch's views as to whether certiorari should be granted. (Such an invitation is known as a "CVSG"—a Call for the Views of the Solicitor General.) Sometimes, the Court issues a CVSG because the justices are genuinely curious about the federal government's position—and are thus likely to follow the "grant" or "deny" recommendation. Sometimes, it's an obvious stalling tactic—when everyone *knows* what the federal government is going to say (like the Biden administration in the race-based affirmative action cases that were argued in November 2022), but it could take them six to eight months to say it. Meanwhile, *amicus* briefs in *opposition* to certiorari are virtually unheard of; the last thing anyone trying to avoid the Court's review wants to do is draw more attention to the case. In all, it is simply impossible to understand the modern Supreme Court without understanding the centrality of certiorari and the various idiosyncratic behaviors that it produces and incentivizes on the part of all comers.[49]

Nor does the strategic maneuvering end once four or more justices have voted to grant certiorari. The norm is that granting certiorari sends a case to the Court's merits docket, where it will receive an additional full round of briefing focused purely on the legal questions under review; full opportunity for participation by friends of the Court; and, once the briefing is complete, at least one hour of oral argument (thirty minutes per side). But there are two important types of cert. grants that do not lead to plenary review, both of which involve rulings that can have significant substantive effects away from the Court's merits docket.

The first category consists of "summary reversals." In these cases, the justices decide the appeal at the certiorari stage through a short opinion for the Court that comes alongside the grant of certiorari. These "summary" rulings are supposed to be for cases in which the lower court clearly and egregiously erred, and so there's no need for the Court to conduct plenary review or hear oral argument before publishing an opinion explaining the error and reversing. To reflect this supposed lack of divisiveness, the norm on the Court is that it takes at least six votes to agree to such a summary disposition, at least in part because any four justices who object to a summary disposition can force plenary review. And to reflect their summary nature, these rulings, even when they speak for a majority, are always unsigned—denominated as *per curiam*, or "for the Court."

In recent years, though, the Court has handed down a growing number of significant and divisive substantive rulings through summary reversals. To take one example, after *Obergefell*, married same-sex couples challenged an Arkansas law that allowed only a legal "husband" of a biological mother, and not a legal "wife," to be listed as a parent on a baby's birth certificate. The Arkansas Supreme Court upheld the law, and the couples petitioned for certiorari. After relisting the petition for six straight Conferences, the Court resolved the case on the same day that it adjourned for its summer recess in 2017, issuing a per curiam opinion in *Pavan* v. *Smith* striking down Arkansas's law. As the unsigned opinion explained, "That differential treatment infringes *Obergefell*'s commitment to provide same-sex couples 'the constellation of benefits that the States have linked to marriage.'" Writing for himself and Justices Alito and Thomas, Justice Gorsuch dissented—not only because he thought the Arkansas law was constitutional, but because he thought the appeal was substantial enough to warrant plenary consideration. Once again, Chief Justice Roberts appeared to be voting strategically. Although he had also dissented in *Obergefell*, he provided a sixth vote at least for the summary disposition in the Arkansas case, if not for its substance, as well. After all, by not objecting to a summary disposition, the chief justice was able to minimize the visibility of a potentially high-profile case concerning *Obergefell*'s impact—even if he ultimately believed the Arkansas law was constitutional.[50]

Two particularly notable categories of cases in which summary reversals have increased in recent years are prisoner and civil rights suits. In those contexts, a plaintiff can usually only prevail if they can show not only that their constitutional rights were violated by a local, state, or federal government officer, but that they were "clearly established" at the time they were violated—where the government's conduct was truly egregious. In one prominent example from 2007, the Supreme Court summarily reversed a lower court that had sided with a Wisconsin prisoner. The prisoner claimed his trial counsel had been ineffective because the lawyer had participated in the prisoner's plea colloquy by speakerphone. The lower court had held that not having a lawyer in the courtroom was automatically a basis for relief regardless of the impact it had, so that the prisoner did not need to prove that he had in fact been prejudiced by his lawyer's remote participation. But although the Supreme Court had suggested in several cases (in which other matters were in dispute) that such conduct was categorically prejudicial, it had never expressly decided as much in a case in which it made a difference, so the prisoner lost.[51]

As legal scholar William Baude has documented, the Court has used summary reversals in those contexts increasingly to hold nothing other than that a lower court was wrong that the plaintiff's rights were, in fact, "clear." (Indeed, it was an uptick in such rulings that led Baude to first use the term "shadow docket" in 2015.) These decisions therefore not only spell doom for those plaintiffs' suits, but fail to make the law any "clearer" for future plaintiffs; it's still not settled today whether criminal defendants have a categorical constitutional right to have their lawyers appear in person when they plead guilty. Unlike cert. denials, summary reversals are at least accompanied by some reasoning and rationale on behalf of the Court. But they still short-circuit the Court's normal process; parties have no advance notice that a specific case is under consideration for summary treatment, and so briefs that were focused on why the Court should (or should not) grant certiorari become the basis for the justices' rulings on the merits. Likewise, because *amicus* briefs opposing certiorari are so rare, there are seldom briefs in support of the party who won below—and, in these cases, that's usually either a prisoner or a civil rights plaintiff.[52]

The second category of grants of certiorari that don't lead to plenary review consists of GVR orders, for "grant, vacate, and remand." A GVR order is an order granting certiorari, vacating a decision below, and remanding for reconsideration in light of some material intervening event. The least controversial of these is a GVR coming after a major new substantive decision, in which the Court returns to lower courts other cases raising the same question. For instance, when the Court in 2018 held that there were circumstances in which law enforcement use of cell phone tower data required a search warrant, the Supreme Court remanded dozens of cases in which lower courts had held to the contrary, formally instructing the lower courts to reconsider their rulings in light of its new analysis.[53]

But GVRs can also be used to send coded substantive messages to lower courts. One illustrative example involves noncitizens detained by the federal government at its military base in Guantánamo Bay. After the United States began detaining "enemy combatants" there in 2002, lawyers sought review of those detentions, not just in the federal district court in Washington, DC, but in Los Angeles as well. Both cases eventually made their way to the Supreme Court. In June 2004, in the DC case (captioned *Rasul* v. *Bush*), the justices held by a 6–3 vote that federal courts had the power to hear the detainees' claims. But the next day, the Court issued a GVR order in the California case (*Bush* v. *Gherebi*), remanding for reconsideration not in light of *Rasul*, but in light of the Court's decision in a non-Guantánamo detainee's case, *Rumsfeld* v. *Padilla*, in which the justices had held nothing other than that a US citizen held as an enemy combatant in South Carolina had filed his challenge to his detention in the wrong federal court.[54]

To outsiders, the order was indecipherable. All it said was "Petition for writ of certiorari granted. Judgment vacated, and case remanded to the United States Court of Appeals for the Ninth Circuit for further consideration in light of *Rumsfeld* v. *Padilla*, 542 U.S. 426 (2004)." But the Ninth Circuit understood the precise message that the justices were implicitly sending: nine days later, the court of appeals transferred the case to Washington, cryptically explaining that "it appears to us that the proper venue for this proceeding is in the District of

Columbia." The Supreme Court's two-line GVR order in *Bush v. Gherebi* is the reason why every Guantánamo case since 2004 has been brought in Washington, DC, and why there has been no opportunity for other judges from other courts to weigh in and perhaps reach different conclusions that, among other things, would require the Supreme Court to resolve more of those disputes. (The Court has not resolved the merits of any Guantánamo-related dispute since 2008.) Just like the cert. denials in the marriage cases, GVRs are cryptic rulings outwardly presented as purely procedural orders even though they can produce significant substantive effects, and often do.[55]

This last point is, as in the marriage cases, the key: With so many of the orders it issues, the Supreme Court is shaping the law at least as it applies on the ground, along with the actions of litigants, lawyers, policymakers, judges, and clerks. Some of these orders are more impactful than others; some are more visible than others; some are more controversial than others. But the entire system reflects strategic behavior by the justices (and, in many cases, the other relevant actors). All of that behavior would look vastly different in a world in which the justices did not completely control their docket.

Put another way, the politics and practices of certiorari drive home the consequences of the Court's accumulation (if not arrogation) of power over the past century. It's not just that the Court sets its own agenda; it's that a significant number of technical line items on that agenda can produce substantive effects even though they are effectively invisible to the layperson. We assume that the bulk of the Court's work involves hearing, debating, and ultimately making the merits decisions that the justices hand down over the course of each term. But that assumption is clearly incorrect as an assessment of volume, and deeply misleading as an assessment of impact. The bottom line is that most of what the Court does is behind the scenes, shrouded in obscurity, driven by norms far more than by rules, and informed by the specter of deeply strategic behavior from all sides to which the public is generally not privy. The rise of certiorari precipitated the rise of the Supreme Court technocracy alongside the decline of the public's ability to understand the vast majority of what the Court actually does. These developments are typified by how the justices quietly but clearly legalized same-sex marriage in eighteen states before they ruled that state marriage bans were unconstitutional, and by the instrumental role that Chief Justice Roberts, who publicly dissented in *Obergefell*, privately played in allowing that to happen.

Finally, the marriage cases illustrate not just how even unsigned, unexplained denials of certiorari can produce significant substantive effects, but also the significant but underappreciated role that stays often play in shaping the conduct of parties as the appeals process plays out. In that respect, the marriage cases represent a bridge from the largest body of unsigned, unexplained Supreme Court orders by volume (denials of certiorari) to a smaller one that has risen in significance in recent years: orders respecting requests for emergency relief pending appeal. What the marriage cases underscore is that there are circumstances in which whether the Supreme Court allows a challenged law to operate while the challenge works its way to the justices can be just as important as, if not more important than, how the Court ultimately resolves that challenge. This trend, which started long before *Windsor* and *Obergefell*, did not have its roots in marriage, though; it started with death.

## CHAPTER 3

# THE MACHINERY OF DEATH

## HOW CAPITAL PUNISHMENT GAVE RISE TO THE MODERN SHADOW DOCKET

In the long history of the Supreme Court, there may never have been a more macabre internal memorandum than the one Justice Felix Frankfurter privately circulated on October 23, 1942, in a transparent attempt to bring his wavering colleagues back into line with the Court's soon-to-be-released decision in a case known as *Ex parte Quirin*.[1]

At issue in *Quirin* was the trial of eight Nazi saboteurs who had surreptitiously entered the United States in the late spring of 1942 on a mission of industrial sabotage. Unintentionally, the saboteurs had exposed stunning vulnerabilities in the United States' coastal defenses and galling incompetence on the part of the Federal Bureau of Investigation, which had rebuffed multiple efforts by two of the saboteurs to surrender themselves and the others, behavior that has been described as "a Keystone Kops–worthy farce." To avoid the public exposure and embarrassment that would likely result from a civilian trial, President Franklin D. Roosevelt authorized prosecution of the saboteurs before a closed-door military commission. Keeping the proceedings secret, Roosevelt believed, would protect both US national security and the FBI's reputation at a moment when the outcome of World War II remained very much in doubt.[2]

The problem for the government was a Civil War–era Supreme Court decision, *Ex parte Milligan*. That 1866 ruling had held that the Sixth Amendment's right to jury trial in criminal cases barred military trials of non-soldiers when and where civilian courts were open and functioning, as they had been in Indiana at the time of Milligan's trial, and as they were in Washington in the late spring of 1942. Because two of the saboteurs were US citizens to whom the Sixth Amendment clearly applied, *Milligan* seemed to bar the saboteurs' military commission trial, too.[3]

Pointing to *Milligan*, the saboteurs' lawyers convinced the Supreme Court to return to Washington in the middle of both the trial and the justices' summer recess to hold a rare "Special Term" to decide whether the seventy-five-year-old precedent applied, thus foreclosing the possibility of the military commission taking the case. After hearing two full days of oral argument on July 29 and 30, the Court issued a cryptic, unsigned order on July 31. The order blessed the military commission, notwithstanding *Milligan*, while announcing that "a full opinion" setting forth the justices' reasoning would be released at an unspecified later date. Their work finished for the moment, the justices returned to their summer vacations. Four days after the Supreme Court ruled, the military commission convicted all eight defendants and sentenced them to death. President Roosevelt commuted the sentences of the two defendants who had turned themselves in to terms of imprisonment; the other six were sent to the electric chair on August 8.[4]

But when the justices reconvened in October, the promised "full opinion" proved elusive. The Court was down to seven justices,* and at least two of the remaining seven had growing concerns about some of the thorny statutory and constitutional questions the unprecedented military prosecution had raised. Meanwhile, Justice Robert Jackson, increasingly convinced that the Court should never have heard the case in the first place, circulated a draft of a proposed concurring opinion to that effect. In his memo, titled "F.F.'s Soliloquy," Frankfurter excoriated his colleagues for their eroding resolve. Recounting a fictional conversation between himself and the six dead saboteurs, Frankfurter suggested, not very subtly, that a divided ruling—or worse, one in which a majority of the Court expressed doubt about the validity of the military trial and the completed executions—would not just make the justices look bad, but also hamper the war effort, delivering a blow to Allied morale and a propaganda boon for the United States' enemies.[5]

Frankfurter's memo had its intended effect, cowing his colleagues into submission. Six days later, the Court issued a unanimous opinion in the name of Chief Justice Harlan Fiske Stone affirming the validity of the military trial, ducking the harder questions, and avoiding any separate statements from the other six justices. The Court had dodged a bullet. But in hindsight, Frankfurter was deeply chastened by the episode; he would later describe *Quirin* as "not a happy precedent." (In 2004, Justice Scalia would call it "not this Court's finest hour.") For Frankfurter, like Scalia, the problem was not what Chief Justice Stone wrote in October; it was the effect of the Court's terse ruling in July. By clearing the way for six executions and promising to provide a rationale only after the fact, the justices had committed themselves to writing an opinion that reached a foreordained result no matter how much their views might

* Justice Frank Murphy had already recused from hearing the case because of his ongoing service in the Army; and Justice James Byrnes, who had participated in the July argument and decision, had resigned from the Court on October 3 to run the newly created wartime Office of Economic Stabilization.

have changed in the interim. After all, it just wouldn't do for the Court to change its mind about whether a defendant could have been executed once he was already dead.[6]

Eleven years later, Frankfurter would draw on the unpleasant memories from *Quirin* to try to persuade his colleagues to take a different course in the sensational case of Julius and Ethel Rosenberg, the first American civilians ever sentenced to death by a US court for spying (and the only ones who were executed). Because death sentences, once carried out, could not be undone, the justices needed to fully resolve any appeals before that happened. And if they didn't have enough time, suggested Frankfurter, the right approach was not to undertake a maneuver like the one the justices had used in July 1942 in *Quirin* (bless first and resolve later); it was to temporarily halt the execution by issuing a stay until and unless the Court reached a consensus about the execution's legality. *Quirin* had taught Frankfurter that the irreversible finality of death required procedural accommodations. Those accommodations would eventually lead to the rise of the modern shadow docket, and, ironically, a return to the Court allowing executions to go forward before resolving legal challenges to them.[7]

Every legal system distinguishes between trials and appeals. Trials are complex, multistep processes designed both to sharpen the parties' legal claims and to resolve any factual disputes. That development happens first through "discovery," which attempts to build an undisputed factual record, and then, if necessary, through a trial, at which remaining factual disputes can be resolved by a neutral fact finder, whether the trial judge or a jury. But both the law-sharpening and fact-finding tasks take time, and the more involved the legal arguments, or the more voluminous and contested the factual record, the longer trial (and pretrial) proceedings are likely to stretch on. The typical appeal happens only after the trial process has run its course, and it is structured not to retry the case, but to resolve any claimed errors arising out of the trial. Did the trial court allow a witness to testify who should have been precluded? Was a legal challenge to part of the proceeding wrongly rejected? Should the case have never been allowed to go to trial in the first place?

In criminal cases, there is an added layer: even after appealing all the way to the highest state court, or the Supreme Court for federal prisoners or if there's a federal right at issue, criminal defendants have long had a right to bring second and successive civil suits challenging their conviction in both state and federal courts. Such a collateral attack on a criminal conviction is often (but not always) known in shorthand as a habeas petition—a petition for a writ of *habeas corpus ad subjiciendum*. Meaning "That you have the body" in Latin, a writ of habeas corpus was historically issued by a court to a jailer as an order to physically produce a prisoner, so that the judge could inquire into the factual and legal basis for his detention. Since the 1940s, the modern procedure typically has been to resolve the petition first, with the jailer producing the body of the prisoner only once the court has decided that his or her detention was unlawful. Because of habeas, criminal cases don't just have direct appeals after convictions; they usually have at least one round of "post-conviction" litigation as well.[8]

The hard question, as we saw in the Cambodia bombing dispute and in the same-sex marriage cases, is what the status quo should be while these legal processes play out. It's one thing to send a criminal defendant to jail while he appeals his conviction; it's quite another to execute him before an appellate court can resolve his challenges, exactly the problem that beguiled the Supreme Court in *Quirin*. Wrongful imprisonment has a remedy; wrongful execution does not. With that concern in mind, when Congress first authorized the federal courts to hear habeas petitions from state prisoners in 1867 (the first time that lower federal courts were expressly allowed to review state convictions), it provided that, once a habeas petition was denied by a district court, the filing of an appeal automatically froze any further proceedings by the state. Because of that proviso, the state could only proceed with the execution of someone convicted of a capital crime after their federal appeals had run their course. There was no discretion for courts to exercise based on the strength (or lack thereof) of the prisoner's claims; executions would just have to wait.[9]

Lawyers for prisoners condemned to death soon began to take advantage of this procedure, filing federal habeas petitions even when they had no serious federal challenges to their clients' convictions or sentences, and then appealing when they lost, solely to delay their clients' executions. By 1908, Congress had seen enough. In a short statute, it limited the language of the 1867 law to cases in which a federal judge found that there was a good reason to allow the prisoner to appeal in a habeas case. Although the statute did not elaborate on what this reason might be, courts would interpret it as requiring prisoners to make a "substantial showing of the denial of [a] federal right." In other words, prisoners had to show not just that they might have a federal objection to their trial or sentence, but that there was a "substantial" argument that their federal claim would prevail.[10]

Even under the 1908 statute, though, once prisoners received permission to appeal, they were still entitled to an automatic stay. But a little-noticed statute that Congress passed in 1934 without much explanation provided that, in cases in which a prisoner received permission to appeal, courts "may" issue a stay, but didn't have to do so. In other words, prisoners were not automatically entitled to stays even when they received permission to appeal; it was left to the courts' discretion. This opened the door to the possibility that prisoners who received permission to appeal, because they had made a "substantial showing" that their rights had been violated, could still be executed before their appeals were resolved. For the first time, whether (and when) executions should be stayed pending appeal became more than an academic question.[11]

How should courts decide whether to exercise their discretion to stay an execution? The 1934 statute didn't say. And because stays in such cases had previously been mandatory, there wasn't a lot of precedent on which to rely. It would not be until decades later that the justices coalesced around four factors to consider in deciding whether to grant a stay—factors that applied to any lower-court judgment, including a state-ordered execution. First, parties seeking stays had to show that there was a good chance the Supreme Court would eventually grant certiorari and agree to take up their full appeal. Second, they had to show not only that the Court would hear their case, but that there was a "fair prospect" that the justices would agree with them and reverse the lower-court ruling. Third, they had to show that they would suffer "irreparable harm" without a stay. Finally, they had to show that the "balance of equities"—to the parties and to the public—favored the issuance of a stay, that is, that all things being equal, it made more sense to all interested players to pause the underlying judgment than to allow it to go into effect.[12]

At first, Congress's decision to make stays of execution discretionary had little real-world impact. Into the 1960s, there just weren't many federal grounds on which death-row inmates could plausibly object to their executions. *Quirin* and the Rosenbergs aside, federal executions remained relatively rare (there would be only three between 1963 and 2020). And criminal defendants in state courts still had few rights under the federal Constitution, so that there weren't that many cases in which the justices could weigh in on state executions even if they wanted to. Perhaps most famously, at least three different justices turned away last-minute efforts to stop Massachusetts from executing Nicola Sacco and Bartolomeo Vanzetti in August 1927. Despite widespread concerns over the propriety of their trial, federal law, at least as it was then understood, furnished no basis for Supreme Court intervention. Instead, states and the federal government retained significant discretion both in choosing which offenses would be capital and in prescribing procedures to follow in imposing and carrying out the death penalty.[13]

It was not until 1961 that the Supreme Court, with Chief Justice Earl Warren at the helm, held that states had to comply with the Fourth Amendment's ban on unreasonable searches and seizures. The next year, the Court first applied the Eighth Amendment's ban on cruel and unusual punishments to states. And it was only in 1963 that the justices recognized that state criminal defendants had a constitutional right to court-appointed counsel for all serious offenses. Without access to those constitutional claims, few death-row inmates could make the necessary showing to get the Court's attention. What's more, those few emergency applications that did make it to the Court were typically resolved "in chambers"—by the individual justice responsible for handling applications from the lower courts from which the application came, just like Justice Marshall in the Cambodia bombing case. During the October 1960 Term, for instance, twenty-five of the twenty-nine stay requests that the Court received in capital cases were resolved by a single justice. Even when the circuit justice wrote a brief opinion explaining his reasoning, those opinions had no effect beyond the case at hand, since they spoke only for one justice, not the full Court.[14]

Another critical factor in the paucity of such cases was the declining prevalence of the death penalty, some of which was a reaction to the Warren Court's jurisprudence, but more of which reflected declining public support for capital punishment amid a successful public relations and litigation campaign by the NAACP Legal Defense and Educational Fund (LDF) to challenge capital punishment in any and all forms. In the midst of the civil rights movement, LDF argued—persuasively—that the death penalty was inseparable from race and racial discrimination, and that efforts to eradicate the latter required reining in the former. In 1963, for instance, only twenty-one executions were carried out nationwide. That number slipped to fifteen in 1964; seven in 1966; and two in 1967. With so few executions scheduled in the first place, there was, quite obviously, little need for last-minute emergency litigation to stop them.[15]

Everything changed on June 29, 1972, when the Supreme Court, in *Furman* v. *Georgia*, imposed what was effectively a nationwide constitutional moratorium temporarily banning all capital punishment. The five justices in the majority could not agree on the exact constitutional defect with the death penalty. But the narrowest view, embraced by Justice Potter Stewart, was that the death penalty was unconstitutional because it was imposed arbitrarily. States had too much discretion to decide which offenses and offenders should receive the death penalty, and the resulting arbitrariness violated the Eighth Amendment's ban on cruel and unusual punishment. In Stewart's words, "These death sentences are cruel and unusual in the same way that being struck by lightning is cruel and unusual. For, of all the people convicted of rapes and murders in 1967 and 1968, many just as reprehensible as these, the petitioners are among a capriciously selected random handful upon whom the sentence of death has in fact been imposed."[16]

Stewart thought that the Court had thereby sounded the death knell for capital punishment in the United States. In fact, the ruling in *Furman* had the opposite effect. It provoked a sharp public backlash and galvanized immediate legislative efforts to rectify the defects that Stewart had identified, so that executions could continue. Congress and thirty-five states quickly modified their death penalty statutes in a series of attempts to make the imposition of capital punishment more uniform and objective. And on July 2, 1976, two days before the nation's bicentennial, the Supreme Court reversed course, lifting the moratorium by approving of reforms adopted by Georgia, Florida, and Texas in rulings often referred to by the name of the lead case, *Gregg* v. *Georgia*. Six months later, Utah would be the first state to carry out a post-*Furman* execution; by 1983, there would be more than 1,200 inmates nationwide on death row. That number would pass 2,000 by 1988.[17]

The Court's 1976 course change not only heralded the return of capital punishment in the United States but ushered in a new era of judicially supervised death sentences and executions. Because of the constitutional rules the Court had imposed in reinstating the death penalty, there were now numerous procedural steps and substantive requirements that states had to follow in capital cases. Adherence to these new rules was mandated by the federal Constitution, and departures from them could and would be the subject of litigation. To take just two examples, it was now a constitutional requirement that the prosecution prove to a jury beyond a reasonable doubt that a capital offense—such as a murder—had involved objectively discernible aggravating factors that distinguished it from other murders. For instance, had the defendant previously committed a violent felony? Was the murder committed as part of another felony? Was the victim a witness or a police officer? And so on. Likewise, defendants had to have had meaningful opportunities to present evidence of mitigation at sentencing, such that their lawyers' failure to put on such evidence could be considered grounds to overturn a death sentence sufficient to require, at a minimum, resentencing.[18]

As death penalty scholars (and siblings) Carol Steiker and Jordan Steiker have written, "The 'new' American death penalty differed in a fundamental respect from its previous incarnation; it would be subject to ongoing extensive regulation by the federal courts, particularly the Supreme Court." The justices had authorized the resurrection of capital punishment, but "sought to tame its arbitrary, discriminatory, and excessive applications through a growing set of constitutional doctrines,"

doctrines that, for better or worse, had little if anything to do with the morality of capital punishment in the specific case at issue, or even in general. Put another way, the Supreme Court judicialized the death penalty, but at the same time largely sanitized it, shifting the focus of the litigation away from the substance of the case (was this an offender and offense deserving capital punishment?) or broader concerns that the administration of the death penalty was irrevocably infected with racial prejudice, and toward the procedures the states followed in imposing and carrying out capital punishment.[19]

All of these developments came through merits decisions, handed down after multiple rounds of briefing and oral arguments. But what they precipitated was a dramatic uptick in requests for emergency relief in capital cases—and, with them, the dawn of the modern shadow docket. Criminal defendants were still free to appeal their convictions and sentences, and they could bring habeas petitions if and when those appeals failed. But the 1976 rulings had directly resulted in three changes in the procedural contours of death penalty cases, each of which dramatically increased the number of requests and the need for emergency relief.

First, thanks to the 1976 rulings, there were far more grounds on which capital trials and sentences could be challenged. Critically, some of these new claims were objections that could be raised only after the direct appeal had concluded, or arguments that could be made only once a state had set an execution date—a step that did not automatically follow from a conviction and sentence. As a result, a growing number of constitutional objections to capital convictions and sentences could only be brought through post-conviction habeas review, and not on direct appeal. And even for those new constitutional rules that were supposed be litigated through direct appeals going forward, there was the separate issue of whether death-row prisoners whose direct appeals had already concluded would be allowed to raise these claims in post-conviction review, and if so, to what extent—that is, how these new procedural and substantive rules would apply retroactively.[20]

Second, at least partly in response to this newfound flood of post-conviction claims, state and federal courts adopted new procedural hoops for prisoners to jump through before they could challenge convictions either on appeal or through habeas petitions. Those new obstacles added still another layer of procedural issues for courts to resolve. In 1977, for instance, the Supreme Court held that if a state prisoner had a valid federal constitutional objection to his conviction or sentence, but had failed to fully present it to the state court, the prisoner had to show "cause and prejudice" before raising that objection in a habeas petition. In other words, the prisoner had to provide a good excuse for why the claim wasn't first raised in state court, and also had to provide reason to believe that, had the issue been fully presented, the outcome of the appeal might have been different. This created something of a paradox for capital defendants (and their lawyers), who were simultaneously faced with a higher burden to raising some constitutional claims on direct appeal and a higher burden for explaining why they *didn't* raise those claims on direct appeal.[21]

Third, and most significantly, states weren't just imposing more death sentences; they were also moving to carry those sentences out much more quickly than before. Because of the backlash to *Furman*, capital punishment had become a highly visible political issue in many states (especially in the South). Local prosecutors and state attorneys general were often eager to have executions carried out on their watch. This led to an array of aggressive behaviors, including setting early execution dates—in many cases, long before post-conviction review had concluded. And once an execution date was set, the only way a court could stop it from being carried out was by issuing a stay of execution. Thus, there was little downside to envelope-pushing behavior by state officials; the worst-case scenario was that the courts might slow them down a little.

One especially notorious example came in Texas, where the state pushed aggressively to execute Ronald Clark O'Bryan (who had been convicted of killing his eight-year-old son with cyanide-laced Pixy Stix on Halloween in 1974) on the eighth anniversary of the crime. The trial judge even offered to drive O'Bryan to the execution chamber if it would help. When the federal appeals court, on October 27, 1982, stayed O'Bryan's execution to resolve a claim that had arisen late in his post-conviction proceedings, Texas asked the Supreme Court to lift the stay, citing not only its interest in carrying out O'Bryan's sentence in general, but its interest in executing him on Halloween specifically. The Supreme Court rejected Texas's request, but it was a sign of the times that the state even asked. Indeed, then-justice Rehnquist would have allowed Texas to proceed.[22]

Together, these developments produced a sharp uptick in requests for emergency relief—for stays of execution—while direct appeals or post-conviction claims ran their course. As Supreme Court journalist Linda Greenhouse documented in her book *Becoming Justice Blackmun*, the justices received eighty-three applications for stays of execution during the October 1983 Term alone. Compared to the October 1960 Term, in which, as we saw, the full Court had considered a total of *four* applications for stays of execution, this was a staggering shift.[23]

The volume became so onerous that the Supreme Court's Clerk's Office, which supervises all paper coming into and out of the Court, designated the chief deputy clerk, Chris Vasil, as the "death clerk." His job was to be on top of every scheduled execution in the country and to give the justices as much heads-up as possible about the claims they could expect to receive in last-minute applications, either from prisoners seeking stays or from states seeking to vacate a lower-court stay. And it was his call to the prison once the Court ruled that either stopped an execution from going forward or cleared the way for it to proceed.[24]

The dramatic uptick in the number of emergency applications in capital cases was complicated by one additional factor: as their 1972 and 1976 decisions reflected, the justices themselves were bitterly divided over even the most basic questions about the death penalty—so that the pre-*Furman* norm of handling virtually all emergency applications in chambers, where one justice could be trusted to speak for the full Court, proved increasingly inadequate. Before 1980, it was rare to have orders of the full Court denying *or* granting applications for emergency relief, at least when there had been no prior action by a circuit justice from which the losing party sought full-Court review. And because individual justices dealt with most such applications, it was common for them to hold oral argument in chambers on applications that presented a close question, and to write "in-chambers" opinions setting forth their reasoning, as Justices Marshall and Douglas had both done in the Cambodia bombing case.

But starting in 1980, the Court's behavior changed in three related respects: The Court stopped formally adjourning during its summer recess, a move that ensured that emergency applications could be resolved by the full Court even when the justices were not physically in Washington. Death penalty applications, specifically, were almost always referred to, and resolved by, the full Court, rather than individual justices. And the practice of in-chambers oral arguments quickly died out—and was not replaced by arguments on emergency applications before the full Court. Indeed, there would be no arguments on emergency applications, either in chambers *or* before the full Court, between 1980 and 2022. In response to the rise in execution-related stay requests, in other words, the justices started resolving a greater total and higher percentage of emergency applications as a collective body, with less process and less explanation than had often been provided by individual justices acting in chambers.

These common features of today's shadow docket, unheard of before 1980, were a direct response to the flood of emergency applications in capital cases. Almost overnight, the number of rulings by the full Court on applications for emergency relief skyrocketed. But while the Court resolved such claims, it did so without committing itself to holding arguments on the questions they presented, or to providing rationales to accompany its dispositions. In other words, by moving from in-chambers resolution of emergency applications to resolution by the full Court, the justices as a whole came to provide less process—and less reasoning—than individual justices had previously.[25]

Then and now, a common critique of emergency applications in capital cases is that desperate lawyers and inmates abuse the process. The argument is that death-row inmates or their (usually pro bono) lawyers file eleventh-hour claims that they can't possibly expect to succeed, and then use the pendency of those claims as a basis for delaying the execution. And they do this, according to the critique, on the not-implausible theory that, with enough delay, they can require the state to keep setting new execution dates. And if that keeps up long enough, they might even avoid the outcome altogether: a future governor or president might grant the defendant clemency, or a change might be made in the underlying law. The criticism may well be deserved in a minority of cases. But it also radically understates the opposing argument. The litigation process itself makes it impossible for prisoners to bring even some undeniably meritorious claims until the last minute, whether because of rules limiting which claims can be brought when or because most death-row inmates lack good (or even competent) legal representation until the later stages of their cases. In 1908, Congress made it harder to stay executions out of concerns that most end-stage challenges to the death penalty were frivolous attempts to abuse the process. By the 1980s, end-stage challenges, in a growing number of cases, had become the only way to raise meritorious objections to many capital convictions or sentences.[26]

Sometimes, the Supreme Court will hand down a new decision that provides a prisoner with a new basis for challenging a conviction or sentence, but only after the direct appeal and post-conviction process has concluded. Sometimes, a prisoner or the defense lawyers will uncover potentially exculpatory evidence, perhaps from a new witness, or discover information that should have been disclosed by the prosecutor but wasn't. Sometimes, lawyers who specialize in the death penalty will discover that an overworked, underpaid trial lawyer failed to conduct the kind of investigation to which his client was constitutionally entitled. And sometimes, the execution itself will raise legal questions—the prisoner may seek to challenge the method of execution, for example (such as the pharmaceuticals used in a lethal injection protocol), or to challenge the execution procedures (such as the right to have a religious officiant present in the execution chamber). Because of a long line of Supreme Court decisions, these challenges—along with others, such as claims that a death-row inmate is not mentally competent to be executed—aren't considered "ripe," and so aren't subject to judicial review, until an execution date is set. It is difficult to accuse a prisoner of sandbagging the courts when he's not allowed to even bring a claim (or be represented by a lawyer remotely versed in the labyrinthine idiosyncrasies of post-conviction capital litigation) until a death warrant is issued.[27]

Regardless of who bears ultimate responsibility for this state of affairs, what cannot be denied is that, since 1976, virtually every execution in the United States has been conducted against a backdrop of ongoing emergency litigation. And as the volume of constitutional issues that could arise in capital cases rose so precipitously in the years after 1976, the question the Court had to resolve was when emergency relief was warranted. Having the justices resolve these applications on a case-by-case basis, and often by themselves, was, at least in the Court's view, simply not sustainable.

The Court's first wholesale attempt to address the problem came in 1983. In *Barefoot* v. *Estelle*, Texas had already scheduled the execution of Thomas Barefoot before his habeas appeal reached the New Orleans–based federal appeals court. Rather than stay the execution, the Fifth Circuit gave Barefoot's lawyers only two days to write and file their briefs and prepare for oral argument, instead of the months-long process that typically accompanies federal appeals. This rushed process was especially problematic because Barefoot's claims were strong. At his sentencing, state psychiatrists had testified that he posed a 100 percent risk of "future dangerousness"—a critical factor in imposing a death sentence under Texas's post-1976 regime—despite having never examined him. Indeed, one of Texas's psychiatrists, Dr. James Grigson, became known as "Dr. Death," and was eventually expelled from the American Psychiatric Association, for routinely testifying in capital trials to the future dangerousness of defendants, such as Barefoot, whom he had never met.[28]

By a 5–3 vote (with Justice John Paul Stevens concurring on narrower grounds), the Supreme Court not only blessed the Fifth Circuit's actions but encouraged other courts to follow suit. Although the majority opinion reaffirmed that stays of execution should be issued to any prisoner who met the traditional standard for permission to appeal in a federal habeas case, the Court's analysis encouraged lower courts to truncate the review they provided to prisoners in such cases by directly approving what the Fifth Circuit had done. After all, as the majority explained, the purpose of a stay pending appeal was only to provide the court of appeals with enough time to fully resolve the merits of the prisoner's claims. If the court of appeals could resolve those merits quickly, a stay would (under *Barefoot*, anyway) be unnecessary. Of course, this only increased the risk that meritorious claims would go unaddressed or misaddressed by lower courts that were moving too quickly, which would only increase the need for emergency intervention by the Supreme Court.[29]

And so, although *Barefoot* was, in the words of lawyer and former Supreme Court clerk Edward Lazarus, "aimed at the lower courts," one of its major (if unintended) results was in fact to make the *justices'* lives harder. "By encouraging expedited appellate review and discouraging the granting of lower court stays," Lazarus wrote, "*Barefoot* guaranteed that capital cases would reach the Court more rapidly and with executions already pending," simply because there would be fewer executions stayed by lower courts. Thus, "the agony of last-minute, last-ditch appeals, thus far unusual at the Court, was about to become a terribly draining and divisive part of its routine." Exacerbating the problem was that, after *Barefoot*, many death penalty states began to set execution dates as soon as a court of appeals ruled against a prisoner, putting that much more pressure on the Supreme Court's shadow docket.[30]

*Barefoot* had one other indirect but undeniable impact on the shadow docket. By articulating circumstances in which lower courts should (and should not) stay an execution while an appeal was pending, the Supreme Court had also armed states with new arguments for seeking their own emergency relief from the justices: not to stay an execution, but to *un*-stay it. Through the end of the 1970s, the justices would routinely deny requests to vacate a stay of execution imposed by a lower court, insisting that such relief was justified only in truly extraordinary circumstances. After all, regardless of how substantial a prisoner's claims were, there was little support for the argument that a stay of execution irreparably harmed the state, especially in contrast to the irreparable harm of prematurely allowing a potentially unlawful execution to go forward.[31]

But Justice O'Connor's confirmation to Justice Stewart's seat in 1981 gave the Court a more strident, pro-death-penalty majority, and, among other things, it was more willing to vacate lower-court stays of execution. This trend kicked off in 1984 with a high-profile 5–4 ruling in *Woodard* v. *Hutchins*, in which the justices quickly vacated a stay entered by a lower court even while a prisoner's second habeas petition was pending in the district court. The justices had never even seen the lower court's ruling; they proceeded solely on the basis of "a short summary" of the order provided to the death clerk via telephone. And, critically, they offered no explanation for why they were vacating the lower court's order. Writing in dissent, Justice William Brennan did not pull his punches: "The most disturbing aspect of the Court's decision," he wrote, "is its indefensible—and unexplained—rush to judgment. When a life is at stake, the process that produces this result is surely insensitive, if not ghoulish." It was bad enough, in Brennan's view, for the justices to decline to intervene in favor of an eleventh-hour appeal by a death-row inmate; it was even worse for the justices to intervene to wipe away a lower court's stay in such a case and not provide any explanation for why they did so. Justice Marshall agreed, calling the majority's haste "outrageous." *Barefoot*, though, had opened the door.[32]

The post-*Barefoot* surge of emergency Supreme Court filings from both prisoners seeking to block executions and states seeking to unblock them revealed two more procedural anomalies in how the Court was handling the increased volume of emergency applications. First, in one case in which Justice Lewis Powell was a likely vote for relief, but was also unavailable (having recently undergone a medical procedure in which he had nearly died), the Court evenly divided, 4–4. That equipoise meant that it lacked the votes to overturn the lower court, which had denied a stay. In response, the *New York Times* ran a critical editorial titled "Kill Him, 4–4." Calls to require that a majority of justices sign off before an execution could proceed quickly followed, but went unheeded.[33]

Second, although Powell's absence was a one-off, it also highlighted the awkwardness of having different vote thresholds for different kinds of relief: The four increasingly reliable votes in favor of death-row inmates (Justices Brennan, Marshall, Blackmun, and Stevens) could combine to grant certiorari in any single case, and to thereby force the Court to give a prisoner plenary review of his appeal. But they lacked enough votes to stay an execution while that appeal ran its course. Would the justices in the majority really allow a state to execute a prisoner whose merits appeal the Court had agreed to hear?

Matters came to a head just after Labor Day, 1985. Willie Jasper Darden was a Black man convicted by a Florida court of killing a white man during a furniture store robbery. Darden had come close to convincing the lower federal courts to grant him a new trial because the prosecutor's closing argument in his case had been racially inflammatory and prejudicial (including twice calling Darden an "animal" who belonged on a leash), but ultimately came up short. As soon as he lost in the court of appeals, Florida scheduled his execution for 7:00 a.m. on Wednesday, September 4. Just after 6:00 p.m. on Tuesday, September 3, the Supreme Court denied his application for a stay by a 5–4 vote.[34]

With the execution looming, Darden's lawyers tried one last tack, faxing a letter to the Court at 9:11 p.m. asking the justices to treat the already denied stay application as a request for plenary review via certiorari. Although he did not see any merit to Darden's claims, once the Brennan bloc had voted to grant certiorari, the Court's swing vote—the increasingly frail Justice Powell—belatedly and begrudgingly agreed to cast a fifth vote for a stay. One minute before midnight, Darden had his reprieve. As Powell wrote in what for him was a rare public concurrence, because four justices had voted to take the case up on the merits, "and in view of the fact that this is a capital case with petitioner's life at stake, and further in view of the fact that the justices are scattered geographically and unable to meet for a Conference, I feel obligated to join in granting the application for a stay." In an even rarer move, Chief Justice Warren Burger, clearly irked by the last-minute maneuvering, filed a *dissent* from the grant of certiorari.[35]

Darden's reprieve would turn out to be temporary; over a blistering dissent from Justice Harry Blackmun, he would lose on the merits, 5–4, and be executed in March 1988. But in voting to stay Darden's execution, Powell inaugurated a practice known as the "courtesy fifth," where at least one justice who voted against granting certiorari would nevertheless support a stay if four justices wanted to hear the case (Powell regularly provided such a vote in his remaining two years on the Court). Indeed, the courtesy fifth was more than just a collegial move by a collegial justice. It was, more fundamentally, the Court living up to one of the promises that Chief Justice Taft had made to Congress in pushing through the Judges' Bill in the mid-1920s—that a substantial minority of justices could force the Court to hear a case. Against that backdrop, the courtesy fifth simply protected the "rule of four." Without it, the vote of four justices to take up a case would be meaningless; the appeal would be mooted by the prisoner's execution before the Court could actually resolve the merits.[36]

But the courtesy fifth had another critical effect on how the Court approached the shadow docket in cases in which there weren't four votes for granting certiorari. Before *Darden v. Wainwright*, the question of whether to grant a stay of execution was focused almost entirely on the force (or lack thereof) of the prisoner's claims, because everyone agreed that the other considerations, including the potential for irreparable harm and the public interest, all weighed against allowing the execution to go forward. After *Darden*, whether to grant emergency relief was tied not just to the likelihood that the Court would grant certiorari, but to whether it in fact granted certiorari. If no petition was even pending, perhaps because it was procedurally premature, a stay would typically be denied.

This technical point is one of immense real-world significance. By tying a courtesy fifth to a cert. grant, *Darden* tied the propriety of granting an emergency stay not to the likelihood that the applicant's claims were valid, let alone that they were "substantial." Rather, a stay would be granted if the Supreme Court chose to exercise its discretion to recognize the significance of the applicant's claims—discretion that, as we've seen, the justices are under no obligation to exercise, and that different justices might choose to exercise differently. Just two and a half years after *Barefoot*, the Court had abandoned its explicit commitment to staying executions in any case in which a prisoner raised a "substantial showing of the denial of [a] federal right," and replaced it with an unspoken commitment to stay an execution if and only if a majority was willing to grant discretionary review via certiorari, a far higher—and far more subjective—bar.[37]

Powell's compromise in *Darden* did little to end the bitter divisions within the Court over the death penalty, or between the Supreme Court and the lower courts, as illustrated in the 1992 case of Robert Alton Harris. Harris was scheduled for execution by cyanide gas on Tuesday, April 21, in California. On Friday, April 17, on behalf of Harris and every other death-row inmate in California, the American Civil Liberties Union (ACLU) brought a class-action suit challenging the use of such gas as cruel and unusual punishment under the Eighth Amendment. One day later, a San Francisco–based district judge granted a temporary restraining order—giving Harris a ten-day reprieve. On Monday afternoon, after a brief pause for Easter and the second night of Passover, a divided three-judge panel of the Ninth Circuit reversed the lower court's restraining order, only to have the full court of appeals restore that ruling and impose two separate stays of Harris's execution just before midnight. Three hours later, close to 6:00 a.m. Tuesday morning in Washington, the Supreme Court vacated both stays, over dissents from Justices Blackmun and Stevens. Harris was brought to the execution chamber within the hour, and was strapped to one of the chairs, when the proceeding was stayed again, this time by Ninth Circuit judge Harry Pregerson. Unamused, the Supreme Court responded by not only vacating Pregerson's stay, but also stating that "no further stays of Robert Alton Harris' execution shall be entered by the federal courts except upon order of this Court." California could have dropped Harris from a helicopter at that point; the Supreme Court wasn't going to let anyone else intervene. At 6:21 a.m., Pacific time, Harris was dead. Four years later, the Ninth Circuit would agree with the ACLU and hold that the use of cyanide gas as the method of execution was unconstitutional.[38]

The continuing divisiveness aside, the courtesy fifth did take some of the pressure off of emergency applications, as did shifts in the Court's jurisprudence that further raised the procedural obstacles to relief in post-conviction habeas cases. As Lazarus wrote, "As the nineties wore on, the terrible battles over emergency stays gradually abated." Applications to stay executions or to vacate lower-court stays would still regularly divide the justices, but the norm of granting a stay of execution, at least in any capital case in which four justices voted to grant certiorari, persisted—albeit with some notorious exceptions*—into the mid-2010s. Indeed, at his 2005 confirmation hearing, then–DC Circuit judge John Roberts specifically committed to following the practice.[39]

Instead, the biggest obstacle to the courtesy-fifth practice (and thus to any relief the shadow docket could provide death-row prisoners) would be interposed by Congress. Having sat on the sidelines as the Supreme Court's habeas jurisprudence ebbed and flowed from the 1930s into the 1990s, Congress finally asserted itself in April 1996, enacting the Antiterrorism and Effective Death Penalty Act (AEDPA, pronounced "ED-pah"). As the statute's name suggests, one of Congress's central goals was to streamline post-conviction review in capital cases. Among numerous other reforms, the statute forbids all

* In one especially awkward 1993 case, *Herrera* v. *Collins*, four justices voted to grant certiorari to decide whether it was unconstitutional to execute a prisoner who was "actually innocent," but who could not identify any specific constitutional error in his conviction or sentence. No courtesy-fifth vote was provided for a stay—a particular irony given the question presented. But the ultraconservative Texas Court of Criminal Appeals granted a last-minute stay of its own after the Supreme Court's grant of certiorari—fortuitously (and surprisingly) taking the justices off the hook.

"second-or-successive" federal post-conviction petitions unless they are based on a very narrow set of new facts or a very specific type of new law as espoused by the Supreme Court. More than that, prisoners may only bring such claims if they receive permission from a court of appeals, and the statute specifically bars the Supreme Court from reviewing a denial of permission via certiorari. In practical terms, then, AEDPA made it far harder for death-row inmates to ask the Supreme Court to even hear eleventh-hour challenges to their executions, since most of them had long since filed their first federal habeas petitions. And if the Court was powerless to grant certiorari, then the availability of a courtesy-fifth vote for a stay was all but irrelevant.[40]

Soon after AEDPA was enacted, the Supreme Court upheld those limits, largely because prisoners still had one last avenue for appeal—an extremely rare habeas petition filed *directly* in the Supreme Court instead of in the lower federal courts, which Congress had not specifically barred the justices from granting. But such "original" habeas relief was entirely illusory; the Court had not granted such a petition since 1925 and would not begin doing so again even after it became the last way for prisoners to bring at least some of their claims to the Court. Instead, because of AEDPA, emergency litigation over the death penalty in the Supreme Court increasingly shifted toward the small class of claims that AEDPA did not doom.[41]

Especially once Justice Alito replaced Justice O'Connor in 2006, the only claims within that already small subset that had any chance of succeeding were those that had the support of Justice Kennedy. In general, those fell into one of three categories: claims that the prisoner was entitled to relief because of an intervening Supreme Court decision; claims based upon new and previously undiscoverable facts that clearly would have changed the outcome, such as recently processed DNA evidence or a critical prosecution witness recanting testimony; or claims of misconduct by the prisoner's (prior) lawyers. In other words, the declining frequency of emergency applications in capital cases was not because of a declining frequency in potentially meritorious legal objections to capital convictions and sentences; it was because of the justices' declining ability to hear them and declining interest in doing so, which coincided with a reduction in the number of executions carried out into the 2010s.* Based on those trend lines, when Justice Kavanaugh succeeded Justice Kennedy in 2018, one might have expected the death penalty to recede even further from the shadow docket. Instead, it came back to the fore in two deeply contentious sets of cases, both of which helped to underscore just how much had changed with regard to the Court's approach to emergency relief in general.

The first involved the justices' seemingly inconsistent treatment of requests from death-row inmates to have religious officials in the execution chamber. On February 7, 2019, a 5–4 majority vacated a lower-court stay of (and thus cleared the way for) Alabama's impending execution of Domineque Ray. Ray had challenged a state policy that allowed Christian chaplains in the execution chamber, but not a Muslim imam. The court of appeals had blocked Ray's execution after concluding that there was a substantial likelihood that the policy discriminated on the basis of religion in violation of the First Amendment. In wiping that ruling away, the justices offered no majority opinion. Instead, the Court offered two terse sentences of justification accusing Ray of waiting too long before requesting relief. In an angry dissenting opinion, Justice Kagan (joined by Justices Ginsburg, Breyer, and Sotomayor) argued not only that Ray had indeed brought his claim in a timely manner, but

* According to the Death Penalty Information Center (DPIC), across the United States a record 315 death sentences were imposed in 1996. By 2019, that number had fallen to 34. The record year for executions was 1999—with 98 carried out by 20 states. In 2019, 22 executions were carried out by 7 states. See "Executions by State and Region Since 1976," DPIC, https://deathpenaltyinfo.org/executions/executions-overview/number-of-executions-by-state-and-region-since-1976.

that the Court should have left the lower court's ruling alone. "Instead," she wrote, "this Court short-circuits that ordinary process—and itself rejects the claim with little briefing and no argument—just so the State can meet its preferred execution date."[42]

The justices' late-night ruling in *Dunn* v. *Ray* provoked a sharp—and sharply critical—public reaction, including charges that a Court that had increasingly bent over backward to protect religious liberty in recent years had gone the other way when it was a Muslim claiming discrimination. Those charges only grew louder eight weeks later, when the Court granted a stay of execution to Patrick Henry Murphy in *Murphy* v. *Collier.* Murphy was a Buddhist prisoner who likewise challenged his inability to have a religious official in the execution chamber, this time in Texas, which allowed Christian and Muslim religious officiants in the chamber, but no others. The only justice to attempt to explain the differential treatment was Justice Kavanaugh, who appended a brief footnote to a concurring opinion emphasizing that Murphy "made his request to the State in a sufficiently timely manner," even though there were good arguments that Ray had moved even faster. To the public, it looked like the justices had ruled for a Buddhist but against a Muslim.[43]

The *Ray-Murphy* imbroglio struck a nerve. Just four days after *Murphy*, the Court handed down its ruling in *Bucklew* v. *Precythe*, a merits docket case about the constitutionality of Missouri's lethal injection protocol that had been argued the previous fall. *Bucklew* had started as a last-minute case, because, thanks to the Supreme Court's own prior decisions, Russell Bucklew's challenge to Missouri's execution protocol could not even be brought until Missouri set an execution date. But the issue before the justices was about the substance of Bucklew's challenge to his method of execution; it had nothing to do with timing. In the Court's decision, a 5–4 majority ruled that a prisoner complaining about the constitutionality of a particular method of execution must propose an alternative. As Justice Gorsuch argued for the majority, because the Constitution expressly sanctions capital punishment, it must follow that there is at least one constitutional means of carrying that punishment out. But Justice Gorsuch also went out of his way to further call into question the propriety of emergency relief itself, at least in favor of prisoners: "Last-minute stays should be the extreme exception, not the norm," he wrote. And, expressly invoking *Ray*, the Court suggested that the mere fact that a death-row inmate had brought a claim close to his execution date that could theoretically have been brought earlier "may be grounds for denial of a stay," entirely without regard to the claim's merit. Again, this language was not just a promise from the justices; it was a warning to lower courts.[44]

Justice Breyer, writing on behalf of the four dissenters, pushed back on that point: "It might be possible to end delays by limiting constitutional protections for prisoners on death row," he wrote. "But to do so would require us to pay too high a constitutional price." Justice Sotomayor, writing only for herself, was more direct in her criticism of the majority's attempt to create a new presumption against emergency relief in death penalty cases, writing, "There are higher values than ensuring that executions run on time. If a death sentence or the manner in which it is carried out violates the Constitution, that stain can never come out. Our jurisprudence must remain one of vigilance and care, not one of dismissiveness." Thus, Sotomayor suggested, the Court's comments about timing, which were "not only inessential but also wholly irrelevant to its resolution of any issue before us," should not be taken as establishing a new standard. Otherwise, "were those comments to be mistaken for a new governing standard, they would effect a radical reinvention of established law and the judicial role."[45]

If the *Bucklew* decision did not accomplish it, such a "radical reinvention" came to pass just over one year later, in response to the Trump administration's reinvigoration of the federal death penalty. Over the course of six months, the federal government would carry out not only its first execution in seventeen years, but a dozen more (as we saw, between 1963 and 2020, there had been a total of three federal executions). Shadow docket rulings from the Supreme Court would clear the way for all thirteen executions. And in seven of the thirteen cases, the execution was made possible only because of an emergency Supreme Court ruling that wiped away a lower-court stay or injunction. Keeping with the pattern that had emerged in the 1980s, only one of those rulings—the first one, *Barr* v. *Lee*—elicited a majority opinion.[46]

The basic issue in *Lee* was the single-drug protocol that the federal government had decided to use to carry out lethal injections, supposedly in response to concerns about the multiple-drug combination that some states had used throughout the 2010s—and that had led to several botched executions. On July 13, 2020, a DC district judge enjoined four impending executions, including Daniel Lewis Lee's, out of concerns that the hastily adopted protocol was unconstitutional. In her ruling, Judge Tanya Chutkan held, based upon expert declarations, that a pentobarbital-only execution protocol likely violated the Eighth Amendment's ban on cruel and unusual punishment, because there was a "substantial risk" that such a protocol would inflict "extreme pain and needless suffering" on prisoners before it succeeded in killing them. Significantly, Judge Chutkan went out of her way to stress that the proximity of her ruling to the impending executions (Lee's was scheduled for July 14) was not the prisoners' fault, but entirely the result of the government's effort to expedite the executions even while the prisoners' significant and untested legal claims remained pending. The government asked the DC Circuit for a stay to allow it to carry out Lee's execution. By a 3–0 vote, the court of appeals refused, but it also set an expedited, eleven-day briefing schedule to allow for resolution of the Eighth Amendment claim on the merits.[47]

Without bothering to wait for that accelerated review by the DC Circuit, the government then asked the Supreme Court to vacate Judge Chutkan's injunction. A few minutes after 2:00 a.m. on Tuesday, July 14, the Court agreed to do so by a 5–4 vote. In an unsigned, three-page, per curiam opinion, the Court did not resolve the Eighth Amendment issue; it simply noted that the prisoner's experts and the government's experts appeared to disagree on the matter. It also once again railed against late-arising challenges to impending executions, even though the district court had made clear why, in these cases, the timing was entirely the government's fault. In the process, the majority took what had been "irrelevant" language in *Bucklew*, suggesting that last-minute stays should be the exception, and turned it into the law of the land.[48]

As death penalty scholar Lee Kovarsky explained, *Lee*'s late-night language has led lower courts to apply "a context-free presumption against all end-stage claims, irrespective of prisoner fault," and to do so with respect to state executions, not just federal ones. Put another way, the ruling in *Lee* made clear that an execution could go ahead so long as a constitutional challenge to it hadn't been decisively resolved in favor of the prisoner, including those in which there were still unresolved questions with respect to which it was merely possible that the government would prevail.[49]

This is perhaps the broadest legal significance of what Kovarsky called the "Trump executions": the Court not only implemented what had been a passing complaint in its April 2019 ruling in *Bucklew* (in which the matter was not even at issue); and it not only vacated lower-court stays of execution in cases in which there were substantial and unresolved constitutional and statutory challenges to the federal government's execution protocol; but it did all of this in late-night, unsigned, and, with the exception of *Lee*, unexplained orders. The *Lee* ruling came at 2:10 a.m. on Tuesday, July 14. Two nights later, the Court vacated another district court injunction to clear the way for the execution of Wesley Ira Purkey—a sixty-eight-year-old inmate with Alzheimer's disease—in a 5–4 order issued at 2:46 in the morning. Although Justices Breyer and Sotomayor both wrote dissenting opinions (the latter on behalf of all four of the dissenters), this time, the majority offered no rationale whatsoever for overturning the lower court's ruling. It's one thing when the majority writes nothing respecting an order that preserves the status quo. In *Barr* v. *Purkey*, though, the justices were clearing the way for executions that the lower courts had blocked—but providing nary a word as to why.[50]

Between the *Lee* and *Purkey* decisions and a series of unsigned, unexplained orders clearing the way for the next ten federal executions (from Dustin Lee Honken on July 17 to Corey Johnson on January 14, 2021), the Court thus used a series of shadow docket rulings to effect a broader substantive change in its own procedures without changing any of the underlying substantive legal doctrines. None of these orders altered the circumstances in which a challenge to a particular execution protocol would or would not violate the Eighth Amendment. Instead, it was the clustered use of the shadow docket in a specific subset of cases that was novel, seemingly designed to put into practice (albeit not fully unpack) the majority's hostility to end-stage challenges to executions without regard to the merits of the condemned prisoners' claims one way or the other. Expedition was the watchword, even when the lower courts were already moving quickly. Even conservative law professor William Baude, who expressed sympathy for the Court's mounting frustration with last-minute challenges to executions, wrote, in the context of the 2019 cases, that the Court's use of emergency orders to effectuate these outcomes was "no way to run a railroad."[51]

But it was the Court's treatment of the thirteenth (and last) Trump execution that leaves perhaps the darkest impression of all. The federal death penalty statute requires that the death sentence be carried out according to the procedures in the state in which the federal court sits. If a person is sentenced to death by a federal court in a state that doesn't have the death penalty, the court is supposed to designate a different state's procedures to follow at the time of sentencing, so that there's no question as to the next steps. But Dustin John Higgs had been sentenced to death by a federal court in Maryland in 2001, *before* the Old Line State abolished the death penalty in 2013. By the time of his impending execution, it was unclear, at best, which procedures the federal government was supposed to follow.[52]

With Higgs's execution set for January 16, 2021, the government asked a Maryland district court to go back and "amend" the 2001 sentencing judgment so that, instead of Maryland, Indiana would be listed as the implementing state, since the federal government's execution chamber is located at the United States Penitentiary in Terre Haute. On December 29, 2020, the district court held that it lacked the power to make that change. The government simultaneously appealed to the Fourth Circuit and sought expedited merits review in the Supreme Court. The Fourth Circuit expedited the appeal and agreed to hear arguments on January 22, but the Supreme Court moved even faster. On January 15, the Court issued a two-paragraph order clearing the way for Higgs's execution. The first paragraph summarily resolved the government's appeal—granting a writ of certiorari "before judgment" in the court of appeals, and cryptically remanding the case to the district court "for the prompt designation of Indiana" as the relevant jurisdiction for purposes of the execution protocol. The second paragraph vacated a stay of execution imposed by the lower courts.[53]

Certiorari "before judgment," which allows the Supreme Court to review a federal district court decision before even the court of appeals has done so, is supposed to be reserved for truly extraordinary cases. The Supreme Court's rules emphasize that it "will be granted only upon a showing that the case is of such imperative public importance as to justify deviation from normal appellate practice and to require immediate determination in this Court." In other words, the issue presented must not just be of national importance, but its resolution must be urgent to justify bypassing the court of appeals. To drive home the rarity of such a procedural move, between August 2004 and February 2019, the Court did not grant certiorari before judgment even once.* By any measure, the government's *United States* v. *Higgs* appeal met neither of these criteria. The statutory question (what to do when a state abolishes the death penalty after a federal death sentence is handed down in one of its district courts) affected a vanishingly small subset of an already tiny set of cases. And the Fourth Circuit was moving with remarkable dispatch to resolve it.[54]

What's more, unlike other grants of certiorari before judgment, which have allowed the Court to conduct expedited plenary review and hand down a lengthy opinion, here the Court acted summarily, issuing a two-paragraph order after no merits briefing or argument. In the ninety-eight years that the Court has had the authority to grant certiorari before judgment (it was also one of Taft's innovations in the 1925 Judges' Bill), there had been no prior instance in which it did so just to issue a summary ruling on the merits. Because summary adjudications effectively require six votes, the *Higgs* move was only possible once Justice Barrett had replaced Justice Ginsburg.[55]

So why did the Court move heaven and earth to resolve the *Higgs* case before the Fourth Circuit could, granting certiorari before judgment, only to resolve the dispute summarily rather than after plenary briefing and argument? The only plausible explanation for the rushed timing is sobering: Five days later, and two days before the Fourth Circuit was set to hear

---

* In another telling sign of how much the Court's docket has changed in recent years, *Higgs* was just one of the *seventeen* cases in which the justices granted certiorari before judgment between February 2019 and the end of the October 2021 Term. In other words, the Court went from no grants of such expedited merits review in fifteen years to seventeen grants in three and a half years

argument in the government's appeal, President Biden would be sworn in. And unlike his predecessor, Biden was publicly opposed to the death penalty. The emergency justifying such extraordinary measures, then, appeared to be the possibility that President Biden would commute Higgs's death sentence, a step all agree he would have had the constitutional authority to take. Perhaps the justices in the majority were convinced that the Fourth Circuit was acting in bad faith by scheduling its own expedited oral argument for two days *after* President Biden's inauguration. But that was still an unusually quick turnaround for a federal court of appeals; and, in any event, because there was no opinion for the Court, there was no way for the public to know the reason for the justices' unprecedented reaction.

Thus, the Supreme Court had not just enabled the Trump executions in general; it had invented a brand-new shadow docket procedure to allow the Trump administration to execute one last prisoner on its way out the door, all while ignoring the limits that its own rules supposedly imposed on such relief. The point was not lost on Justices Breyer and Sotomayor, who each lashed out at the majority in blistering dissents. As Sotomayor concluded, "This is not justice. After waiting almost two decades to resume federal executions, the Government should have proceeded with some measure of restraint to ensure it did so lawfully. When it did not, this Court should have. It has not."[56]

In that respect, *Higgs* was a fitting bookend to an overview of the Court's death-penalty shadow docket jurisprudence. What started in the 1980s as a series of accommodations to handle the flood of emergency applications that the justices themselves had provoked slowly morphed into orders increasingly reflective of the majority's contentment with capital punishment, as well as its frustration with last-minute litigation that could thwart, or at least postpone, scheduled executions. What started as litigation that assumed that executions should be delayed if there was any meaningful chance the prisoner would prevail ended as litigation that expressly endorsed the opposite presumption, and the assumption that last-minute claims were abusive even if they might succeed on the merits. But, perhaps most tellingly, what started with a merits decision (*Barefoot*)—and efforts even on the shadow docket to provide coherent explanations for individual justices' (and, later, the full Court's) behavior—ended as cryptic and unexplained full-Court orders even in those cases in which the justices were overturning a lower-court decision and were divided 5–4.

As a case in point, in September 2022, the justices offered no explanation in support of a 5–4 decision to vacate lower-court decisions that had blocked Alabama's scheduled execution of Alan Miller. The district court had written sixty-one pages explaining why Miller was likely to prevail in his challenge to being executed by lethal injection (Miller claimed that he had requested to be executed by nitrogen hypoxia, as Alabama law allows; the state argued that it never received his election form; the district court found Miller more believable). The court of appeals wrote thirty-two pages in leaving that ruling intact. The five justices in the Supreme Court majority—Chief Justice Roberts and Justices Thomas, Alito, Gorsuch, and Kavanaugh—wrote nothing about why those rulings were wrong. Indeed, they wrote nothing at all.[57]

The absence of explanations in these orders obscured not just the grounds on which the justices were allowing executions to go forward but also the bitter divides behind the scenes over the specific questions presented and the Court's institutional role more broadly. As Kovarsky put it, by the end of the Trump cases, "the Supreme Court established that it would intervene aggressively against method-of-execution claims, using procedural vehicles ordinarily reserved for emergencies. Because the emergency intervention was so often unreasoned, however, the Court's collected work product reads more as primal scream than as meaningful judicial guidance." Unlike Justice Frankfurter, whose regrets about the Nazi saboteurs' case had led him to push the Court to change its ways, this time around the complaints of the more progressive justices fell on deaf ears.[58]

And yet, for all of the problems and pathologies that the Supreme Court's approach to emergency death penalty orders reveals, these shadow docket cases were necessarily limited to the unique context of capital punishment. Whatever one thinks of the Court's death penalty jurisprudence, it tends to be death-penalty-specific. As the Court itself has put it, "Death is different." The legal questions are, increasingly, unique to capital punishment. The procedural questions are limited to contexts in which all agree there is a clear and approaching deadline—the execution itself. And even as the Court made new procedural law in some of its shadow docket orders respecting executions, it has generally shied away from resolving any broader substantive statutory or constitutional questions about the death penalty. Indeed, the Breyer and Sotomayor dissents in *Higgs* went out of their way to catalog the myriad substantive questions that the Court had pointedly *declined* to answer in the federal execution cases of 2020–2021. That was certainly a fair (and significant) criticism of the majority's actions in those cases, but the narrow compass of these rulings also blunted their broader impact. Norman Mailer had it exactly right in 1981 when he wrote, "Capital punishment is to the rest of all law as surrealism is to realism."[59]

Beyond the death penalty, the Trump execution cases also provided further evidence of the Court's willingness not only to use the shadow docket in ways it never had before, but to do so, as in *Higgs*, for the all-but-undeniable purpose of allowing the Trump administration to carry out its policy agenda before the Biden administration came along and reversed it. The shadow docket was becoming a place to achieve political victories, not legal ones. In that respect, the death penalty cases were just the latest in a series of examples of the justices using the shadow docket to enable the implementation of aggressive new federal policies that, in many cases, may not have even been lawful. And, as in the Trump execution cases, they did so at the repeated request of an actor who, to this point, has not played a significant role in the story: the so-called "tenth justice," the solicitor general of the United States.[60]

# CHAPTER 4
# THE TENTH JUSTICE

## HOW THE TRUMP ADMINISTRATION BLEW UP THE SHADOW DOCKET

The modern shadow docket may have its origins in the death penalty cases of the 1980s. But any narrative of how the shadow docket (and the Supreme Court's use and abuse of it) has exploded in recent years has to start in 2017, with President Trump's travel ban.

Early in his presidential campaign, then-candidate Donald Trump had made headlines by suggesting he would pursue a "total and complete shutdown" of the entry of Muslims into the United States "until our country's representatives can figure out what is going on." Trump's invective was based upon a deeply bigoted and never substantiated claim that soft immigration policies were making it too easy for potential terrorists to enter the country. One week after taking office in January 2017, President Trump signed an executive order that appeared to follow through on his patently unconstitutional campaign promise, barring the entry of all foreign nationals from Iran, Iraq, Libya, Somalia, Sudan, Syria, and Yemen into the United

States for 90 days; indefinitely barring the entry of all Syrian refugees; and prohibiting any other refugees from coming into the country for 120 days. The government justified the restrictions with amorphous and evidence-free claims that they were necessary to protect national security. But given Trump's ugly campaign rhetoric, and because the populations of all seven named countries were predominantly Muslim, critics called Trump's order a "Muslim ban."[1]

Whatever its name, the ban as initially implemented caused chaos at international airports across the United States. It had been put into effect without any apparent preparation or notice to the relevant government stakeholders, to airlines, or to travelers; and its text was open-ended and overbroad. Among other things, it applied even to dual US citizens and lawful permanent residents of the United States ("green card" holders) returning from one of the seven countries, even though they had a well-settled constitutional right to reenter the United States. Because of its many procedural flaws and the fact that it applied to those to whom it could not possibly apply lawfully, within forty-eight hours of Trump's order, it had been blocked by five different federal judges. Several of those orders were described in the media as "nationwide injunctions"—barring implementation of the ban anywhere in the country.[2]

As we've already seen, injunctions are especially coercive judicial orders, requiring a party to start (or stop) doing something. A party that fails to comply can be held in contempt—which can include escalating fines, and, in extreme cases, imprisonment, until the contempt is cured. The typical injunction is party-specific, directing a defendant to act (or stop acting) in a particular way toward the plaintiff. Usually, there are no geographic limits on such relief; if a court in Los Angeles orders a stalker to stop following a celebrity, that mandate is not limited to the physical boundaries of Los Angeles. In that respect, many injunctions are "nationwide," or, at least, statewide.

That understanding doesn't stop the defendant from pursuing the same unlawful behavior against others, though. Obtaining that kind of injunction has historically required a lawsuit known as a "class action," in which plaintiffs sue as representatives of others just like them—think Apple customers challenging alleged price-fixing, or female Walmart employees protesting allegedly discriminatory wages. If a class of plaintiffs representing individuals across the country obtains an injunction, that order would, by default, have nationwide effect; the defendant would be barred from acting unlawfully against anyone *like* the named plaintiffs, and not just against the named plaintiffs themselves.

In a series of decisions in the 2000s and 2010s, though, the Supreme Court made it much more difficult for plaintiffs to bring class-action suits. In response, lower courts began issuing a rarer kind of injunction, which barred the defendant from carrying out the challenged policy against *anyone*, whether or not they were plaintiffs (or represented by the plaintiffs) in the case at hand. Although these orders are commonly referred to as "nationwide injunctions," that misleading term misses both what is different and what is controversial about them; the legal issue is not their geographic scope, but rather that they constrain the defendant's conduct not just against the plaintiffs, but against nonparties as well. These rulings became far more common toward the end of the Obama administration. And in response to the travel ban and an array of other controversial policies, they proliferated even more during the Trump presidency, starting with a February 3, 2017, ruling blocking the travel ban by Seattle-based judge James Robart, who had been appointed to the district court in 2004 by President George Bush.[3]

The Trump administration immediately asked the Ninth Circuit to pause Judge Robart's order and put the travel ban back into effect. But on February 9, the court of appeals unanimously refused. The three-judge panel explained that the government had not shown that it was likely to win on appeal, and that, even if it was, it could not show that leaving the travel ban on hold in the interim would cause the government irreparable harm, especially since the district court's ruling merely returned the law to where it had been the day before the travel ban was imposed.[4]

Rather than appeal that decision to the Supreme Court, the Trump administration went back to the drawing board. On March 6, President Trump signed a new executive order, replacing the first travel ban with a somewhat more nuanced version. The order still restricted travel from six predominantly Muslim countries (Iraq was, with no explanation, removed from the list). But, in direct response to one of the constitutional problems the courts had found with the original travel ban, the second version expressly allowed entry to anyone who already had a visa, regardless of their country of origin. And the order would be in effect only for six months, so that it had a short shelf life. Even with those modifications, the order was subject to two different nationwide injunctions before it could go into effect—one from Hawaii and one from Maryland. Once again, the government asked the courts of appeals to stay those rulings. Once again, the courts of appeals declined, and then eventually affirmed the injunctions on the merits.[5]

This time, the Trump administration decided to take the cases to the Supreme Court—albeit with a bit of a twist. On June 1, 2017, Acting Solicitor General Jeff Wall asked the justices to stay both injunctions (that is, to allow the second travel ban to go into effect) and to agree to hear the government's appeals of the lower-court decisions that had affirmed the injunctions on the merits. Curiously, although the government stressed the urgency of the matter and requested that the justices expedite the appeal briefing, it did not ask the Court to expedite oral arguments. This technical distinction was not an accident; it had enormous real-world significance: The justices were set to take their annual summer recess at the end of June, from which they would not ordinarily return before the last week of September. Without expedited arguments, there would be no way for the justices to even hear the merits of the government's appeals before October, let alone to resolve them.[6]

It would be one thing if the government was simply looking to delay the justices' consideration of the travel ban; as we have already seen, parties often behave strategically when it comes to the timing of Supreme Court review, especially around the justices' lengthy summer recess. But it wasn't. The second travel ban was set to expire on its own in late September, at which point the challenges to it would become moot—leaving the Supreme Court without a live dispute to decide. By not pushing for oral arguments sooner, the government ensured that they would never happen; the justices would simply dump the cases once there was no policy left to review. The government's strategy therefore would have had the Supreme Court allow the ban to take effect from June through September, but never actually resolve whether it was constitutional. Among other things, such a strategy bespoke a Justice Department that was less than optimistic about what that resolution would be. The low-stakes shot at a short-term political win, then, was far more worth it than the high-stakes risk of losing the long-term legal principle.[7]

At the heart of that strategy was a claim not only that the second travel ban had fixed the constitutional problems with the first one, but that, contra the Ninth Circuit's February ruling, the government *was* suffering irreparable harm every day that the injunctions were in effect. Relying on a 2012 opinion that Chief Justice Roberts had written as a circuit justice, the government argued that any injunction against a government policy causes irreparable harm, because it deprives the government of the ability to carry out the democratic will. As Roberts had written in 2012, "Any time a State is enjoined by a court from effectuating statutes enacted by representatives of its people, it suffers a form of irreparable injury."[8]

This argument derived from an idea known as the "presumption of constitutionality," a term that captures the unremarkable proposition that, all things being equal, courts ought to assume that legislative enactments are constitutional, and should put the burden on challengers to show otherwise. A core tenet of judicial restraint, the presumption dates to the late 1930s, when, shortly after President Franklin D. Roosevelt threatened to add six seats to the Supreme Court, the justices endorsed a recalibration of their role vis-à-vis the political branches in suits challenging government action. Rather than approach economic regulation with skepticism (as the Court had for a generation), the justices suggested that, as a general matter, unelected judges ought to defer to laws enacted by democratic legislatures.[9]

Historically, though, the presumption comes with two critical, baked-in limits, both of which should have cut against its invocation in the travel ban cases. First, the presumption is about statutes, not executive branch policies. It's one thing to defer to the text of legislation that has worked its way through the cumbersome gauntlet of state or federal political processes; it's quite another to apply it to executive orders that may represent nothing more than the fleeting whim of a single person. Second, and just as importantly, the presumption is supposed to give way in the face of substantial claims that the challenged action violates individual constitutional rights, a context in which the government ought not to be entitled to the benefit of the doubt. In the travel ban cases, where the central claim was that an executive order was discriminating against Muslims, the presumption should have been a nonstarter, all the more so where the only "harm" the government could claim was the harm of not being able to enforce a *new* policy—as opposed to an order blocking it from enforcing a long-standing one.[10]

Nevertheless, on June 26, 2017, the Supreme Court sided with the government, at least in part. In an unsigned, thirteen-page opinion, the Court "narrowed" both lower-court injunctions to reflect a new distinction between those foreign nationals with a "bona fide relationship with a person or entity in the United States" and those without such a relationship. (The former category included relatives of US residents, employees of US companies, students or faculty associated with US universities, and others on whom the ban imposed significant hardships.) As applied to those with such a "bona fide relationship," the travel ban remained on hold, meaning that the noncitizens at issue were free to travel to the United States so long as they had visas or did not need to obtain them. As applied to those without such a relationship, the Court allowed the travel ban to go into effect.[11]

What is especially telling about this compromise ruling is that no party had sought it. Instead, the justices appeared to be drawing the line that they believed they would ultimately draw on the merits, distinguishing between those foreign nationals with stronger constitutional claims (those with "bona fide relationships" to Americans) and those with weaker claims. To that end, the Court also granted certiorari in both cases and set them for argument "during the first session of October Term 2017." In a statement that registers as a subtle—but intentional—rebuke on the Court's part, the opinion stressed that "the Government has not requested that we expedite consideration of the merits to a greater extent." There would be no reason for the justices to point that out if they didn't think it was noteworthy. And although the justices could still have chosen to hold an expedited argument, they certainly weren't going to do so if no one was asking them to.[12]

In the moment, the ruling was largely considered a setback for the Trump administration. (Justice Thomas, joined by Justices Alito and Gorsuch, had dissented in part; they would have allowed the entire travel ban to take immediate effect.) As applied to those to whom it mattered the most—foreigners with family, friends, or employers in the United States, including the plaintiffs in the cases before the Court—the travel ban remained on hold. The lower courts were vindicated, not just for blocking the ban, but for doing so on a nationwide basis. But beneath the surface, there was a lot for the government to like. The Court had partially granted two applications for stays without offering, and perhaps without even performing, a detailed assessment of the government's likelihood of prevailing on the merits; it had seemingly accepted the argument that the injunctions necessarily caused irreparable harm to the government; and, perhaps most importantly, it had agreed to push resolution of the cases off until after the travel ban was set to expire, so that the government would never have to actually defend the second iteration of the ban on its dubious merits.[13]

Sure enough, just over one week before the scheduled oral argument on the merits that fall, the Trump administration hit the reset button one more time. On September 24, 2017, it replaced the second travel ban with another new executive order, which was commonly called "Travel Ban 3.0." Again, the government incorporated into the new iteration lessons it had learned from litigation over the previous version. For instance, Travel Ban 3.0 added North Korea and Venezuela, which don't have Muslim majorities, to the list of countries from which entry was suspended. The order didn't explain why those two countries were now included, a curious omission given that, as countries with which the United States lacks diplomatic relationships, travel from them directly to the United States was already practically impossible. Travel Ban 3.0 also created a new "waiver" process for would-be travelers to request an individual exemption from the ban due to hardship, albeit without any requirement that such waivers ever be granted. And it reinforced the very distinction that the Supreme Court had invented in June—between those with bona fide connections to the United States, who were largely exempted from the ban, and those without.[14]

The legal challenges to Travel Ban 3.0 followed a pattern similar to those that had arisen in response to the second travel ban. Once again, district courts in Hawaii and Maryland entered preliminary nationwide injunctions against the policy.

This time, though, the government immediately sought stays of the district court injunctions pending appeal, first in the courts of appeals (both of which refused), and then in the Supreme Court. The justices granted both applications in their entirety. Thus, Travel Ban 3.0 had been in full effect for over six months by the time a 5–4 Court finally reached the merits on June 26, 2018, and upheld it. Justice Sotomayor's caustic dissenting opinion from the 2018 merits ruling criticized the travel ban as being "rooted in dangerous stereotypes," and criticized the majority for making the same mistake in upholding it that the Court had infamously made in *Korematsu* v. *United States*, a 1944 case that had sanctioned Japanese American internment camps during World War II, largely by accepting at face value dubious (and, it turned out, affirmatively false) representations from the executive branch about the "threat" those individuals posed. We'll never know how many noncitizens were stopped from traveling to the United States as a result of the Supreme Court's 2018 decision, known as *Trump* v. *Hawaii*. But any estimate would have to be in the tens of thousands.[15]

The merits ruling aside, the travel ban litigation set the tone for much of what followed on the shadow docket after 2017. First, the government was allowed to put into effect at least part of a policy (the second version of the travel ban) that no court would ever actually uphold. Second, a majority of the justices seemed to accept the deeply contestable proposition that any injunction of government action causes irreparable harm weighing in favor of emergency relief. Third, the Court's 2017 ruling allowing part of the second version to go into effect seemed to turn entirely on a predictive judgment of how the justices might rule on the merits of the government's appeal (by creating a distinction tied to "bona fide relationships") rather than a more traditional assessment of whether the government had truly made the extraordinary case for emergency relief.[16]

But, most significantly, the government's litigation strategy and tactics operated together to produce what was almost certainly the optimal political result for the Trump administration. Without risking having the Court strike down the second travel ban on the merits (a scenario the government avoided by not pushing for an earlier argument), the solicitor general's behavior allowed the president and his defenders to claim victory. It allowed the second version of the travel ban to (largely) go into effect, and it set a precedent for the government to expand and exploit in new cases going forward—to change the law on the ground without changing the law on the books. Not only would the travel ban cases set a precedent for new, controversial immigration policies, but they proved that the solicitor general could use aggressive litigation tactics to sidestep legal challenges to the administration's policies, in the immigration sphere and elsewhere, while avoiding definitive Supreme Court rulings. It was a strategy of winning simply by not losing.[17]

Credit for that strategy belongs not just to Noel Francisco, who served as the forty-seventh solicitor general, from September 19, 2017, to July 3, 2020, but to his principal deputy, Jeff Wall, who served as acting solicitor general in the Trump Justice Department both until Francisco's confirmation and after his resignation. It was Wall who spearheaded the split-the-difference approach to Travel Ban 2.0, and who was also at the helm as that approach spread from the travel ban cases to other disputes. Indeed, winning by not losing quickly became the dominant story of the shadow docket during the Trump administration. Francisco and Wall took a hyperaggressive approach to emergency litigation in the Supreme Court (and to the role of the solicitor general in pursuing that litigation) unmatched in the Court's history. In that respect, it was some of the most overtly political behavior in the 150-year history of an office that, at least historically, has prided itself on its independence from the political leadership of the Justice Department and even the president.

Just as important, though, is that the justices—at least, a majority of them—enabled and invited that behavior, using emergency orders to give the federal government a series of political victories in cases it was destined to lose on the merits. The solicitor general might have been responsible for pushing the envelope, but none of the justices in the majority ever expressed so much as a hint of disapproval of the government's aggressive litigation behavior—even when turning away some of the solicitor general's more outlandish requests. In that respect, the Trump administration may have been responsible for blowing up the shadow docket, but its efforts succeeded only because five of the justices allowed it to.

When Congress created the federal court system in the Judiciary Act of 1789, it also created the position of US attorney general. Buried in the last sentence of the last section of the statute, the job was almost an afterthought. The attorney general was to be "a meet person, learned in the law," and was given exactly two duties: representing the United States before the Supreme Court, and providing legal opinions when asked for advice by the president or other government actors.[18]

The First Congress's brief reference to the attorney general was also deliberately vague about where in the government that officer would sit. Weeks earlier, when the legislature had created the "great departments" of Foreign Affairs (now State), the Treasury, and War (now Defense), it was clear that these were executive departments, and that their heads—"secretaries"—were to be appointed by, and directly answerable to, the president. In contrast, the 1789 Judiciary Act said nothing at all about establishing a legal department. And it provided only that an attorney general "shall also be appointed," without bothering to specify by whom.[19]

The passive voice was deliberate. The judiciary bill that had initially passed the Senate earlier that summer would have given the power to choose the attorney general to the Supreme

Court, reflecting the drafters' view that the attorney general's principal responsibility was to the justices, not the president. Congress decided to muddle the language, with some members suggesting (with their implicit approval) that the ambiguity would allow President Washington to name an attorney general himself. Washington did so, nominating Edmund Randolph just two days after signing the bill into law. Still, it was hardly self-evident that the attorney general should—or would—be wholly subordinate to the chief executive. Most states at the Founding decided to have their attorneys general chosen and supervised by others. To this day, the attorneys general of forty-five states are independent of the chief executive: Tennessee's is appointed by its supreme court; Maine's is appointed by the state legislature; and the attorneys general of forty-three other states are directly elected by the people. Only five states follow the federal model.[20]

The 1789 statute's ambiguity about the location of the attorney general's office was also a reflection of Congress's deep ambivalence about the office's purpose. Was the attorney general a political adviser to the president? Was he an officer of the Supreme Court? Was he the chief legal adviser to the entire government, with duties and obligations to the courts and Congress that were independent of his relationship with his effective (if not formal) boss? The Judiciary Act seemed to contemplate some awkward hybrid. But as was true of so many other important early statutes, Congress left significant room for interpretation. Part of the reason for the ambiguity appears to be that, as with many of those other early laws, the representatives couldn't agree on a more specific vision for the office. But part of it was also because, at least in this case, many of them just didn't care. As legal historian Susan Low Bloch has explained, "The First Congress did not expect this part-time attorney, with no staff and little power, to play a major role in the emerging federal government." It was not until 1818 that the attorney general was even authorized to hire a clerk; 1821 that he was allowed a physical office; 1853 that Congress provided a salary commensurate with a full-time position; and 1861 that the attorney general was given full authority over US Attorneys—the lawyers principally tasked with representing the government in each of the lower federal district and circuit courts, who previously answered directly to the president.[21]

In tandem with the workload of federal courts, though, the Civil War exploded the docket of lawsuits involving the United States. By the end of the war, there was widespread consensus on the need to centralize the federal government's rapidly expanding legal efforts under one roof, rather than having the government's legal business conducted by lawyers from seemingly every different federal office—and, increasingly, by private counsel retained by the government at mounting expense.[22]

So it was that, on June 22, 1870, President Ulysses S. Grant signed into law "an Act to establish the Department of Justice." Debate remains today as to whether the creation of the department was simply a bureaucratic expedient (to consolidate federal legal practice), a civil-rights-driven substantive policy reform (to expand the government's ability to directly enforce the myriad new laws that Congress passed during Reconstruction), or some combination of both. But either way, one of the central innovations of the 1870 act was the creation of a new office, Solicitor General of the United States, to take over the first duty that Congress had given to the attorney general back in 1789: to represent the United States before the Supreme Court.[23]

From that day onward, the solicitor general (or "SG") has typically been one of the nation's top appellate lawyers. Of the forty-six men and two women to have held the position throughout the nation's history as of the end of 2022, five (including William Howard Taft, Thurgood Marshall, and Elena Kagan) have gone on to serve on the Supreme Court, and many more have gone on to distinguished judicial careers in the lower federal courts. The Office of the Solicitor General has been referred to as "the finest law firm in the nation"; even its highly coveted junior positions are viewed as stepping stones to the most prestigious private law practices or academic positions in the country.

Part of that reputation stems from the quality of the work that typically comes out of the office. But part of it reflects a deeper ethos. "There is a widely held, and I believe substantially accurate, impression," wrote Rex Lee, solicitor general from 1981 to 1985, "that the Solicitor General's Office provides the Court from one administration to another . . . with advocacy which is more objective, more dispassionate, more competent, and more respectful of the Court as an institution than it gets from any other lawyer or group of lawyers."[24] Its lawyers even dress differently: male lawyers in the Solicitor General's Office are the only advocates who are still expected to appear before the Court in formal "morning" dress, which includes a single-breasted jacket with a link closure and tails that go down to the knees, along with a waistcoat and striped pants.*

In other words, the influence of the solicitor general has derived, to a large degree, from its perceived *independence*—from the belief that it represents the interests of the United States as a whole, and not just the current policy preferences of the incumbent president. Indeed, one of the principal reasons for having a solicitor general distinct from an attorney general was to separate the political and judicial responsibilities that had previously been combined in one office. As Simon Sobeloff, solicitor general from 1954 to 1956, explained, "The Solicitor General is not a neutral, he is an advocate; but an advocate for a client whose business is not merely to prevail in the instant case. My client's chief business is not to achieve victory, but to establish justice." (Sobeloff famously refused to sign the government's brief or argue on the government's behalf in one case about a

---

* When she became the first woman to serve as solicitor general in 2009, Elena Kagan (who thought the woman's version of a morning coat looked "ridiculous") is said to have received the justices' approval, through intermediaries, to argue in a business suit.

McCarthy-era loyalty review board's dismissal of a federal government employee, in which he thought that principle had been neglected.) Frederick Lehmann, solicitor general under President Taft, was even more blunt, remarking that "the United States wins its point whenever justice is done its citizens in the courts." Or, as Francis Biddle, one of President Roosevelt's six solicitors general, put it, "The Solicitor General has no master to serve except his country."[25]

Reinforcing that independence, the solicitor general is the only federal officer other than the vice president with formal offices in two branches of the federal government, one in the main building of the Department of Justice and one in the Supreme Court. This arrangement reflects the unique role that the solicitor general is supposed to play in serving two masters. The solicitor general does not just have a physical presence at the Supreme Court, either; the Court's rules and traditions both formally and informally credit the solicitor general as being the de facto leader of the Supreme Court's bar—the unofficial representative of all lawyers who appear before the justices. Thus, although solicitors general have developed a "special relationship" with the Court, in the words of former solicitor general Seth Waxman, that relationship "is not one of privilege, but of duty—to respect and honor the principle of stare decisis, to exercise restraint in invoking the Court's jurisdiction, and to be absolutely scrupulous in every representation made."*[26]

One of the many ways in which successive solicitors general have "exercise[d] restraint in invoking the Court's jurisdiction" has been in deciding which lower-court rulings against the government should be appealed to the Supreme Court and when. Most of the time, if the government loses in the lower courts, it does not ask the justices to weigh in. Such selective behavior

---

* *Stare decisis* means "to stand by things decided" in Latin. It is the principle that, all things being equal, courts will—and should—follow their precedents, and should overrule prior decisions (even those with which the current court disagrees) only in rare and exceptional circumstances.

preserves at least the appearance that government petitions for certiorari are not automatic, but rather reflect an exercise of discretion on the SG's part—highlighting those cases believed to be especially worthy of the Court's attention. Related to that historical pattern, the government has also been stingy in seeking emergency relief from the justices, seldom asking for stays of adverse lower-court rulings while appeals have run their course. To take one illustrative data point, from 2001 to 2017, across the (very different) two-term administrations of Presidents George W. Bush and Barack Obama, the solicitors general sought emergency relief from the Supreme Court a total of eight times—an average of one request every two years. Four of those requests were granted; four were denied—but, at least publicly, seven of the Court's eight orders in those cases were unanimous. Thus, when the solicitor general took the rare and extraordinary step of asking for emergency relief, the justices were generally all on the same page.[27]

All of that changed during the Trump administration. Starting with the second iteration of the travel ban and ending with the execution of Dustin John Higgs, in just four years Trump's solicitors general sought emergency relief from the Supreme Court a total of forty-one times—a more than twentyfold increase over Bush's and Obama's SGs combined. That would be a story unto itself. But even more striking is that, as in the travel ban cases, in most of the others the justices largely acquiesced, granting at least part of the government's request in twenty-eight of the thirty-six applications that resulted in an up-or-down decision. What's more, after the June 2017 travel ban ruling, twenty-five of the remaining twenty-six grants of emergency relief to the Trump administration would come with no opinion from the Court, and thus no explanation for why the justices were either putting policies blocked by lower courts back into effect or freezing lower-court mandates: no explanation of how the lower court erred; no explanation of why the policy was likely to be upheld; no principles to guide future judges and decision-makers. Over and over throughout the Trump administration, policies that no court ever upheld (and that multiple lower-court judges had held to be unlawful) were allowed to remain in effect for years thanks to one-sentence orders from the Court.[28]

Unlike the rulings on emergency applications from the Bush and Obama administrations, the Trump orders were increasingly divisive as well. Twenty-seven of the thirty-six decisions included at least one public dissent; ten were publicly 5–4 (perhaps others were behind the scenes). And because the Biden administration discontinued most of the policies in question soon after coming into office in January 2021, challenges to them became moot before the Supreme Court was ever able to conduct plenary review, so that the stay rulings were typically the justices' only involvement in these disputes.[29]

Defenders of the Trump administration's aggressive litigation tactics point to their success as evidence that they were justified—a necessary response by the Supreme Court, in their view, to lower-court judges running amok in their desire to subvert Trump's policies. The reality, though, is not nearly as straightforward, or as complimentary to the efforts of either the justices or the solicitor general. In the Trump cases, the Office of the Solicitor General advanced radical new theories justifying broad usage of the Supreme Court's power to grant emergency relief, theories that the conservative justices repeatedly bought into. As in the travel ban cases, the goal appeared to be to rack up short-term victories even (if not especially) when long-term legal wins were unlikely. It would be problematic enough if the Court formally embraced such an approach, whether by adopting new procedural rules that applied only to emergency applications by the federal government or new substantive principles of deference to federal executive officials. Then, at least, future solicitors general, including those of a different party, could benefit from the same problematic but principle-driven shifts in the Court's jurisprudence.

But in order after order, the Supreme Court gave the Trump administration most of what it wanted *without* endorsing principles that the justices would be bound to apply to future presidents, so that the justices could (and ultimately did) refuse to provide the same relief when a Democratic president took office. Looking at the cases as a whole, the conclusion is all but inescapable that the Court was just as responsible for enabling the rise of the shadow docket as the Trump administration—and that it did so in a manner that specifically tended to advance Republican policies rather than conservative legal principles.

Consider, for example, the "transgender ban"—the government's response to two July 2017 tweets by President Trump that "the United States Government will not accept or allow . . . Transgender individuals to serve in any capacity in the U.S. Military." Four different district courts—in the Central District of California, the District of Columbia, the District of Maryland, and the Western District of Washington—entered nationwide injunctions against the ban. But after those rulings, Secretary of Defense James Mattis introduced a substantially more nuanced framework, known as the "Mattis Policy," in lieu of a categorical ban on military service by transgender individuals. The government then moved to dissolve each of the injunctions in light of the changed circumstances. Three of the district courts denied the government's motions; the fourth deferred its ruling.[30]

The government then filed appeals to the DC and Ninth Circuits (in both the California and Washington cases), which refused to stay the district court's orders pending appeal. While those appeals were pending, the government filed petitions for certiorari before judgment in each of the three cases, asking the Supreme Court to take up the merits of the disputes before the courts of appeals could. Hedging against the possibility that the justices would decline to leapfrog the courts of appeals, the government separately asked the Court to stay the district court rulings while those appeals unfolded. In each case, the argument for bypassing the courts of appeals, or at least allowing the Mattis Policy to go into effect pending their review, was similar: "Absent a stay, the nationwide injunction would thus remain in place for at least another year and likely well into 2020—a period too long for the military to be forced to maintain a policy that it has determined, in its professional judgment, to be contrary to the Nation's interests." In other words, the harm from the nationwide injunction was simply the harm of being unable to carry out the policy (and thereby having to allow more transgender individuals to join the military)—and this justified not just emergency relief, but also expedited plenary review on the merits.[31]

On January 22, 2019, the Supreme Court denied the three petitions for certiorari before judgment but granted two of the applications for stays, each over four dissents. The justices declined to take up the merits of the Mattis Policy before the courts of appeals could do so, but allowed it to go into effect while those appeals ran their course. Although the justices had not written a single word in defense of the stays, the message was clear: the harm caused by injunctions necessarily outweighed the harm caused by the underlying policies—meaning that the government would obtain relief in any case in which it had a decent chance of winning on the merits. Thanks to the intervening adoption of the Mattis Policy, that included the transgender ban cases, too.[32]

Government lawyers and their defenders repeatedly portrayed district court abuse of nationwide injunctions as the bogeyman justifying these interventions. But the reality was decidedly to the contrary; the justices blocked injunctions that applied only locally, too. One telling example involved litigation challenging the Trump administration's "public charge rule," which affected immigrants who utilized public benefits such as Medicaid or food assistance, or who were deemed likely to utilize them in the future. A public charge rule had long been in place. However, the new rule expanded what kinds of benefits could be considered as grounds to deny applications to change immigration status or enter the country. Critics worried the new rule would discourage those who needed it from getting medical care and accessing other essential public benefits. When the Supreme Court in January 2020 stayed a nationwide injunction that had prevented the rule from going into effect, it did so largely, according to Justice Gorsuch's concurring opinion (which Justice Thomas joined), because of the nationwide scope of the injunction. In his words, "the real problem here is the increasingly common practice of trial courts ordering relief that transcends the cases before them." Just twenty-five days later, however, the Court also stayed a district court injunction against the same rule that applied only in Illinois—an injunction Gorsuch had specifically distinguished in the prior ruling. Perhaps the justices found some additional problem with the Illinois-specific injunction, but we'll never know; all the majority said was that "the application for stay presented to JUSTICE KAVANAUGH and by him referred to the Court is granted."[33]

Even when the government had little chance of winning on the merits, the Court was still willing to intervene. Consider one of the more controversial limits on asylum imposed by the Trump administration. The United States has obligations under both domestic and international law to allow anyone entering the country, even those who enter surreptitiously and without legal status, to seek asylum if they have a credible fear of persecution in their home country. In 2019, the Trump administration imposed an additional requirement barring applications for asylum from anyone who transited through a "third country" before entering the United States, but did not apply for asylum there. In effect, the rule forbade asylum for virtually anyone (other than Mexican nationals) who entered or sought to enter the United States across the southern border, since all of them necessarily transited through Mexico.[34]

As both a San Francisco–based federal district judge and a unanimous panel of the Ninth Circuit concluded, this "third-country rule" was flatly inconsistent with the statutory authority Congress had delegated to the executive branch. That authority included the power to enter into "safe third country agreements" with countries through which asylum applications had transited before entering the United States, but not the power to unilaterally impose a third-country rule by executive order. (Indeed, there was every reason to believe that Mexico was *not* a "safe third country.") The district court blocked the policy on a nationwide basis, but the Ninth Circuit narrowed the scope of the injunction to cover only those states under its jurisdiction, including Arizona and California. Still, the government asked the Supreme Court to stay even that narrowed injunction. And in *Barr* v. *East Bay Sanctuary Covenant*, the Court, once again, agreed.[35]

Joined by Justice Ginsburg, Justice Sotomayor dissented, emphasizing all of the respects in which the government was likely to lose on the merits. She was right. In July 2020, the Ninth Circuit held on the merits that the third-country rule violated federal law. Once again, the government used clever litigation tactics to avoid having that decision heard by the Supreme Court—asking the full Ninth Circuit to rehear that ruling, a process that (as the government well knew) would take months and almost certainly fail. By the time the court of appeals finally and predictably rejected the government's request on April 8, 2021, it was a moot point; the Biden administration had come into office and rescinded the rule. For eighteen months, though, the Trump administration had succeeded in unlawfully preventing potentially tens of thousands of Central Americans and others from seeking asylum at the southern border through a policy that no federal judge or Supreme Court justice ever endorsed as legal. And all because of an unsigned, unexplained order on the Supreme Court's shadow docket.[36]

Justice Sotomayor's dissent did not just criticize the majority on the merits; it also called out the majority's increasing willingness to grant emergency relief to the solicitor general. "Granting a stay pending appeal should be an 'extraordinary' act," Sotomayor wrote. "Unfortunately, it appears the Government has treated this exceptional mechanism as a new normal. Historically, the Government has made this kind of request rarely; now it does so reflexively." Although Sotomayor directed her criticism to the solicitor general, it was implicitly aimed across the bench. In her view, the problem wasn't just how often the solicitor general was asking for emergency relief; it was how often the Court was answering in the affirmative, and the manner in which it did so. Sotomayor returned to this view five months later in objecting to the stay of the lower-court injunction in the Illinois public charge case. As she wrote, "The Court's recent behavior on stay applications has benefitted one litigant over all others"—the government. Such preferential treatment of the solicitor general, she warned, "erodes the fair and balanced decisionmaking process that this Court must strive to protect."[37]

That the solicitor general had increasingly come to view emergency applications as a means of scoring political points rather than legal ones was reinforced by *Garza* v. *Hargan*, a lawsuit arising out of the Trump administration's refusal to allow minors in immigration detention to have access to otherwise legal abortions. After the district court entered a preliminary injunction, and the DC Circuit, sitting en banc, rejected the government's application for a stay, the solicitor general filed a highly unusual petition for certiorari. The petition did not ask the Court to take up the merits of the dispute, but rather to vacate the lower courts' rulings, which, in the government's view, were mooted when the original plaintiff obtained an abortion in the interim. Moreover, the solicitor general asked the justices to impose sanctions against the American Civil Liberties Union for allegedly misleading the government in order to help the minor in question to procure an abortion. As unusual as it was for the Justice Department to ask the Supreme Court to sanction opposing counsel (even the most knowledgeable historians of the Court could not remember if it had ever happened before), it was especially aggressive in *Garza*, because the allegedly unethical behavior had occurred in the lower courts, not the Supreme Court. Marty Lederman, a former senior Justice Department lawyer and Georgetown University law professor, described the petition as "fundamentally a press release" rather than a legal pleading on par with the high standards set by prior solicitors general.[38]

While that petition was pending, the government became aware of another pregnant teenager ostensibly covered by the lower courts' rulings, and it applied to the Supreme Court for a stay of the injunction as applied to her as well. In other words, the government sought a stay not because it was hoping to preserve its ability to have the Supreme Court reach a different conclusion on the merits (again, the pending petition wasn't asking the justices to even resolve the merits), but simply to prevent one particular minor from obtaining an abortion. When the government subsequently determined that the plaintiff was not actually underage (and was therefore not subject to detention by the Department of Health and Human Services), it withdrew the application.[39]

Of course, all these cases involved immigration and/or national security policies, contexts in which, historically, the Supreme Court has shown significant deference to the executive branch. But perhaps the best example of just how much the Supreme Court watered down the standard for emergency relief during (and in response to) the Trump administration came in a case involving mifepristone, known somewhat better as "RU-486," and even more widely as "the abortion pill."

In 2000, after years of debate and controversy, the US Food and Drug Administration (FDA) approved the use of mifepristone in combination with misoprostol as a means of inducing abortion up to the seventh week of pregnancy—or, where needed, to help manage a miscarriage. To mitigate potential complications from taking the two-drug combination, the FDA at that time required that mifepristone not only be prescribed by specially certified physicians or other medical providers, but that it be administered only in a hospital, clinic, or medical office under that provider's direct supervision. The FDA eventually relaxed the in-person administration requirement, but as of 2020, obtaining mifepristone still required the patient to have a series of in-person contacts with licensed medical professionals (misoprostol, in contrast, could be obtained through retail or mail-order pharmacies).[40]

In response to the COVID pandemic in 2020, the FDA suspended many of its regulatory requirements relating to in-person treatment and authorized telemedicine on a previously unprecedented scale. But it did not change any of the requirements for mifepristone, even though COVID-related closures made it impossible for many providers to comply with them, and COVID-related disruptions made it much harder for pregnant patients to travel to those medical facilities that were even open for in-person care.[41]

Against that backdrop, a federal district judge in Maryland in July 2020 granted a preliminary injunction against the FDA's enforcement of all in-person requirements related to mifepristone until thirty days after the end of the public health emergency caused by the COVID pandemic, setting out his reasons for doing so in an eighty-page opinion. Specifically, Judge Theodore Chuang concluded that the government's refusal to relax the in-person dispensation requirements for mifepristone imposed a substantial obstacle to the right to a previability abortion recognized by *Roe* v. *Wade* in 1973 and reaffirmed in *Planned Parenthood* v. *Casey* in 1992. Moreover, he said, the FDA's willingness to relax other in-person requirements during the COVID pandemic undermined any argument that its refusal was based on concern for the health of the patient, rather than on hostility to abortion as a practice.[42]

After the Fourth Circuit unanimously denied the government's application for a stay, the government once again went to the Supreme Court, applying for a stay of the district court's injunction on August 26, 2020. This should have been a straightforward case; whatever the merits of Judge Chuang's analysis, there was simply no emergency justifying a stay. But when Justice Ginsburg died on September 18, the Court still had not ruled. Apparently, her death had complicated matters. On October 8, the Court issued a bizarre order noting the government's argument that COVID-related circumstances had changed; suggesting that "a more comprehensive record would aid this Court's review"; directing the district court to reconsider the injunction "within 40 days of receiving the government's submission"; and holding the government's application "in abeyance" in the interim. Presumably because they were now tied 4–4, the justices (all except Thomas and Alito, who publicly dissented from what appeared to be a compromise among the other six justices) had agreed to punt.[43]

The issue returned to the (once again full) Court in December, when, after the district court had reaffirmed its July ruling, the government renewed its request for a stay. Finally, on January 12, 2021, the Court granted the government's application, over the public dissents of Justices Breyer, Sotomayor, and Kagan. The majority once again offered no analysis of the merits—let alone any explanation for what emergency justified such relief. This was especially galling because, by that time, the district court's injunction had been in effect for over six months, and yet the government had no evidence that mifepristone prescribed via telemedicine had caused harm to a single patient. The absence of any such evidence certainly seemed to undermine the government's central justification for reinstating the in-person dispensation requirement. Nevertheless, twenty weeks to the day after the government asked the Court to step in, the justices agreed.* In another strongly worded dissent, Justice Sotomayor, joined by Justice Kagan, emphasized not only that "the FDA's policy imposes an unnecessary, unjustifiable, irrational, and undue burden on women seeking an abortion during the current pandemic," but also that "the Government has not demonstrated irreparable harm from the injunction." It didn't matter; eight days before the end of the Trump administration, the idea that the government had to show harm more specific than simply being subject to an injunction had gone by the wayside.[44]

It would be one thing if the Trump-era cases were simply emblematic of a broader shift in the Supreme Court's approach to emergency relief. Perhaps the justices were just categorically opposed to nationwide injunctions. In a 2018 concurrence, Justice Thomas wrote that "universal injunctions are legally and historically dubious," concluding, "If federal courts continue to issue them, this Court is dutybound to adjudicate their authority to do so." And in his opinion concurring in the January 2020 stay in the public charge case, Justice Gorsuch criticized the practice while expressing "hope . . . that we might at an appropriate juncture take up some of the underlying equitable and constitutional questions raised by the rise of nationwide injunctions." Or perhaps the justices now agreed about extending the presumption of constitutionality, so that all injunctions of federal (and state) government action would be disfavored

* To underscore how long the Court sat on the emergency application in the mifepristone case before granting it, during the same time period that the government's application remained on the docket, the justices (1) agreed to conduct plenary merits review of a dispute over whether reapportionment data provided by the secretary of commerce could exclude undocumented immigrants; (2) received full briefing from the parties and numerous friends of the Court; (3) heard oral argument; and (4) handed down a decision on the merits. That whole process took eighty-seven days.

whatever their scope. On that view, the government would be entitled to appellate stays of lower-court decisions if it had *any* chance of winning on appeal. Or maybe it was all about showing special deference to the president in the subject-matter-specific areas of immigration and national security. Maybe the mifepristone case was just an outlier, as abortion cases so often were.[45]

In the abstract, these explanations seem plausible. Taking account of all the Court's work, though, they each run into two separate problems. First, the Court never actually articulated these new understandings of the appropriateness of nationwide injunctions, or the proper deference courts should grant to the political branches of government. Only two of the twenty-seven orders granting emergency relief to the Trump administration were accompanied by a majority rationale—one related to the second travel ban, and the other to the first federal execution since 2003. Thus, if district courts kept getting the same things wrong in enjoining the government, or if appellate courts kept getting the same things wrong in refusing to stay those injunctions, the justices did not identify such a pattern or provide any guidance to prevent those errors from recurring, or suggest that, in fact, the relevant doctrinal rules had changed. We—and, more importantly, lower courts and government actors—are simply left to speculate about why the Supreme Court, having shown such reticence about granting this kind of emergency relief in the past, all of a sudden decided to issue it on such a regular basis. Worse, without written opinions setting forth the Court's rationales, nothing prevents the justices from acting inconsistently in the future, since there's no analysis that binds the future Court to rule the same way.

Second, and bearing that out, none of these behaviors persisted after January 20, 2021. Like the Trump administration, the Biden administration saw a rash of district court rulings subjecting its policy initiatives to nationwide injunctions, especially where immigration and COVID mitigation were concerned. But unlike the Trump administration, the very first time the Biden administration sought an emergency stay of such an injunction, the justices denied the application, with only Justices Breyer, Sotomayor, and Kagan publicly dissenting. (In that case, a suit by Texas challenging the Biden administration's rescission of the Trump-era "Remain in Mexico" asylum protocol, the Court would eventually side with the Biden administration and reverse the district court on the merits, making its unexplained refusal to stay the injunction that much harder to defend.) Apparently, the objections by Justices Thomas and Gorsuch to nationwide injunctions against Trump policies did not apply to similar district court rulings freezing Biden policies; both would dissent in January 2022 when a 5–4 majority voted to stay a nationwide injunction against the vaccination mandate for health-care workers at facilities receiving federal Medicare or Medicaid funding. And when the Biden administration asked the Court in July 2022 to stay a nationwide district court injunction blocking its enforcement priorities for immigrants subject to removal, Thomas and Gorsuch again refused to support a stay, silently joining the 5–4 majority against granting relief. That same order saw the first public vote by Justice Ketanji Brown Jackson—joining Justices Sotomayor, Kagan, and Barrett in dissent (the first 5–4 male-female split in the Court's history).[46]

Likewise, the notion that executive action is generally entitled to a presumption of constitutionality is not just irreconcilable with these votes, but with the Court's broader pattern of behavior in cases challenging COVID-based gathering restrictions on religious liberty grounds. In those rulings, as we'll shortly see, the justices regularly defied their own procedural rules to block a series of blue-state executive orders after lower courts had declined to do so.

Instead, the only explanation that ties these seemingly disparate results together is that, whether because of the solicitor general's new aggressiveness under the Trump administration or merely by coincidence around the same time, the justices came to believe that the underlying merits of the dispute were all that mattered when considering emergency applications. Under the traditional standard, the merits have been a significant part of the analysis, but not the sum total. The Court is also supposed to take into account the harms the parties stand to suffer depending upon which rule governs while the appeal unfolds, and the public interest more generally. But the conclusion that government suffers irreparable injury whenever any of its conduct is enjoined would seemingly justify ignoring any irreparable harm others will suffer if that conduct is allowed to persist, so that the only thing that matters is whether what the government is doing, in the justices' preliminary views, is legal.[47]

Consider, in this regard, the Court's July 2019 stay of lower-court rulings that had blocked President Trump from building a wall at the country's southern border. After Congress expressly refused to fund the endeavor, Trump declared a national emergency, solely so he could attempt to take advantage of an obscure pot of money appropriated for military construction, which could be repurposed only "in the event of a declaration of war or the declaration by the President of a national emergency." Once again, lower courts held that Trump's actions were unlawful, and enjoined them. Once again, the government asked for (and received) a stay from the Supreme Court, which this time cryptically suggested not that the president acted lawfully, but that the plaintiffs in the case—the environmental group Sierra Club and a coalition of communities along the southern border—might not have the right to sue him. Justices Ginsburg, Sotomayor, and Kagan dissented in full, but Justice Breyer dissented only in part. As he wrote, he would have split the difference, allowing the government to finalize construction contracts while leaving the injunction in place as applied to the construction itself, which was not scheduled to begin soon in any case. This kind of balancing of the equities was, historically, the dominant principle governing emergency relief. In *Trump* v. *Sierra Club*, though, it was irrelevant; all that mattered to the five justices in the majority was whether they were ultimately going to rule for the plaintiffs.[48]

The Court made this implicit theme of the Trump-era cases explicit in January 2022. In an unsigned ruling granting emergency relief against a Biden administration policy (the COVID vaccination-or-testing rule imposed on large employers by the Occupational Safety and Health Administration, or OSHA), the justices noted that both sides had identified a series of harms that would result from granting or denying emergency relief. The per curiam opinion then concluded, "It is not our role to weigh such tradeoffs."

If all that mattered were the merits, that would be true enough; an OSHA regulation is either lawful or it isn't. But, at least historically, when faced with an application for emergency relief pending appeal as opposed to plenary review on the merits, weighing such tradeoffs was precisely the Supreme Court's job. The core purpose of the enterprise was to balance the equities as a way of deciding whether it made more sense to leave a lower-court ruling on hold while it was challenged or to allow it to go into effect. Otherwise, as Justice Kagan put it in an April 2022 dissent, "that renders the Court's emergency docket not for emergencies at all. The docket becomes only another place for merits determinations—except made without full briefing and argument." Once again, perhaps the justices in the majority believed that such a balance of the equities should no longer be part of the analysis in such cases. But the OSHA decision nowhere suggested as much, and at least some of the Court's subsequent rulings continued to apply the traditional balancing analysis as if nothing had changed.[49]

This leads to the final—and perhaps most surprising—irony of the Trump administration cases: for all of the government's successes on the shadow docket from 2017 to 2021, almost none of those orders translated into victories on the merits docket. Travel Ban 3.0 was the *only* Trump-era policy the justices originally allowed to go into effect on the shadow docket and later upheld on the merits. By the time the litigation challenging other policies came to the Court via plenary review, President Biden had come to office and rescinded the policies, rendering the legal disputes moot. During the Supreme Court's October 2020 Term alone, the justices dismissed five different challenges to Trump-era policies that they had previously agreed to resolve on the merits—after the policies were unwound by the Biden administration.* Thus, the justices were never forced to revisit their predictive judgments when staying lower-court injunctions of Trump policies; the unexplained stays were, in almost every case, their last word on the subject.[50]

The rise of the shadow docket during the Trump administration was a demonstration of brilliant strategic and tactical litigation by the solicitors general. The men in that position, Noel Francisco and Jeff Wall, salvaged as much of the government's controversial policies as they could for as long as possible, even in the face of a Court that was largely hostile on the merits to the president's more extreme initiatives. Indeed, shadow docket activity became such a staple of the Office of the Solicitor General that a new deputy position was created, principally to handle the government's emergency applications. And so long as the justices acquiesced, some may find it difficult to fault advocates within that office for acting like lawyers, and taking all ethically permissible steps to vindicate the

* The Supreme Court has long recognized that, when an appeal becomes moot while it is still pending through no fault of the party that lost below, it would not be fair to require that party to abide by a ruling it wasn't able to challenge. Instead, the Court in such instances issues what's known as a "*Munsingwear* vacatur" (named after the 1950 decision that first proposed such a solution). Such a ruling summarily wipes the lower-court decision off the books and remands the matter so that it can be dismissed. As the Trump-Biden transition cases underscore, these rulings are yet another example of technical, procedural orders that can produce significant real-world impacts.

underlying interests of their client—even if such an approach went against the historical traditions of the office.

However, so framed, the story of the solicitor general during the Trump administration is a story about using the shadow docket "to prevail in the instant case" at the expense of broader principles, exactly the opposite of how the position had previously been described by both its creators and many of its holders. The shadow docket had become a place for the government's lawyers to achieve short-term wins, even if they compromised longer-term institutional interests. Put another way, the solicitor general's own behavior tacitly conceded that the shadow docket was a place to score political victories as much as (if not more than) legal ones. The point was not to make new law that would apply going forward; it was to use procedural machinations to keep as much of the president's agenda in effect for as long as possible—even (if not especially) those policies that no court would ultimately uphold. After all, if the solicitor general had been confident that these policies truly were lawful, there would have been no need for the government to repeatedly take procedural steps in these cases that slowed down—and eventually frustrated—merits review. Given the shifts in the Court's composition during the Trump administration toward a majority that was more likely to be sympathetic to any Republican administration's initiatives, such skepticism about the government's likelihood of success on the merits in these cases is especially telling.

In that respect, the solicitors general during the Trump administration blew up the shadow docket in two distinct senses of the term. Their aggressive behavior was directly responsible for an unprecedented number of applications for emergency relief being granted by the justices. But the government's litigation behavior also drove home the precise problem with the justices handing down so many unsigned, unexplained rulings that altered the status quo for so many people: the Court's behavior appeared to be transparently political, if not overtly partisan. It's easy to understand why private lawyers bent on winning will take advantage of that trend so long as it favors them. It's much harder to understand how it could be appropriate for the government's principal advocate before the Supreme Court, whose loyalties and responsibilities were supposed to transcend the politics of the moment, to repeatedly and publicly illustrate—and exploit—that pattern.

If there was a silver lining to these efforts, it was how much they were *not* focused on making new law. For all of the other flaws in how the Supreme Court used the shadow docket during the Trump administration, at least the justices stuck to a tacit understanding that emerged from the surge of death penalty cases in the 1980s: these unsigned, unexplained orders, no matter how divisive or significant they were, were meant only to address the status quo; the articulation of new, forward-looking legal rules would have to come on the merits docket. For the more cynical, the shadow docket thereby provided the justices with a means of controlling executive branch policies without having to take a position on their legality—policy without law. But even that situation would soon be overtaken by events. And the next shift would come not from the Court's reaction to Trump administration policies, but from its reactions to the COVID pandemic, especially after the confirmation of Trump's final appointment to the Court, Justice Amy Coney Barrett.

## CHAPTER 5

# COVID AND THE COURT

### HOW THE COURT ABUSED THE SHADOW DOCKET TO EXPAND RELIGIOUS LIBERTY

On Monday, May 4, 2020, the Supreme Court did something it had never done before: It heard oral argument by telephone. Traditionally, the Court was the one institution in Washington that refused to close—even when inclement weather (or, more often, the mere threat of it) shut down the rest of the federal government. Among other things, the Court's obstinacy has led to some well-worn anecdotes about lawyers scheduled to argue on snow days. Lacking any other means of reaching the Court's Capitol Hill building, counsel would often trek through snowdrifts in their formal attire to the nearest justice's house to catch a ride downtown. (The real challenge, as it turns out, was getting a ride home afterward.)[1]

But it wasn't weather that forced the justices in March and April 2020 to postpone their regularly scheduled argument sessions for the first time in over a century; it was the

COVID-19 pandemic.* Starting with a dispute about whether the company "Booking.com" could legally trademark its rather generic corporate name (the Court would eventually say yes), the justices heard arguments and handed down decisions on the merits docket from afar for the rest of the October 2019 Term and the entire October 2020 Term. They would not conduct business in person again for over a year, and would not physically return to the bench until October 2021. (Oral arguments were not reopened to the public until October 2022.)[2]

As with the rest of the world, COVID necessitated changes to the justices' long-standing habits and internal procedures. But far more significantly, it provoked an array of novel legal questions about just how far government officials at every level could go in responding to a global public health emergency. Although COVID cases of all kinds came to the Court, those touching on religious liberty would be the ones in which the justices were the most active. In the immigration and death penalty cases that had come to the shadow docket during the Trump administration, the Court had demonstrated a new willingness to intervene in controversial political battles. As we've seen, though, it had consistently refrained from making new law—from handing down decisions that changed the meaning of federal statutes or constitutional provisions.[3]

With the religious liberty cases, that changed. In these cases, the justices used the shadow docket to expand the religious liberty protected by the Constitution. In the end, these efforts resulted in an understanding of the First Amendment under which far fewer government regulations will now be allowed to burden religious practice, even if the burden is unintentional, than in the past. More starkly, the five-justice majority

* During the fall 2001 anthrax attacks (which, among other things, caused the first closure of the Supreme Court building in its sixty-six-year history), the justices heard oral argument a few blocks away at the DC federal courthouse. But even then, the Court kept to its preset argument schedule.

accomplished that shift by breaking not only the Court's internal norms, but also the rules set by Congress limiting their power to provide such relief, deliberately choosing to make new law on the shadow docket rather than the merits docket.[4]

The turnabout in religious liberty cases happened virtually overnight, and was made possible only by the unexpected death of Justice Ruth Bader Ginsburg in September 2020 and her replacement one month later by Justice Amy Coney Barrett. That shift solidified the Court's conservative majority and marginalized Chief Justice Roberts's vote, which had been decisive in COVID cases up to that point. Barrett would write her first opinion on the Court in one of the COVID-related shadow-docket religion cases, and her vote would allow legal arguments that had been made only in dissent as late as July 2020 to become the law of the land within a month of her confirmation. It was a stunningly impactful debut for a brand-new justice—albeit one that was largely overlooked because it came entirely on the shadow docket.[5]

The First Amendment to the US Constitution protects religious liberty in two respects. First, the Establishment Clause prohibits Congress from enacting any law "respecting an establishment of religion." That language bans any state religion or government-endorsed preference for any particular sect, or even for religion over the lack thereof. Second, the Free Exercise Clause bars laws that "prohibit the free exercise" of religion, keeping the government from interfering in religious practice. In a society founded largely on the principle that those of different faiths (or no faith) should be able to live side by side in peace, these two guarantees, which have long been understood to apply to all government actors in the United States, and not just Congress, prevent the government from doing either too much or too little with respect to religion.

But what is "too much," and what is "too little"? Consider zoning regulations and fire codes, for instance. Is it unconstitutional for local governments to enact rules that impact both where and how houses of worship can be constructed? What about religious employers? Can they be required to follow federal antidiscrimination laws when it comes to the hiring and firing of ministers? Of janitors? Can states refuse to allow religious schools to participate in educational grant programs out of concern that public tax dollars will end up subsidizing religious education? From the Founding onward, questions like these have been left largely to the courts. And for decades, the Supreme Court's answers were, to put it mildly, inconsistent.

In its landmark 1990 ruling in *Employment Division* v. *Smith*, the Court consciously attempted to bring some degree of clarity to its doctrine. *Smith* upheld Oregon's refusal to provide unemployment benefits to an individual who was fired for using peyote in violation of state law, even though it was undisputed that his use of the drug was part of a religious ritual. In an opinion written by Justice Antonin Scalia, the majority held that laws that burden religious practice should not be subject to especially rigid judicial scrutiny unless they single out religion. Otherwise, Justice Scalia wrote, courts would be in a difficult position because of America's dual commitment to religious freedom. After all, if all laws burdening religious exercise were constitutionally problematic, that "would open the prospect of constitutionally required exemptions from civic obligations of almost every conceivable kind." Governments would have to walk on regulatory eggshells if every single law had to accommodate every single religious belief. Thus, *Smith* was understood to establish that the Free Exercise Clause is not offended merely because a law impacts religious practice. Rather, the Constitution is violated only if that was the law's purpose.[6]

From the day it was decided, *Smith* was controversial. Because the rule Justice Scalia articulated in *Smith* was generally deferential to democratic majorities in the political branches of government, liberals worried that it would unduly burden minority religions, perhaps even forcing members of those religions to relocate to parts of the country more tolerant of their religious practices. As time went on, though, and more and more jurisdictions across the United States enacted laws that appeared to burden widely held Christian beliefs, as well, conservatives also began to turn on *Smith*.[7]

In 1993, while this shift was in its early stages, Congress passed the Religious Freedom Restoration Act (RFRA). "RIFF-ruh" represented a compromise between liberals and conservatives, and an overt attempt to undermine *Smith*. The new law did not purport to redefine the Free Exercise Clause; Congress can neither overrule the Supreme Court's constitutional interpretations nor amend the Constitution by statute. But it did attempt to require, as a matter of federal law, that courts hearing challenges to laws burdening religious practice apply what is known as "strict scrutiny," that is, uphold only those laws that are narrowly tailored (neither overbroad nor underinclusive) to achieve a compelling governmental interest. This was a far cry from *Smith*, under which laws incidentally burdening religious practice needed only a "rational basis" to survive. Strict scrutiny, the saying goes, is often "strict in theory, but fatal in fact," because, relative to their goals, laws of general applicability are invariably based upon generalizations, and tend to therefore be both overbroad and underinclusive. RFRA thus appeared to restore the law to what it was before *Smith*; that is, governments would need both special justifications and precisely calibrated rules for any laws that imposed even incidental burdens on religious practice. If the government couldn't adequately explain why a church of a particular size had to have fifteen fire exits rather than ten, then the fire code would be preempted by RFRA.[8]

In 1997, however, the Supreme Court held that RFRA exceeded Congress's constitutional authority to pass laws directly regulating local and state governments. The decision in *City of*

*Boerne* v. *Flores* did not affect the federal government, which is still bound by RFRA's more exacting standard today. And in response to the ruling, at least twenty-one state legislatures enacted some analogue to RFRA as a matter of state law, while the supreme courts of several other states derived similar principles from their state constitutions. But that still left *Smith*'s deferential standard in place as the governing baseline in just under half of the states. The courts in those states upheld laws burdening religious practice so long as the law applied to secular and religious activities alike and the burden on religion was not intentional. Those RFRA-free jurisdictions, where the governments tended to be controlled by Democrats, would be the focal point for the cases arising out of the COVID pandemic.[9]

By the end of the 1990s, both *Smith* and the interference with religious practice that it tolerated had become the bête noire of conservative commentators and jurists. Religious liberty gradually appeared to provide conservatives with a cudgel against the growing scope of federal antidiscrimination rules—protecting the right of a cakeshop owner to refuse to bake a cake for a gay wedding, for example; or the right of a corporation to refuse to include contraceptive coverage in the health insurance it provided to its employees. Whether as cause or effect of that evolution, disagreements about the scope of the Free Exercise Clause increasingly broke neatly along partisan political lines.[10]

As this shift crystallized in the early 2000s, conservatives relied in part on an important precedent stemming from a 1999 opinion for the Philadelphia-based Third Circuit written by then circuit court judge Samuel Alito. At issue in that case, *Fraternal Order of Police Newark Lodge No. 12* v. *City of Newark*, was a Newark Police Department policy prohibiting male officers from having beards unless justified for medical reasons or when going undercover. Two Sunni Muslim officers sued, challenging the no-beard policy on the ground that it violated the First Amendment insofar as they had a religious obligation to grow a beard. Writing for the court of appeals, Alito agreed, because the policy included at least one secular exception. In his words, "the Department's decision to provide medical exemptions while refusing religious exemptions is sufficiently suggestive of discriminatory intent so as to trigger heightened scrutiny," which it did not survive. To Alito, the issue wasn't just that the policy had a secular exception with no corresponding religious exception; it was that this dichotomy appeared to be intentional, which is why heightened scrutiny was appropriate even under *Smith*.[11]

Under this view, which scholars have dubbed the "most-favored-nation" theory of the Free Exercise Clause, neutral laws that burden religious practice will still be constitutionally suspect if they include any secular exceptions without exceptions for "comparable" religious activities. And although Alito attempted to explain why this understanding was not inconsistent with *Smith* (to him, treating comparable secular and religious activities differently was itself evidence of discriminatory intent), the practical impact would be to turn *Smith* on its head. After all, almost every government regulation has at least some exceptions. Speed limits, to take just one example, do not apply to properly signed police, fire, or other emergency vehicles in appropriate circumstances. And a zoning regulation that prevents commercial establishments from being located in a particular neighborhood might have a carve-out for a therapist who sees patients in a home office.

Judge Alito's *Fraternal Order of Police* opinion wasn't the only one to apply heightened scrutiny to cases in which *Smith* appeared to counsel deference. Additional efforts to chip away at *Smith* followed, especially in the lower federal courts. The Supreme Court moved more slowly. Although it handed down a series of decisions in the mid-2010s that at least outwardly favored religious liberty claims, those cases often produced fractured results or rested on narrow grounds, reflecting the lack of a majority, at least so long as Justice Kennedy was the swing vote, for any broader reconsideration of *Smith*.[12]

But by the time Kennedy retired in 2018, no justice remained who had been on the Court when *Smith* was decided. Six months later, Kennedy's successor, Justice Kavanaugh, joined Justices Thomas, Alito, and Gorsuch in a brief opinion hinting that the Court should revisit *Smith* in an appropriate case. And on February 24, 2020, the Court appeared to find such a case on its merits docket, granting certiorari in *Fulton* v. *City of Philadelphia*. At issue in *Fulton* was Philadelphia's 2018 decision to cut off referrals of prospective foster-care children to Catholic Social Services after learning that the agency categorically refused to certify unmarried couples or same-sex married couples to be foster parents. Represented by the Becket Fund for Religious Liberty, Catholic Social Services and two prospective foster parents sued, claiming that Philadelphia's decision discriminated against them because of their religious beliefs. And one of the questions the Court agreed to answer when it granted certiorari in the *Fulton* appeal was whether, insofar as Philadelphia's decision did not violate *Smith*, *Smith* itself should be overruled. Ordinarily, the case would have been scheduled for argument that fall, producing a decision by the following summer. But before any of that could happen, the pandemic came along.[13]

Although state COVID restrictions were challenged on a dizzying array of grounds, the suits that garnered the most attention were challenges to restrictions on religious services in states without their own RFRAs. The first of those cases to reach the Supreme Court, in May 2020, involved the South Bay Pentecostal Church in Chula Vista, California, just south of San Diego. At issue in *South Bay United Pentecostal Church* v. *Newsom*, which would become known as *South Bay I*, was California's effort to relax its original COVID-based ban on indoor public gatherings, which, as modified, effectively limited attendance at indoor religious services to either 25 percent of the building's capacity or one hundred attendees, whichever was fewer. The church argued that, because it had a capacity of six hundred congregants, and usually had roughly two hundred or three hundred congregants in attendance, California's limits would impair religious exercise, especially in light of the state's failure to likewise impair what the church described as "comparable" secular activities, such as small businesses. After all, the church could only be at one-sixth capacity, whereas small businesses under the same limits could operate at one-quarter capacity. California responded by noting the numerous instances in which COVID had been spread to large groups of people during a religious service; flagging the different but also strict limits on secular indoor gatherings, such as concerts, movies, plays, and spectator sports; and stressing that it was attempting to relax the restrictions as quickly as public health experts deemed reasonable.[14]

The lower courts refused to put California's restrictions on hold while the church pursued its case. That made this case unlike the Trump-era cases, for instance, in which the government so often asked the Supreme Court for a stay to put an adverse lower-court injunction on hold while it was challenged on appeal. There was no injunction for the Court to freeze in the church's case, and courts can't issue a stay of nothing. Instead, the church had to ask the justices for a more aggressive form of emergency relief—an "emergency writ of injunction," through which the justices themselves could pause California's rules while the church fought its case in the lower courts.[15]

The problem for the church was that the distinction between an emergency stay and an emergency injunction is far more than semantic. A stay pending appeal is simply an appellate court pausing the effect of a lower court's ruling. But an injunction pending appeal is an appellate court directly halting the defendant's ongoing conduct in circumstances in which the lower courts had necessarily refused to do so. Thus, a stay pending appeal restores the status quo that existed prior to a ruling by a lower court; an injunction pending appeal disrupts that status quo. That's why, as Justice Scalia had explained in 1986, an emergency injunction "demands a significantly higher justification" than a stay: appellate courts need a stronger case for restraining the parties to a lawsuit than they do for restraining the courts from which those parties are appealing.[16]

Emergency injunctions and emergency stays do not just serve different functional purposes, but the Court's formal authority to issue them comes from entirely different sources. The former rely on a statute called the All Writs Act that was part of the original Judiciary Act of 1789, whereas the latter are based on the Judiciary Act of 1925. That distinction matters—the Court's formal power under the older law is far more limited than its more flexible authority deriving from the later reforms. Unless parties seeking emergency injunctions pending appeal can show that their right to relief is "indisputably clear," the justices lack the authority to issue such orders. (A stay, in contrast, requires the applicant to show, among other things, only a "reasonable likelihood of success on the merits," which means it can be based upon new law as well as old.) Another way of thinking about this distinction is that for relief to be justified under the All Writs Act (so, for an injunction pending appeal), there has to be some showing that a lower court not only erred, but made a mistake that no reasonable judge could have made. In contrast, relief under the 1925 stay provision, which appears in the US Code at 28 U.S.C. § 2101(f), merely requires that the traditional factors for pausing a lower-court ruling weigh in favor of doing so—factors that can be satisfied even, in some cases, if the lower court did not err at all. That distinction helps to explain why the Court had not issued an emergency injunction in any case since 2015. That was in a Hawaii election dispute, and was one of only four injunctions the Court had issued in the nearly fifteen years since Chief Justice Roberts's appointment in September 2005.[17]

The technical but meaningful distinction between a stay and an injunction loomed large when, over four dissents, the justices turned away the South Bay Pentecostal Church's request in a summary, one-sentence order filed on May 29, 2020. There was no majority opinion to explain the 5–4 ruling. But Chief Justice Roberts, whose vote was decisive, wrote a solo opinion concurring in the denial of relief that rested on this exact procedural point—that the Court applies a stricter standard for emergency injunctive relief than it does for a stay pending appeal. In his words, "The precise question of when restrictions on particular social activities should be lifted during the pandemic is a dynamic and fact-intensive matter subject to reasonable disagreement," all the more so "while local officials are actively shaping their response to changing facts on the ground." Invoking the Court's high standard for an emergency injunction, Roberts concluded that "the notion that it is 'indisputably clear' that the Government's limitations are unconstitutional seems quite improbable." Over a dissenting opinion by Justice Kavanaugh (joined by Justices Thomas and Gorsuch), and an unexplained dissent by Justice Alito, California's restrictions were allowed to remain in place.[18]

History repeated itself two months later, when Calvary Chapel Dayton Valley (a small church about forty-five minutes southeast of Reno) sued to challenge Nevada's restrictions on indoor gatherings. In *Calvary Chapel Dayton Valley* v. *Sisolak*, the specific problem the church identified was that, true to form, Nevada (and its governor, Steve Sisolak) had exempted casinos from its rules but not houses of worship. Thus, even if California's indoor gathering rules could have been justified on the ground that small businesses can't easily be analogized to large churches, the same didn't hold for casinos, which were nonessential indoor businesses in which large numbers of people tend to closely congregate for extended periods of time. Once again, the lower courts refused to block the state restrictions. Once again, the church applied to the Supreme Court for an injunction pending appeal. Once again, by the same 5–4 vote, the justices declined.[19]

In his dissent in the Nevada case, Justice Kavanaugh attempted to explain why, even if the California church did not deserve relief in May, the Nevada church did in July. As Justice Alito put it in his dissent, "The Constitution guarantees the free exercise of religion. It says nothing about the freedom to play craps or blackjack, to feed tokens into a slot machine, or to engage in any other game of chance." None of the dissenting opinions, however, specifically argued that Calvary Chapel had met the very high standard for an emergency injunction pending appeal. Without Chief Justice Roberts (who, unlike in *South Bay I*, did not write separately in the Nevada case), that argument was, quite clearly, insufficient to produce a majority. The battle lines, as they were, appeared to be drawn.[20]

Then, on September 18, 2020, eighty-seven-year-old justice Ruth Bader Ginsburg lost her battle with pancreatic cancer, becoming only the third justice to die in office since 1954. Ginsburg's death, among many other things, left what had been a stable 5–4 majority against emergency relief in the COVID religious liberty cases as a 4–4 deadlock. As we saw in the death penalty cases, the lower courts' rulings under these circumstances, whether granting or denying emergency relief, would automatically be left intact. But this deadlocked state of affairs wouldn't last very long.

With the presidential election less than six weeks away, President Trump and the Republican-controlled Senate hustled to name and confirm Ginsburg's successor, forty-eight-year-old Seventh Circuit judge and former Notre Dame law professor Amy Coney Barrett. Barrett, a devout Catholic who had written extensively about her faith before taking the bench, was confirmed by the Senate on October 26 and took office the next day, just one week before the 2020 presidential election. Although she would join her colleagues on the phone for oral arguments in regularly scheduled merits cases the following Monday, her first publicly revealed vote would not come until religious liberty challenges to COVID restrictions returned to the shadow docket, as they would just before Thanksgiving. And her vote would flip the Court.

Just three weeks after Ginsburg's death, the Roman Catholic Diocese of Brooklyn and the Agudath Israel Synagogue filed separate lawsuits challenging New York's complicated and evolving COVID restrictions, which imposed varying attendance limits at houses of worship depending upon the recent prevalence of new cases in surrounding neighborhoods. Everyone agreed that the New York restrictions treated houses of worship and businesses differently. The complication was that, in a majority of cases, it treated them more favorably than nonessential secular businesses. For instance, in so-called "red zones" (those with the highest rates of infection), houses of worship could hold no more than 25 percent of their maximum occupancy or ten people, whichever was fewer. In contrast, the order simply closed nonessential secular businesses in those areas ("essential" businesses were allowed to remain open, albeit with their own restrictions). The diocese and the synagogue both claimed that the order thereby singled out religious practice in violation of the Free Exercise Clause.

On October 9, 2020, Brooklyn district judge Eric Komitee refused the diocese's request for a temporary restraining order. Citing Chief Justice Roberts's concurring opinion in *South Bay I*, Komitee wrote that "the government is afforded wide latitude in managing the spread of deadly diseases under the Supreme Court's precedent." On the same day, a different district judge likewise denied Agudath Israel's request for a temporary restraining order on similar grounds. After a bit of procedural wrangling in the district court, both parties challenged those decisions in the Second Circuit.[21]

On November 9, the court of appeals agreed to speed up the merits of both appeals but declined to put New York's restrictions on hold while those appeals were resolved. Also citing Chief Justice Roberts's concurrence in *South Bay I*, the court explained that "COVID-19 restrictions that treat places of worship on a par with or more favorably than comparable secular gatherings do not run afoul of the Free Exercise Clause." Judge Michael Park dissented from the Second Circuit's ruling. His objection focused not on the distinction between houses of worship and nonessential secular businesses, but on the distinction between those religious institutions and *essential* secular businesses. Because the New York restrictions were more restrictive of houses of worship in red zones than of essential secular businesses such as banks and grocery stores, he argued, they ran afoul of the Constitution.[22]

Three days later, the diocese applied to the Supreme Court for an emergency injunction pending appeal. The application, which would shortly be joined by a similar application from Agudath Israel, picked up on Judge Park's dissent. Its central claim was that, compared to at least some essential secular businesses, New York was treating houses of worship unfavorably. In its response filed on November 18, New York explained that, already, the decrease in cases in the relevant neighborhoods had automatically loosened the restrictions on churches operated by the Roman Catholic Diocese. Indeed, as of Friday, November 20, none of the diocese's churches remained in red or orange zones, so none of them were actually subject to gathering-size limits.[23]

The diocese's challenge therefore appeared to be moot, which would usually be a reason to dismiss its lawsuit altogether. The churches were no longer subject to the restrictions they were challenging. Even if the courts still had the power to resolve the underlying dispute (mootness doesn't apply to cases in which defendants have voluntarily ceased their complained-of conduct), the diocese's request for an emergency injunction pending appeal seemed, at the very least, unnecessary. But the diocese responded that the New York restrictions were a "Sword of Damocles" over its head because they could go back into effect at any time, were the number of positive cases in surrounding neighborhoods to rise again.[24]

Although the diocese and Agudath Israel had urged the Court to act by Friday, November 20, no orders came down through the close of business on the day before Thanksgiving, Wednesday, November 25. Then, four minutes before midnight, the Court, with no public warning, handed down its rulings. With Justice Barrett silently joining the four dissenters from *South Bay I* and *Calvary Chapel*, the new majority voted 5–4 in both cases to block New York's restrictions.[25]

In *Roman Catholic Diocese of Brooklyn* v. *Cuomo*, the majority joined together to write a short, unsigned per curiam opinion purporting to explain its rationale. But even though the Court's precedents for emergency injunctions pending appeal were well settled (and, as noted, required a showing that the applicant's entitlement to relief was "indisputably clear"), the majority instead analyzed the diocese's claims under a different rubric. The analysis focused entirely on the traditional (and far weaker) standard that *trial* courts use to decide whether to issue a preliminary injunction at the outset of a new lawsuit. The justices never explained why they'd chosen to take that approach. Instead, all that the opinion considered was whether the diocese was likely to succeed on the merits and whether it would be irreparably harmed if the restrictions were to remain in place while its legal challenge worked its way through the courts. Echoing Judge Park, the majority said yes on both counts.[26]

The irreparable harm analysis was especially ironic given that the diocese's churches were no longer subject to *any* capacity restrictions. The Supreme Court majority responded, though, by invoking the hypothetical specter that they might be in the future: "The Governor [Andrew Cuomo] regularly changes the classification of particular areas without prior notice. If that occurs again, the reclassification will almost certainly bar individuals in the affected area from attending services before judicial relief can be obtained." The justices had long interpreted the Constitution to bar federal courts from remedying future injuries unless they were "certainly impending." But here, the new conservative majority was not only willing to provide a remedy for a hypothetical future scenario, but to provide the extraordinary remedy of an emergency injunction pending appeal. And all of this was only possible because of Justice Barrett, who joined the majority opinion without comment.[27]

Although the majority opinion in *Roman Catholic Diocese* focused its analysis on the debatable claim that New York was singling out religious worship for especially discriminatory treatment, Justices Gorsuch and Kavanaugh each wrote separately to suggest an even broader objection to New York's restrictions. In their concurring opinions, both justices nodded more aggressively toward the "most-favored-nation" view of the Free Exercise Clause. As Justice Kavanaugh put it, the central problem with the New York restrictions was that "in a red zone, for example, a church or synagogue must adhere to a 10-person attendance cap, while a grocery store, pet store, or big-box store down the street does not face the same restriction." The deferential standard articulated in *Smith* was nowhere to be seen.[28]

The three more liberal justices dissented. They disagreed with the majority's analysis of the Free Exercise Clause issue and argued, in detail, that injunctive relief was inappropriate because the diocese's churches were no longer subject to capacity restrictions. As Justices Breyer and Sotomayor each noted in separate dissenting opinions (both of which were joined by Justice Kagan), it was pointless to issue an emergency injunction (and impossible to meet the standard for one) because the relief the majority had voted to issue would have no immediate effect.[29]

It was on this last point that Chief Justice Roberts focused his separate dissent, just the second time in his fifteen years on the Court in which he wrote a dissenting opinion for only himself. Noting that he agreed with Justice Kavanaugh's concurrence (that New York's rules were distinguishable from, and more problematic than, the ones he had voted not to block in the California and Nevada cases), the chief justice nevertheless focused once again on procedure. Even though he apparently had the same problems with the New York rules as his colleagues in the majority, he was not prepared to use the rare remedy of an emergency injunction, or the shadow docket more generally, to address them. Just as in his concurring opinion in *South Bay I*, the chief justice emphasized the proper limits on the Court's power to provide emergency relief. The only difference was that, with Justice Barrett having replaced Justice Ginsburg, his view was no longer controlling.[30]

Not long after the rulings in *Roman Catholic Diocese* and its companion case, *Agudath Israel of America* v. *Cuomo*, the Court's new majority made clear that its First Amendment concerns with capacity restrictions on religious gatherings were not limited to New York. What's more, rather than writing additional majority opinions to carefully explicate why these other cases from different states raised similar concerns, the justices sent that message through a new form of summary, unexplained shadow docket procedure.[31]

In *Harvest Rock Church* v. *Newsom*, for instance, another California church (this one in Pasadena) challenged the evolving capacity restrictions the state had imposed on churches under Governor Gavin Newsom and asked the Supreme Court for an emergency injunction after lower courts, ruling before *Roman Catholic Diocese* and relying on *South Bay I*, had refused to provide one. Unlike in the New York cases, the justices declined to grant such relief. Instead, they took the church's application for an emergency injunction and treated it as something else. In a short order, the Court transmogrified the church's application for emergency relief into a petition for a writ of certiorari "before judgment," that is, for plenary review before the court of appeals was given a chance to rule on the church's appeal.

But whereas "cert. before judgment" has historically been a means of expediting merits consideration in important and time-sensitive disputes, here the justices combined it with another procedural device—the "GVR" order we saw earlier, which summarily grants a petition, vacates the lower court's order, and remands for reconsideration in light of a recent development. In this instance, that intervening development was the Thanksgiving-eve ruling in *Roman Catholic Diocese.* In other words, with one (rather long) sentence, the justices took the church's application for an emergency injunction, turned it into a petition for cert. before judgment, wiped away the district court's ruling denying the church's request for a preliminary injunction, and commanded the lower courts to reevaluate whether Harvest Rock Church was entitled to relief in light of the Supreme Court's cursory (and New York–specific) shadow docket analysis in *Roman Catholic Diocese.* Without issuing any relief directly, and without agreeing to conduct plenary review of the church's appeal, the Court instead used the shadow docket to compel the district court to take a do-over.[32]

Perhaps because no justice publicly dissented, the order in *Harvest Rock Church* went largely unnoticed. But it's worth pausing for a moment to reflect on how remarkable and unprecedented the justices' unorthodox procedural move truly was. Recall that the 5–4 majority in *Roman Catholic Diocese* had focused on the uniquely problematic nature of New York's restrictions, treating houses of worship in "red" and "orange" zones more harshly than "essential" secular businesses. And yet, eight days after the *Roman Catholic Diocese* ruling, the Court invoked it to wipe away a district court ruling that had refused to block California's less onerous restrictions. In other words, the justices effectively ordered the lower courts to try to sort out for themselves how a brief shadow docket ruling about New York's COVID restrictions could and should apply to California's. The Supreme Court's ruling in *Roman Catholic Diocese* had changed the law in New York; *Harvest Rock Church* implied (but did not actually *say*) that it had thereby meant to change the law nationwide.[33]

Nor were the justices focused only on the nation's two largest blue states. On December 15, the Court issued the same kind of novel relief it had fashioned in the *Harvest Rock Church* case in different disputes arising from New Jersey and Colorado. In both cases, as it had in *Harvest Rock Church*, the Court took applications for injunctions, turned them into petitions for cert. before judgment, and used that to justify wiping the district court rulings off the books and remanding for reconsideration.[34]

The subtext of these machinations may well be lost in their procedural subtlety. Indeed, that was quite possibly the point. These unsigned one-sentence orders from the Supreme Court weren't explicitly compelling the lower courts to block their states' COVID restrictions. But they carried at least *some* meaning. At bottom, they represented a signal to lower courts, state officials, and religious groups that the Court had changed its analysis of the Free Exercise Clause in *Roman Catholic Diocese* far more than what the seven-page majority opinion in that case had actually said. The Court may well have been seeking to use these procedural orders to accomplish the same goals as in *Roman Catholic Diocese*, but without having to expend additional capital and without nearly as much effort or attention.[35]

Without further guidance, in both the *South Bay* and *Harvest Rock* cases, the Ninth Circuit returned the disputes to the district courts. There, not only did California continue to defend its restrictions, but it introduced significant new evidence, including detailed scientific reports and expert testimony supporting the distinctions that its revised restrictions drew. Among other things, California introduced evidence that indoor religious services had become a significant vector for the spread of COVID across the state. As California argued, that data justified more aggressive measures in those areas with the highest positivity rates, including outright bans on indoor religious services in some areas, and a 25 percent capacity restriction and ban on singing or chanting (because of the documented risk of viral spread resulting from those specific activities) in others.[36]

Based on this evidence, separate district courts concluded that the revised California restrictions did not suffer from the same infirmities as the ones the Supreme Court had identified in *Roman Catholic Diocese*. Following the district courts' lead, the Ninth Circuit refused to enjoin most of the restrictions pending the churches' appeals, though it did enjoin attendance caps of one hundred or two hundred persons in some areas. Both churches then returned to the Supreme Court. And just like the religious groups in the New York case, they asked for emergency injunctions pending appeal.[37]

At 10:44 p.m. on Friday, February 5, 2021, the Court largely obliged. In unsigned orders in *South Bay II* and *Harvest Rock II*, the Court issued separate emergency injunctions against many of California's new restrictions. The Court blocked the prohibition on indoor religious services in "Tier 1" (areas with the highest incidence of the virus) but left in place the 25 percent capacity restriction on such services, along with the ban on singing or chanting during indoor services. There was no majority opinion to explain either why the categorical prohibition was being blocked or why the other provisions were being left intact. But there were several separate statements by justices whose votes had created a majority for the bottom line.[38]

Justices Thomas, Alito, and Gorsuch would have blocked the restrictions in their entirety (although Alito noted that he would have given the state thirty additional days to defend the percentage capacity restrictions); Justices Breyer, Kagan, and Sotomayor would have left them all in place. That left Chief Justice Roberts and Justices Kavanaugh and Barrett somewhere in the middle. As in *South Bay I*, Roberts wrote a solo concurrence (this one running two paragraphs), briefly reiterating his view that governments were entitled to deference in responding to COVID, with the terse caveat that "deference, though broad, has its limits." And Kavanaugh joined a separate concurrence by Barrett, whose first signed opinion on the Court ran one full paragraph.[39]

Usually, a new justice's "maiden opinion" is independently noteworthy. By tradition, it's meant to be a straightforward opinion for the Court in an uncontroversial merits case, where the other justices show their support by not publicly disagreeing with their new colleague. It was a sign of the times, then, that Justice Barrett's debut opinion came in a religious liberty case on the shadow docket. One month before her first signed opinion for the Court in an argued case (for a 7–2 majority expanding an exception to the Freedom of Information Act), Barrett penned a short concurrence to a late-Friday-night shadow docket ruling in which the Court granted another emergency injunction pending appeal.[40]

As she explained, the reason that she and Justice Kavanaugh were joining the three more progressive justices to leave the singing ban intact was that it just wasn't clear if the ban singled out religious performances: "Of course, if a chorister can sing in a Hollywood studio but not in her church, California's regulations cannot be viewed as neutral. But the record is uncertain, and the decisions below unfortunately shed little light on the issue." Given that the entire dispute had reached the Justices on an application for an emergency injunction before there was an opportunity for the parties to develop any evidentiary record in the trial court, it could hardly have been surprising that the record was unclear. Indeed, even Justice Gorsuch (who wrote for himself and Justices Thomas and Alito in explaining why he would have blocked the singing restrictions) conceded that the record was unsettled; he just wouldn't give the state the benefit of the doubt. That view might make sense in the abstract, but it did not in the procedurally fraught context of an application for an emergency injunction, where, again, the burden is on the party seeking relief (in this case, the church) to show that the violation of its rights is "indisputably clear," not on the state to show that it isn't. In that context, a lack of clarity in the record ought to be a reason to deny relief, not a reason to grant it.[41]

The majority's decision to block the prohibition on indoor services provoked a strident dissent by Justice Kagan, who opened by noting that "Justices of this Court are not scientists."

The crux of her opinion, which Justices Breyer and Sotomayor joined, was that California had based its restrictions on careful study and detailed testimony from public health experts. This was factual evidence that, at least at that point in the litigation, the majority was supposed to accept as true, and that the justices forming the majority had done nothing to rebut in their separate writings. And, critically, Kagan pointed out, the rules applied to religious and secular assemblies alike, including political gatherings, which were also specifically protected by the First Amendment.[42]

Worse still, Kagan explained, was the fact that the Court had provided no explanation for its decision: "Is it that the Court does not believe the science, or does it think even the best science must give way? In any event, the result is clear: The State may not treat worship services like activities found to pose a comparable COVID risk, such as political meetings or lectures." But what about decision-makers elsewhere, or confronting other regulations? "The Court's decision," Kagan wrote, "leaves state policymakers adrift, in California and elsewhere." She concluded, "It is difficult enough in a predictable legal environment to craft COVID policies that keep communities safe. That task becomes harder still when officials must guess which restrictions this Court will choose to strike down. The Court injects uncertainty into an area where uncertainty has human costs."[43]

Finally, Kagan's dissent closed with what was, for her, an unusually personal swipe at the majority, and the relative safety from which they had issued their unsigned order: "If this decision causes suffering," she wrote, "we will not pay. Our marble halls are now closed to the public, and our life tenure forever insulates us from responsibility for our errors." It was quite a shot for her to take at her colleagues, and unusual for any justice, let alone one who had developed a reputation during her first decade on the Court for collegiality and civility, even, if not especially, in dissent. And it wouldn't be her last.[44]

Just as they had after their November ruling in the New York *Roman Catholic Diocese* case, the justices quickly invoked *South Bay II* as the basis for ordering a district court to reconsider its refusal to enjoin a separate aspect of California's COVID restrictions. But the *Roman Catholic Diocese* order had at least included an opinion for the Court; *South Bay II* had no such majority rationale. That didn't stop the justices, though. Just three days after *South Bay II*, the Court handed down an unsigned order in a case captioned *Gish* v. *Newsom* that shows just how much the pathology of the shadow docket had evolved: there was no majority opinion in *South Bay II* for the lower courts to follow, and therefore no analysis to govern other cases; the justices simply assumed that lower courts would be able to read the tea leaves from the fact that they had enjoined California's restrictions, and from the separate opinions *disagreeing* as to why. The *Gish* order thus "GVR'd" the dispute, wiping away a lower-court decision that refused to block other California COVID restrictions "for reconsideration in light of [*South Bay II*]."[45]

But whereas *Gish* simply wiped away a lower-court ruling and ordered a do-over, three weeks after *South Bay II*, when the Gateway City Church in San Jose challenged not the State of California's restrictions on indoor gatherings, but those of Santa Clara County, the *South Bay II* majority went much further. Santa Clara County's restrictions were carefully and deliberately crafted to avoid the issue that had doomed California's; they specifically avoided drawing any distinction between religious and secular facilities. And yet, although the Ninth Circuit had explained in detail why the county's rules were therefore not subject to the same infirmities as those the justices had identified in their various concurring opinions in *South Bay II*, the Supreme Court, in (yet another) unsigned late-Friday-night order, not only enjoined the county's restrictions without providing any analysis explaining why it was doing so, but criticized the court of appeals in the process. As the unsigned order in *Gateway City Church* v. *Newsom* explained, "The Ninth Circuit's failure to grant relief was erroneous" because "this outcome is clearly dictated by this Court's decision" in *South Bay II*. Of course, the conclusion of the lower court's analysis was that the Santa Clara County restrictions stood on *different* footing from the California restrictions that the Supreme Court had blocked in *South Bay II*. And yet, not only did the Court decline to explain why that analysis was wrong, but for the first time, the Court made explicit what its growing body of remand orders had only implicitly signaled: even unsigned emergency orders, such as *South Bay II*, were to be given precedential effect by lower courts, despite a long-standing tradition to give them no such weight.[46]

The summary, unsigned orders in *South Bay II* and *Gateway City Church* drove home that the justices were not willing to let California's restrictions on indoor religious services in houses of worship, or those of its subdivisions, stand under any circumstances. But what about the state's distinct limits on in-home gatherings? Based upon significant testimony and input from epidemiologists and other public health experts, California had limited all gatherings in private homes to members of no more than three households—with no exceptions. To whatever extent discernible principles could be extracted from the separate opinions in *South Bay II*, they didn't seem to apply to a policy that imposed categorical and religiously neutral capacity restrictions in private residences.

That's why, on March 30, 2021, the Ninth Circuit denied a request for an emergency injunction pending appeal from two pastors claiming that the in-home gathering limits unconstitutionally interfered with their right to conduct Bible study and hold prayer meetings in their personal homes. By a 2–1 vote, the panel of three Republican appointees held that "the record does not support that private religious gatherings in homes are comparable—in terms of risk to public health or reasonable safety measures to address that risk—to commercial activities, or even to religious activities, in public buildings." In other words, even under the "most-favored-nation" view of the Free Exercise Clause, the pastors were likely to lose on the merits, because California treated in-home religious gatherings exactly the same way that it treated in-home secular gatherings. Undeterred, the pastors applied to the Supreme Court for an injunction pending appeal. And in another late-Friday-night ruling, the Court agreed.[47]

Given everything that preceded it, the Court's 5–4 ruling in *Tandon* v. *Newsom* might seem anticlimactic. As in *Roman Catholic Diocese*, the majority wrote a brief per curiam opinion. But this time, the Court finally made clear what it had been hinting at (and, in retrospect, building toward) since the previous November: The prevailing understanding of the Free Exercise Clause adopted by the Supreme Court in *Smith* in 1990 had changed. As the majority wrote, "Government regulations are not neutral and generally applicable, and therefore trigger strict scrutiny under the Free Exercise Clause, whenever they treat *any* comparable secular activity more favorably than religious exercise."[48]

Although the *Tandon* opinion cited the November ruling in *Roman Catholic Diocese* as support for that proposition, it was in this sentence, and not in its prior ruling, where the Court for the first time directly embraced the most-favored-nation theory of the Free Exercise Clause. Because California permitted "hair salons, retail stores, personal care services, movie theaters, private suites at sporting events and concerts, and indoor restaurants to bring together more than three households at a time," it didn't matter that the nation's largest state treated secular and religious in-home gatherings alike. For the first time since *Smith*, a majority of justices struck down under the Free Exercise Clause a facially neutral government regulation entirely because it made no exception for—and *therefore* burdened—religious practice. As Jim Oleske, one of the nation's leading scholars of law and religion, wrote shortly thereafter, *Tandon* was the Court's "most important free exercise decision since 1990." That's a pretty remarkable development to come on the shadow docket.[49]

As if all of that weren't enough, the Court concluded its brief opinion with another parting shot at the court of appeals, noting, "This is the fifth time the Court has summarily rejected the Ninth Circuit's analysis of California's COVID restrictions on religious exercise." Oblivious to the irony of complaining about a lower court's failure to apply an analytical framework that the Court itself had never articulated, a five-justice majority thus put into writing what the *Gateway City Church* order had all but already broadcast as the law: even unsigned and unexplained emergency orders were to be treated as precedent by lower courts. For the sixth time in just over four months, the Court had issued an emergency writ of injunction to block state COVID restrictions on religious liberty grounds while challenges to them proceeded through the lower courts. This time, it did so by explicitly changing the law, all while having the temerity to criticize lower courts for not recognizing the unexplained change sooner.[50]

As in *Roman Catholic Diocese*, Chief Justice Roberts joined Justices Breyer, Sotomayor, and Kagan in dissenting (although this time, he simply registered his dissent without writing separately or joining a dissenting opinion). Justice Kagan again wrote on behalf of the Democratic appointees, and, as in *South Bay II*, did not pull her punches: "As the per curiam's reliance on separate opinions and unreasoned orders signals, the law does not require that the State equally treat apples and watermelons." In other words, it was a damning indictment of the majority's insistence that it was applying existing Free Exercise Clause principles that it couldn't trace any of those principles to the Court's merits docket. She also once again criticized the majority for ignoring the lower courts' factual findings, including the different levels of risk associated with brief visits to secular businesses compared to lengthy gatherings in private homes. "No doubt this evidence is inconvenient for the per curiam's preferred result," she continued. "But the Court has no warrant to ignore the record in a case that (on its own view) turns on risk assessments."[51]

But neither Justice Kagan nor Chief Justice Roberts flagged the most problematic aspect of the ruling in *Tandon*: that it was indefensibly lawless. After all, by formally adopting the most-favored-nation reading of the Free Exercise Clause, the majority indisputably articulated a new understanding of the Constitution. But relief based upon the All Writs Act, as the Court had explained for decades, depended upon the violation of rights that were already "indisputably clear." Even after *Tandon*, the Court would continue to cite that standard as the correct one. So if *Tandon* didn't change the standard for an emergency writ of injunction, how could a decision that itself changed decades of settled law possibly have been based upon a legal rule that was *already* "indisputably clear"?[52]

It's a powerful sign of how desensitized the justices (and their clerks) had become to the shadow docket that, by the time *Tandon* was handed down in April 2021, none of the justices bothered to note that the majority was using it to enshrine a dramatic expansion in the Constitution's protection of religious liberty. The fact that the ruling was clearly in excess of the Court's authority under the All Writs Act was simply immaterial compared to the merits of the Free Exercise Clause analysis. From the perspective of both the majority and dissenting opinions, the posture of the case was irrelevant; the formal limits on the Court's power were beside the point; and the long-standing norms militating against emergency relief were brushed aside. All that mattered was the substantive constitutional issue—on which they sharply divided. The shadow docket had come full circle.

What's particularly galling about this denouement is that there were numerous opportunities for the justices to use cases already pending on their merits docket to accomplish the same doctrinal shift. At the time *Tandon* was decided, for instance, *Fulton* v. *City of Philadelphia*, the case where the petitioners had directly asked the Court to overrule *Smith*, had already been argued. The justices would have voted on the result in *Fulton* at their Conference on November 6, meaning the opinions in that case were well on their way to being drafted when *Tandon* was decided. The opinion in *Fulton*, released the following June, would ultimately leave *Smith*'s holding—that laws of general applicability that incidentally burden religious practice do not violate the Free Exercise Clause—untouched, ruling against Philadelphia on narrower grounds. Thus, when the Court decided *Tandon*, the justices knew they weren't going any further in *Fulton*.

Even if the justices preferred to revisit *Smith* in the specific context of COVID restrictions on religious gatherings, they had already bypassed one opportunity to do so in January, when they denied certiorari on the merits in the *Calvary Chapel Dayton Valley* v. *Sisolak* case from Nevada. And at the time they decided *Tandon*, the justices were sitting on a cert. petition from the South Bay Pentecostal Church, which was finally raising the merits of its challenge to California's capacity and singing restrictions. But rather than using plenary review in the case that had started it all as the vehicle for expanding the Free Exercise Clause, the Court used the rushed shadow docket proceedings in *Tandon*. Only on April 26 (seventeen days after *Tandon*) would the Court issue a GVR in *South Bay III*, sending the case back to the lower courts . . . in light of *Tandon*.[53]

*Tandon* thus shows not only that the five justices in the majority knew they were making significant new constitutional law on the shadow docket late on a Friday night, but that the decision to do so was willful. Faced with a choice of numerous cases they could have used to change the meaning of the Free Exercise Clause, the majority opted to reach that holding on the shadow docket specifically, even though the very statutory constraint that they ignored in *Tandon*—that they could issue an injunction only to protect a right that was "indisputably clear"—didn't apply to cases on the merits docket. Justice Thomas would later argue in a dissenting opinion that "circumstances *forced us* to confront challenges to [COVID mitigation] measures in an emergency posture" (emphasis mine). In reality, whether strategically or just because of inertia, the justices were not forced: they chose the shadow docket.[54]

As with the shift the Court undertook in the Trump cases, it would be one thing if the arrival of Justice Barrett had heralded a shift in the Supreme Court's approach to emergency writs of injunction across the board. But it didn't. With one exception, every application seeking such relief during the October 2020 Term on non-religious-liberty grounds was denied. Those denials included an application that, in some respects, presented an even more compelling case for the Court's intervention than *Tandon*: *Whole Woman's Health* v. *Jackson*. At issue in *Whole Woman's Health* was Texas's controversial "Senate Bill 8" (SB8), known as the Texas Heartbeat Act, which banned virtually all abortions after the sixth week of pregnancy. In *Whole Woman's Health*, the same five justices who'd had no trouble ignoring a procedural bar to emergency relief in *Tandon* relied upon the novel procedural questions raised by SB8 (about who could be sued to challenge the law) as justification for their nonintervention, even though there was no question that, under the precedents of *Roe* v. *Wade* and *Planned Parenthood* v. *Casey*, the substance of the law was (in Justice Sotomayor's words) "flagrantly unconstitutional." The same five justices who ran roughshod over procedural constraints in *Tandon* to make new constitutional law hid behind procedural questions in *Whole Woman's Health* to avoid vindicating existing constitutional law.[55]

As we'll see, the Court's nonintervention in the SB8 case provoked a significant and sustained public backlash. Perhaps as a result, the very next time that the full Court considered an application for emergency relief challenging a COVID-based state measure on religious liberty grounds, it balked. This time, the dispute involved Maine's vaccination mandate for health-care workers, which the plaintiffs challenged as infringing their religious liberty, because cells derived from aborted fetuses had allegedly been used during development of the vaccines. Despite a lengthy dissent from Justice Gorsuch (joined by Justices Thomas and Alito) arguing that Maine was discriminating against the plaintiffs' sincerely held religious beliefs, the majority denied relief. Although there was no opinion for the Court, Justices Barrett and Kavanaugh (whose votes had been critical in *Roman Catholic Diocese* and *Tandon*) filed a short concurrence suggesting that, even when the applicant had made out a case for emergency relief, granting such relief was still an exercise of the Court's discretion. As for what would govern that discretion going forward, the Court's two newest justices wouldn't say. Perhaps, though, their concurrence was a tacit concession that they had exercised that discretion a bit too permissively over the previous eleven months. Indeed, the Maine case would be the first of five shadow docket rulings refusing to block vaccine mandates during the October 2021 Term from which Thomas, Alito, and Gorsuch were the only public dissenters.[56]

~

Why did the Court so consistently favor the Free Exercise Clause, at the expense of every other constitutional right, in the specific and uniquely fraught context of COVID-related shadow docket rulings? Neither of the Court's two majority opinions—in *Roman Catholic Diocese* or *Tandon*—provide any insight into the matter. But the separate opinions of Justices Alito, Gorsuch, and Kavanaugh all insisted, at various points, that policymakers were disguising hostility toward particular religious beliefs behind their COVID-mitigation policies. Thus, perhaps the best that can be said about the Court's aggressive vindication of religious liberty claims on the shadow docket is that it was motivated by a good-faith belief that policymakers were using COVID mitigation simply as cover for a subtle but significant attempt to restrain religious practice.[57]

Of course, this view assumes bad faith on the part of any number of government actors—bad faith that is, at best, inferred from rather limited circumstantial evidence in proceedings in which, unlike most cases on the Court's merits docket, there was little to no opportunity to develop a factual record. Worse still, there is a telling contrast between the willingness of these same justices to carefully scrutinize the motives of government actors when it came to claims of religious liberty in the COVID context and their unwillingness to do so when it came to President Trump's travel ban. Recall that the central constitutional claim in *Trump* v. *Hawaii* (the Travel Ban 3.0 case) was that the president had singled out the countries at issue *because* they were predominantly Muslim. That claim relied upon public statements by President Trump (that the 5–4 majority held to be irrelevant) to the same extent that Justice Gorsuch's dissent from the Court's December 2021 refusal to block New York's vaccine mandate for health-care workers relied upon public statements by Governor Kathy Hochul. Perhaps the implication is that governments require even stronger justifications for acting in a manner that impedes religious liberty during a pandemic than at other times. If that's the theory, though, none of the justices have ever publicly endorsed it.[58]

But even if that *is* the best argument, it doesn't actually hold up: ordinary modes of judicial review should not be abandoned during a public health crisis in either direction. Thus, although governments should not have been entitled to meaningfully more deference when adopting public health measures in response to the COVID pandemic, they should not have been entitled to meaningfully less deference, either. And then there's the additional problem of implementing these views through unsigned, unexplained shadow docket orders in defiance of the statutory limits on the Court's power, rather than in fully and carefully reasoned merits decisions unquestionably within the justices' authority.[59]

If the argument is, instead, about wariness of novel state legislation more generally, again, the same justices have been more than a little inconsistent. In May 2022, for example, the Supreme Court supported a district court injunction against a Texas law that, in the guise of limiting "censorship," prohibited most content moderation by large social media platforms. Although the Fifth Circuit had stayed the district court's ruling, the Supreme Court vacated the stay by a 5–4 vote. In a dissenting opinion joined by Justices Thomas and Gorsuch, Justice Alito argued that "the preliminary injunction entered by the District Court was itself a significant intrusion on state sovereignty, and Texas should not be required to seek preclearance from the federal courts before its laws go into effect." Of course, Alito was part of the majority in almost all of the COVID cases discussed above, in which the justices themselves blocked state laws before—or shortly after—they went into effect. And in September 2022, he wrote a dissent on behalf of Justices Thomas, Gorsuch, and Barrett when a 5–4 majority *refused* to block New York's human rights law on religious liberty grounds after a state court had interpreted it to require Yeshiva University to recognize an LGBTQ+ student group. If there was a principled basis for distinguishing between New York and California laws, on the one hand, and Texas social media restrictions, on the other, Justice Alito did not say.[60]

It is also worth returning to the April 2021 5–4 ruling in *Tandon*, and the fact that the justices reached out to establish an important new principle of Free Exercise Clause jurisprudence on the shadow docket both in defiance of their authority to act in such cases *and* when opportunities to make the same jurisprudential move were pending before them on the merits docket. That ruling, and the broader pattern of which it is emblematic, underscores the extent to which the justices are using the shadow docket *on purpose*—in contexts in which the same questions are already pending before them on the merits docket, and in which review on the merits docket would come with none of the procedural obstacles that are supposed to be part of shadow docket consideration. The subtitle of this chapter—and of this book—implies that the Court's recent misuse of the shadow docket has been more than just an accident. Here is Exhibit A.

Even without a good explanation for these developments, for those to whom religious liberty predominates over other constitutional protections, the Court's use and abuse of the shadow docket to embrace the most-favored-nation theory of the Free Exercise Clause may well seem worth it. But for those who care about the Court as an institution, it is hard to look at the religious liberty cases in contrast to the Court's nonintervention in other contexts and disagree with Justice Kagan's September 2021 dissent from the Court's refusal to block the Texas abortion law, which concluded that "the majority's decision is emblematic of too much of this Court's shadow-docket decisionmaking—which every day becomes more unreasoned, inconsistent, and impossible to defend." Kagan's dissent was the very first time that a justice had directly referred to the shadow docket by name.* And measured against how procedurally and substantively aggressive the same five justices had been in using the shadow docket to expand constitutional protections for religious liberty throughout the October 2020 Term, and what that inconsistency said about the Court's increasingly eroding legitimacy, her critique was—and remains—spot-on. If anything, the objection that the majority was using the shadow docket in ways that were increasingly problematic would become only that much more powerful in the other context in which the justices also started using the shadow docket to make new law—election-related disputes.[61]

---

* In a September 2019 dissent, Justice Sotomayor had cited to a paper that had the term in its title, but hadn't used the term herself.

CHAPTER 6

# THE "*PURCELL* PRINCIPLE"

## HOW THE CURRENT COURT USES THE SHADOW DOCKET TO HELP REPUBLICANS

If it weren't for the shadow docket, you might never have heard of Lyndon Baines Johnson. Nearing the end of his sixth term as a relatively anonymous congressman from the Texas Hill Country, Johnson bet his political career on winning the 1948 Democratic nomination for Texas's open Senate seat—in a state in which whoever won the Democratic primary was all but assured of victory in the general election. On primary day, Johnson finished second, 70,000 votes behind former governor Coke Stevenson. But Stevenson did not have enough votes in a crowded field to avoid a runoff, so the race came down to a head-to-head matchup between the two.[1]

Stevenson was an old-school conservative Texas Democrat—a segregationist and unapologetic racist widely known as "Mr. Texas." Johnson was more closely aligned with the New Deal wing of the Democratic Party, with perhaps even more support in Washington than in his own state. Johnson was also desperate to win, throwing an unprecedented amount of money and influence into the runoff. That included enlisting friendly political bosses in parts of Texas where it was widely believed that elections followed the Joseph Stalin model—that it wasn't the votes that counted, but rather who counted the votes. Johnson's efforts had an impact: when the results came in on the night of the runoff, he appeared to have lost by fewer than 1,000 votes. Over the next few days, "adjustments" closed the margin to just over 100 votes as precincts "corrected" erroneous election-night reports. Still, it appeared that that's where the election (and Johnson's career) would end.[2]

Then, six days after the runoff, 202 additional votes were miraculously reported from Precinct 13 of Jim Wells County in South Texas, in the tiny town of Alice.* Remarkably, 200 of the 202 late-discovered ballots had been cast for Johnson. And, according to Stevenson and a witness who saw the voter roll before it mysteriously disappeared, the names of those last 202 voters on the tally sheet were in alphabetical order, which was a rather improbable coincidence, to say the least. Worse still, they appeared to be in the same pen and handwriting, which were themselves different from the other entries on the list. Stevenson also tracked down the last person listed as having voted before the late-added names, who swore that he had voted twenty minutes before the polls closed, and that no one else had been waiting to vote after him.[3]

The votes from "Box 13" put Johnson ahead by 87 votes out of nearly 1 million cast—a lead of 0.008 percent. This wasn't Johnson's first election-fraud rodeo. In a 1941 special Senate election, he'd had the Democratic nomination stolen from *him* in a similar fashion—via late-reported votes from his opponents'

---

* There is some dispute as to whether there were 201 late-discovered votes rather than 202. All agree that Johnson himself received exactly 200 new votes (allegedly because the local election judge changed the number on the precinct tally sheet from 765 to 965). Whether Stevenson received one or two more votes is—and always has been—a distinction without any real difference.

strongholds. To this day, it's not clear whether Johnson knew in advance about the similar efforts of his allies in 1948. But what *is* clear is that Johnson worked tirelessly behind the scenes afterward, first to block any attempt at a recount in Jim Wells County, and then to get the executive committee of the state Democratic Party to certify the result, which it did the following Monday in a contentious, dramatic, and nail-biting 29–28 vote. Referring to himself as "Landslide Lyndon," Johnson declared victory.[4]

At that time, parties—not states—ran primary elections, and post–Election Day shenanigans in close races were more the norm than the exception, especially in Texas. But even by those low standards, the Box 13 episode was extreme. With witness testimony casting grave doubt on the integrity of the late-reported Box 13 totals, Stevenson persuaded Dallas federal judge T. Whitfield Davidson to issue an injunction blocking certification of Johnson's victory until the electoral fraud claims could be fully investigated. Davidson appointed a special master to conduct a full-scale investigation into the matter (and a second special master to investigate irregularities in neighboring Duval County). Not only would such an inquiry potentially spell doom for Johnson, but it also increased the possibility that, either way, the ballots for the November general election would be printed with *no* Democratic candidate on them, unless the matter could be resolved by the state's October 3 ballot-printing deadline.[5]

The mounting drama in Texas had nationwide implications. Having lost control of Congress in the 1946 midterms for the first time in fourteen years, Democrats were desperate to retake control of the Senate, and holding onto the safe Texas seat was essential to that goal. More than that, the rift between Johnson and Stevenson mirrored the broader schism between the Democratic establishment and the "Dixiecrats"—southern Democrats opposed to the party's turn toward civil rights, who supported Strom Thurmond, rather than the incumbent president, Harry S. Truman, for the party's nomination for president. Thus, across the country, all eyes turned to the legal proceedings in Texas.[6]

On Monday, September 27, 1948, William Robert Smith Jr., formerly the US Attorney for the Western District of Texas and now the special master appointed by Judge Davidson to investigate Box 13, convened a hearing in the local courthouse in Alice, and began to take testimony from witnesses and collect the sealed ballot boxes. By Tuesday afternoon, he was perhaps minutes away from either locating the missing tally sheet from Box 13 (which would presumably prove the fraud) or proving that all three copies of the list had been destroyed. Either outcome would only further inculpate Johnson's local allies. But then, Supreme Court justice Hugo Black intervened.[7]

Johnson's legal team, headed by Abe Fortas (whom Johnson would appoint to the Supreme Court in 1965), had already asked Fifth Circuit judge J. C. Hutcheson Jr. to stay Judge Davidson's injunction. But Hutcheson had ruled on Friday, September 24, that he had no power to act by himself, and that Johnson would have to wait until the full Fifth Circuit reconvened on October 4 (the day after the Texas ballot-printing deadline). The next morning, Fortas called Black, asking him in his capacity as circuit justice for the Fifth Circuit to stay Judge Davidson's injunction and allow Johnson's name to be printed on the ballot. On the morning of Tuesday, September 28, Black, who had been a New Deal–supporting Democratic senator from Alabama before his elevation to the Court in 1937, heard four hours of argument in his Washington chambers. That afternoon, he issued an oral ruling staying Judge Davidson's injunction. As relayed in a firsthand account by a *New York Times* reporter, Black concluded that no statute authorized Judge Davidson to "suspend the process of electing a Senator or Governor." When he formalized the order in writing the next day, he provided even less analysis, simply noting that he was issuing a stay pending further order of the Court, without any explanation as to why. And although the stay only froze the injunction, Judge Davidson understood it, perhaps overbroadly, to also freeze the ongoing investigations into Box 13 and other voting irregularities—which were stopped in their tracks, never to resume.[8]

On Saturday, October 2, Stevenson asked the full Supreme Court to lift Black's stay, arguing that Black lacked the authority to rule by himself. Fortas responded on behalf of Johnson, encouraging the full Court to either affirm Black's order or to stay Judge Davidson's injunction itself. But especially with the ballot-printing deadline on Sunday, the rest of the justices wanted nothing to do with the dispute. On the afternoon of Monday, October 4—the "First Monday" of the October 1948 Term—the justices voted 8–0 to deny both Stevenson's and Johnson's motions (the orders were handed down the following morning; Justice Frank Murphy did not participate due to illness). So the last word belonged to Black.

*Life* magazine called it "the eighty-seven votes that changed history." If anything, that was an understatement. Four weeks later, Johnson won the general election with 66 percent of the vote. Two months later, he was sworn into the Senate. Within two years, Johnson would be the majority whip. Two years after that, he'd be the majority leader. And the rest was, indeed, history—history that would have looked very different without the stay issued by Justice Black. Johnson himself acknowledged as much: when he hosted an eightieth birthday party for Justice Black at the White House in 1966, he concluded, in his toast, that "if it weren't for Mr. Justice Black at one time, we might well be having this party. But one thing I know for sure, we wouldn't be having it here."[9]

The Box 13 affair was an early test case for two distinct sets of questions in election cases: First, what should courts do when faced with challenges to election results after the fact, or with eleventh-hour challenges to the rules by which elections would be conducted? And second, what should appellate courts do when lower courts decided to intervene in those contexts? In *Johnson* v.

*Stevenson*, Justice Black justified his intervention on the ground (although never committed to writing) that no statute gave Judge Davidson a basis for intervening in the first place, even though Stevenson had made deeply credible allegations of result-altering election fraud. Black's conclusion seemed to be that a challenge to a state election was principally a question of state law, to be resolved by state courts, if at all.[10]

In 1948, that understanding made at least some sense. The Constitution itself has very little to say about federal elections, besides generally leaving them to state control unless Congress provides otherwise, and Congress for the most part hadn't.* More than that, the Constitution doesn't expressly confer a right to vote, as such. The Fifteenth Amendment, ratified in 1870, bars states from discriminating at the polls on the basis of race. And the Nineteenth Amendment, ratified in 1920, likewise bars voting-based discrimination on the basis of sex. Whatever else might be said about the Box 13 affair, it wasn't an example of either form of discrimination. What's more, although the Supreme Court in 1941 had recognized a constitutional right to participate in state primaries, Stevenson's claim was that he had been defrauded, not that particular voters had been disenfranchised. In considering that claim, Black had followed the norms for emergency applications that governed the situation at the time, giving the parties an opportunity for lengthy oral argument, ruling by himself, and not providing any written analysis (so that his in-chambers decision couldn't have any impact beyond the Texas Democratic Senate primary). It was an unusually visible shadow docket ruling, but a typically modest one for the era.[11]

Things changed in 1965, thanks—ironically—to President Johnson. Horrified by the violence of "Bloody Sunday," in

* In a handful of statutes, such as the Apportionment Act of 1842 or the Electoral Count Act of 1887, Congress had provided *some* rules to govern how districts were drawn and how elections were conducted. But beyond the specific requirements of those statutes, the rules for local, state, and federal elections were almost entirely governed by state law into the 1960s.

which Alabama state troopers and local police had attacked unarmed protesters marching from Selma to Montgomery in an effort to call attention to the widespread disenfranchisement of Black southerners, Johnson pushed Congress to enact the Voting Rights Act (VRA)—what he would later call the "greatest accomplishment" of his presidency. At its core, the VRA made it much easier for voters to challenge local and state election rules on the grounds that they discriminated, deliberately or not, on the basis of race, national origin, or language. It required jurisdictions with a documented history of discrimination to have any changes to their election rules "precleared" by the federal Justice Department or by the DC federal district court, and abolished literacy tests as a prerequisite for voting. One of the most effective pieces of civil rights legislation in American history, the VRA also reconceived the role of the judicial branch in election-related disputes; the statute's sweeping new protections were meant to be enforced not only by the Justice Department, but also by the federal courts.[12]

At first, Congress's clear legislative goal in the VRA led to an uptick in federal judicial involvement in local, state, and federal elections, including interventions, at least by lower courts, in the run-up to (and immediate aftermath of) Election Day. As the Supreme Court in the 1990s and 2000s became more hostile to the VRA itself, though, it also became more skeptical of last-minute federal judicial interventions in election disputes. The problem is that, rather than offering an objective test for when such interventions were or were not appropriate, the answer the Supreme Court eventually settled on was "sometimes." Making matters worse, the justices eventually used the shadow docket to adopt, and then enforce, a profoundly subjective and underexplained test. Under that approach, politics once again at least appear to have taken precedence over principle.

As *Johnson* v. *Stevenson* suggests, election disputes are a natural source of emergency applications, much like the death penalty cases we've already encountered. The two most common classes of election-related litigation—challenges to voting rules and redistricting *before* Election Day; and challenges to the results afterward—both tend to unfold under highly compressed timetables with a fixed expiration date, whether the election itself or the deadline for certifying the election's results. Just as in death penalty cases, the rule that applies while a dispute is pending is often more important than the ultimate resolution of the legal dispute. And as is also the case with death penalty cases, the disputes in election cases tend to be quite localized, turning on the rules that apply in a single city, county, or state.

But the last parallel to death penalty cases is perhaps the most important one: just as the Supreme Court became wary of emergency applications in capital cases in the early 1980s, it became wary of election-related applications in the mid-2000s. As they did in the capital context with their 1983 ruling in *Barefoot* v. *Estelle*, the justices in their 2006 ruling in *Purcell* v. *Gonzalez* attempted to articulate principles to govern all emergency applications in election cases. This time, though, they did so through a cryptic shadow docket ruling, one that has caused far more mischief than it has prevented.

In 2004, Arizona voters approved a ballot initiative, Proposition 200, that imposed strict new identification requirements for in-person voting on Election Day. Under the VRA, the initiative could not go into effect until it received "preclearance" from the Department of Justice, which DOJ granted in 2005. In May 2006, a group of Arizona voters, Native American tribes, and community organizations sued, claiming that the more stringent voter ID requirements were both a violation of the VRA and unconstitutional because they made it disproportionately more difficult for people of color and members of other minority groups (for whom obtaining the required IDs has been, and generally remains, more difficult) to vote. On September 11, 2006, the district court denied the plaintiffs' request for an injunction, albeit with no accompanying explanation. The challengers quickly appealed that ruling, and also asked the Ninth Circuit to enjoin Proposition 200 pending that appeal. Recognizing that it wouldn't be possible to fully resolve Proposition 200's legality in time for the upcoming 2006 elections, the challengers wanted to prevent the initiative from being enforced at least in that voting cycle. On October 5, in a summary, four-sentence order, the Ninth Circuit agreed to block the new voter ID rule while it considered the merits.[13]

Arizona then asked the Supreme Court to stay the Ninth Circuit's injunction—to put Proposition 200 back into effect in time for Election Day 2006. Rather than just granting Arizona's request for a stay, though, the Supreme Court went further. It treated the state's emergency application as a petition for a writ of certiorari, granted it, and summarily vacated the Ninth Circuit's injunction. In an unsigned, five-and-a-half-page per curiam opinion, which conservative legal scholar Orin Kerr described as "a bolt of lightning," the Court in *Purcell* v. *Gonzalez* articulated what UCLA election law scholar Rick Hasen has dubbed "the *Purcell* principle" (Helen Purcell was the Maricopa County recorder and the nominal defendant in the case). At its simplest, the principle is that, to avoid confusion among voters and election administrators, courts should generally not change the rules governing elections as Election Day approaches, meaning that injunctions against even unlawful election rules are increasingly disfavored as Election Day draws near. *Purcell* is not an argument against the power of lower courts to provide remedies for unlawful election laws; rather, it's an argument against allowing injunctions of election laws to go into *effect* too close to elections. Although it's directed toward district courts, *Purcell* is as much a principle for appellate courts to apply, to justify stays of district court injunctions issued too closely to an election, or, as the Supreme Court held the Ninth Circuit should have in *Purcell*, to justify staying their hand when district courts had, as well.[14]

At first blush, that principle seems reasonable enough: court orders—especially competing court orders—changing the rules in the run-up to Election Day can easily cause chaos, risking not just the potential disenfranchisement of confused voters, but potential headaches for election officials tasked with administering an election and tallying results under shifting legal foundations. Indeed, perhaps the best defense of *Purcell* is that it was an attempt by the Supreme Court to introduce rigidity into an area in which the justices believed there was too much discretion—to tightly circumscribe the power of courts as Election Day approaches. But in the seventeen years since *Purcell* was handed down, numerous problems have emerged with the principle it espoused.[15]

First, on its own terms, *Purcell* never explained when it's "too close" to an election for courts to intervene. In *Purcell* itself, the Ninth Circuit injunction came thirty-three days before the Arizona election—far enough out to seemingly abate any confusion or concern (the Supreme Court's decision, in contrast, came just eighteen days before the election). But if thirty-three days is too close, what about forty-three? Or sixty-three? Indeed, in a 2022 ruling we'll come back to shortly, the Court appeared to rely on *Purcell* to block a district court injunction handed down over nine *months* before the election—and twelve weeks before the primary (which, unlike the general election, could have been moved if necessary). Right off the bat, then, *Purcell*'s seeming nod toward a bright-line rule turns on the grayest of temporal considerations—inviting the very subjective decision-making from judges that the decision claimed it was trying to eliminate.[16]

Second, although *Purcell* justified an election-specific rule for limiting the effects of injunctions by alluding to "considerations specific to election cases," it never explained why such a rule was needed. Why wouldn't the traditional standards for injunctions, and for stays of injunctions pending appeal, suffice? As we've repeatedly seen, when a district court enters an injunction, whether that injunction should be stayed pending appeal depends upon a number of factors, including the harm that the parties might suffer from a ruling in either direction and how the public interest is impacted either way. Those traditional factors are supposed to be "balanced," an invitation to courts to assess which harm is worse: the harm to plaintiffs, for example, of having to comply with potentially unlawful voting rules, or the harm to everyone else of blocking those rules on the eve of the election. Thus, even before *Purcell*, the argument for staying an eleventh-hour injunction that would have wreaked havoc on a state's election procedures would have been powerful, even if the plaintiffs' challenge to those procedures was strong. Likewise, a pre-*Purcell* analysis would have focused on the actual likelihood that a specific law or court order blocking it would cause voter confusion, rather than the more general presumption the Supreme Court articulated in *Purcell*—that all late changes to election rules will confuse voters.[17]

But the flip side of this coin is even more troubling: by departing from the traditional standard, *Purcell* removes from the equation the possibility that, as disruptive as an injunction might be, freezing (or not issuing) it would be worse. For example, say a new state election rule would unlawfully prevent 20 percent of registered voters from actually voting, but that barring the new rule from taking effect would entail the risk that some minority of the remaining voters might be confused on Election Day. The chance of some voters being confused hardly justifies allowing widespread disenfranchisement. Under *Purcell*, though, that analysis becomes irrelevant, even if the plaintiffs' challenge to the new election rule is very likely to succeed.[18]

As such, *Purcell* seemingly invites bad behavior by local and state election officials, who might themselves change the rules on the eve of an election because they know they can do so without worrying about interference from the courts. At the time *Purcell* was decided, such last-minute changes wouldn't have been possible in many jurisdictions, due to the Voting Rights Act's preclearance requirement. But in 2013, the Supreme Court effectively gutted that requirement when it held, in *Shelby County* v. *Holder*, that the formula that Congress had used to identify those jurisdictions to which it applied was itself unconstitutional. Since then, no jurisdiction has had to obtain preclearance from the Justice Department for any changes to its election rules, even eleventh-hour ones. And the rise of election denialism in response to—and since—the 2020 election only increases the risk that relevant local or state officials in some parts of the country might be inclined to attempt such shenanigans.

Even though *Shelby County* vitiated the preclearance regime, nothing in the Court's 2013 ruling prevented the justices from providing clearer criteria for last-minute interventions in election cases, a task that became only that much more urgent in a world without preclearance. *Purcell* could have identified a window (say, sixty days) before the election, and instructed courts to view changes to the rules by *any* relevant actor, whether a local or state politician or a state or federal judge, with presumptive skepticism. By instead treating the election law at the moment it reaches the district court as the operative baseline, even if that law was deliberately changed weeks (or even days) beforehand, *Purcell* makes it even easier for election administrators to get away with unlawful rule changes so long as they're adopted late in the game. And even if a court ultimately strikes down the rule on the far side of the election, *Purcell* would support allowing the rule to remain in effect on Election Day itself, presumably accomplishing the goal of those officials who adopted it. Even in states whose officials don't behave quite so badly, *Purcell* at the very least incentivizes delay. When Georgia governor Brian Kemp waited a full month in late 2021 before signing the state legislature's new congressional district maps into law, it was broadly assumed that, with an eye on *Purcell*, he was simply trying to run out the clock. And it worked: although a Georgia district court concluded in early 2022 that the maps violated the Voting Rights Act, it also held that it wouldn't enjoin them because of the proximity to Georgia's primaries.[19]

Finally, and exacerbating all of these concerns, *Purcell* was itself a shadow docket decision—decided on a compressed schedule, with no argument, and with no advance indication to the parties or anyone else that the Court was going to treat Arizona's emergency application as an opportunity to fundamentally rewrite judicial procedure in election cases. Its thinly reasoned analysis spans just over two pages. One would think, if the justices wanted to dramatically change the nature of judicial review in election cases, that they would have done so a bit more publicly, and in a more comprehensive opinion.[20]

For all of these reasons (and others), *Purcell* has been roundly and repeatedly criticized by election law scholars. Hasen has written that it was both "overdetermined and undertheorized." University of Wisconsin professor Dan Tokaji suggested that the Court's analysis could "charitably be described as careless." And Brooklyn Law School's Wilfred Codrington III has been perhaps the most unsparing in his analysis, describing the decision as a "charade," and dismissing the Court's reasoning as "vacuous, self-contradictory, amorphous, and *more* prone to aggrandizing election-related concerns—including those that the Supreme Court suggested it should mitigate."[21]

Perhaps no set of cases better illustrates these concerns than those the Supreme Court decided in the run-up to the 2020 election. Because of the COVID pandemic, the 2020 election cycle was characterized by an unusual volume of late changes to election rules in response to the perceived risks of in-person, Election Day voting. We also saw an unprecedented number of lawsuits challenging the validity of those changes, and still other lawsuits challenging the refusal of some jurisdictions to do more to facilitate voting given the precarious public health situation.

It started with Wisconsin. Early in the pandemic, with COVID cases exploding across Wisconsin (and long before any vaccine was available), a federal district court in Madison ordered the state, among other things, to extend the deadline for receiving mail-in ballots for the state's 2020 spring election, which included the 2020 presidential primaries plus contests for a seat on the Wisconsin Supreme Court, three seats on the intermediate state court of appeals, and several thousand other positions. Because of delays by the state in processing the record number of applications for mail-in ballots, and by the US Postal Service in delivering those ballots to voters, the district court held that a number of voters who had requested mail-in ballots in a timely fashion risked being disenfranchised through no fault of their own. Thus, the court ordered the state not only to extend the deadline for when mail-in ballots needed to be received (to six days after Election Day), but also to extend the mailing deadline, such that every mail-in ballot received by that date should be counted, even if they were mailed the day after the election.[22]

The Republican National Committee (RNC) asked the Seventh Circuit to stay the district court's ruling. Although the RNC sought to block the entire ruling, it focused especially on the argument that, even if it was appropriate for the receipt deadline to be extended, given the postal delays, the district court should not have also extended the mailing deadline past Election Day. The court of appeals stayed part of the injunction but left the extension of both the mailing and receipt deadlines intact. The Supreme Court, in an unsigned, 5–4 ruling, put the original mailing deadline back into effect. Although the Court went out of its way to take no position on the merits (a punt made possible only by *Purcell*, since the merits *would* be one factor under "normal" stay analysis), it invoked *Purcell* for the proposition that "this Court has repeatedly emphasized that lower federal courts should ordinarily not alter the election rules on the eve of an election."[23]

But as Justice Ginsburg pointed out in her dissent on behalf of all four Democratic appointees, invoking *Purcell* in this context was more than a little ironic. The district court ruling extending the postmark deadline for mail-in ballots posed little risk of voter confusion, since uninformed voters would just return their ballots earlier. The Supreme Court's own ruling was instead the one that risked creating confusion. After all, one day before the election, it was the justices themselves who had moved the postmark deadline back up to Election Day. Worse still, Ginsburg wrote, the tens of thousands of Wisconsin voters who still had not even received their mail-in ballots would now be forced to vote in person, even as COVID cases were increasing dramatically both within the state and nationwide. Under any conventional balancing of the equities, the Supreme Court should (and would) have stayed its hand. Under *Purcell*, it could—and did—ignore those powerful, countervailing considerations.[24]

The inconsistency pervading the Court's approach to *Purcell* was made even clearer three months later in a case arising out of Florida. In 2018, Florida voters had amended the state constitution to restore the right to vote to convicted felons who had fully served their sentences, an amendment that would re-enfranchise as many as one million voters. Florida's Republican-controlled political branches vehemently opposed the amendment; because the population to whom it applied was overwhelmingly poor and nonwhite, the widespread assumption was that it would favor Democrats. Thus, the governor and state legislature interpreted the amendment as only applying to those released felons who had also cleared all outstanding fines, fees, and restitution, even if they could not afford to do so, or even if, as was usually the case, Florida wasn't sure how much they even owed, because of faulty recordkeeping or a lack of clarity in the underlying judgments. When those interpretations of the felon re-enfranchisement amendment were challenged in

2019, in *Jones* v. *DeSantis* (naming Florida's new governor, Ron DeSantis), a federal district court temporarily blocked them, holding that they were likely unconstitutional violations of due process (because many convicted felons did not and could not know how much they owed); equal protection (because they imposed a wealth barrier to voting); and the Twenty-Fourth Amendment (which prohibits poll taxes). In May 2020, the district court issued a final judgment after an eight-day trial, striking down the pay-to-vote requirements.[25]

On July 1, 2020, the Eleventh Circuit, which had previously refused to stay the district court's preliminary injunction, stayed the district court's permanent injunction. With the voter-registration deadline only nineteen days away, the court of appeals changed the rules that had been in effect since the previous summer while offering no explanation as to why it was doing so. The plaintiffs then asked the Supreme Court to lift the court of appeals' stay by invoking *Purcell*, arguing that the Eleventh Circuit had changed the rules for an election on the eve of the relevant deadline, and had failed to either justify its ruling or explain why the district court ruling that it blocked was wrong. Under any reading of *Purcell*, this should've been an easy case for vacating the stay.[26]

Instead, in a one-sentence order, the Supreme Court denied the application. Justice Sotomayor, joined by Justices Ginsburg and Kagan, wrote a fiery dissent, noting the inconsistency between the Court's April intervention in Wisconsin and its nonintervention in Florida: "Ironically," Sotomayor concluded, "this Court has wielded *Purcell* as a reason to forbid courts to make voting safer during a pandemic, . . . because any safety-related changes supposedly came too close to Election Day. Now, faced with an appellate court stay that disrupts a legal status quo and risks immense disfranchisement—a situation that *Purcell* sought to avoid—the Court balks."[27]

The July 16 ruling in what was now *Raysor* v. *DeSantis* was the last time the justices would publicly dispute how to apply

*Purcell* before Justice Ginsburg died on September 18. But in the thirty-nine days between Ginsburg's death and the swearing in of her successor, Justice Amy Coney Barrett, on October 27, an eight-justice Court was left to handle a flurry of last-minute election-related challenges.

The first post-Ginsburg case came from South Carolina. A South Carolina district court had blocked the state's requirement that absentee ballots include witness signatures, holding that the rule could not be justified when balanced against the risk voters faced from having close personal contact with unrelated witnesses in the midst of the pandemic, a risk that implicated voters' rights under the First and Fourteenth Amendments. The district court's ruling came on September 18, forty-six days before the election. But after the full court of appeals refused to stay the injunction, the Supreme Court agreed to do so, at least in part, on October 5. The only justice to write an opinion justifying the decision was Justice Kavanaugh, whose solo concurring opinion relied largely on *Purcell*. In his words, "For many years, this Court has repeatedly emphasized that federal courts ordinarily should not alter state election rules in the period close to an election. By enjoining South Carolina's witness requirement shortly before the election, the District Court defied that principle and this Court's precedents."[28]

Two things stand out about the Court's decision in the South Carolina case, known as *Andino* v. *Middleton* (Marci Andino was executive director of the State Election Commission, and thus the defendant in the challenge to the signature requirement). First, three justices—Thomas, Alito, and Gorsuch—noted that they would have stayed the district court injunction in full, even as applied to absentee ballots that had already been cast without the required witness signature. In other words, those three justices would have disenfranchised hundreds (if not thousands) of South Carolina voters who had already returned their absentee ballots based on the rules that were in effect at the time that they cast their votes. The other five justices, in contrast, agreed that "any ballots cast before this stay issues and received within two days of this order may not be rejected for failing to comply with the witness requirement." It's fairly stunning that this conclusion wasn't unanimous.[29]

Second, Justice Kavanaugh's invocation of *Purcell* appeared to turn the 2006 decision on its head. Not only did the district court's ruling come well in advance of the November 3 deadline for returning absentee ballots, but, once again, confusion was far more likely to result from the Supreme Court's intervention than from the district court's. Under the district court's ruling, absentee ballots would be valid whether or not they had a witness signature. Thanks to the Supreme Court's intervention, whether the ballot had to be signed by a witness depended on when the ballot was received, a matter largely beyond the control of voters who had already, or would shortly, return their ballots.[30]

At least the South Carolina ruling included some explanation, even if only from a single justice. The Court's next major election ruling came with no explanation whatsoever. On September 30, an Alabama district court had blocked the state's decision to ban curbside voting, holding after a lengthy trial that, given the COVID pandemic, the state's action likely discriminated against physically disabled individuals in violation of the federal Americans with Disabilities Act. The court of appeals rejected Alabama's application to stay the district court order, so Alabama asked the justices to intervene.[31]

On October 21, the 5–3 conservative majority agreed with the state, staying the district court injunction without either a majority or a concurring opinion. Justice Sotomayor, dissenting on behalf of herself and Justices Breyer and Kagan, stressed that the district court's injunction carried no risk of voter confusion because it "lifts burdensome requirements rather than imposing them, and permits county officials to help educate voters about whether curbside voting is available in their county." If the majority had a response to that argument, it declined to provide it publicly.[32]

Finally, in the last week before the election (with Justice Barrett shortly to join the Court, but not yet participating in cases), Chief Justice Roberts introduced a new wrinkle into the *Purcell* analysis. Across a series of cases from North Carolina, Pennsylvania, and Wisconsin (all of which were expected to be battleground states on Election Day), Roberts, still the swing vote on the Court, split the difference. In cases where a state court had sanctioned a late, COVID-related change to the relevant election rules, the chief justice sided with the three more liberal justices to leave that ruling in effect. But in cases where a federal court had sanctioned such a change, he sided with the conservatives to block it. And in one of the Wisconsin cases, he wrote to make this distinction explicit: "While the Pennsylvania applications [which the Court denied, 4–4] implicated the authority of state courts to apply their own constitutions to election regulations," he wrote in a brief concurring opinion, "this case involves federal intrusion on state lawmaking processes. Different bodies of law and different precedents govern these two situations and require, in these particular circumstances, that we allow the modification of election rules in Pennsylvania but not Wisconsin."[33]

Like *Purcell* itself, the distinction the chief justice proposed makes some sense on first impression, but withers under more rigorous scrutiny. If the problem *Purcell* seeks to solve is voter confusion, why is that concern any less present when a state court is responsible for it than a federal court? And if the answer is the technical one, that *Purcell* is an interpretation of the equitable powers of *federal* courts, specifically, well, the Supreme Court is also a federal court, and should be bound by those principles even if the state courts aren't. In other words, even under Roberts's reading, lower state courts may not be bound by *Purcell*, but the justices were—so that they had an obligation to minimize judicial interference with an impending election even if that interference had been caused by others. That's presumably why the other four conservatives dissented in the Pennsylvania cases. More explicitly, in March 2022, Justice Kavanaugh expressly invoked *Purcell* in a concurring opinion to justify *non*intervention by the Supreme Court when it was asked to stay a redistricting decision by the North Carolina Supreme Court pending appeal—a move that simply ignored the distinction the chief justice had made less than two years earlier.[34]

That's where the Supreme Court's affirmative involvement in the 2020 elections ended.* Unlike 2000, when the Supreme Court's deeply controversial merits decision in *Bush* v. *Gore* halted the Florida recount and effectively handed the election to President George W. Bush, this time around the justices' interventions had all come in advance of Election Day and on the shadow docket.[35]

The Court's interventions, in retrospect, reinforced two distinct—but equally problematic—impressions. First, they powerfully illustrated the inherent subjectivity of *Purcell*, and the extent to which its oversimplistic principle can and does crowd out some of the most important, competing concerns in election cases, including those rooted in the Constitution and federal law. Second, with the exception of the 4–4 Court's refusal to intervene in Pennsylvania and North Carolina in the last fortnight before the election, the Court's rulings tended to benefit Republicans and hurt Democrats. The April intervention in Wisconsin was at the behest of Republicans. The July refusal to intervene in Florida precluded thousands of ex-felons

---

* On Friday, November 6, Justice Alito, acting alone as circuit justice for the Third Circuit, issued an order requiring Pennsylvania election officials to segregate mail-in ballots that were received after the polls had closed on Election Day but before the extended Friday receipt deadline that the Pennsylvania Supreme Court had imposed. The full Court would eventually turn away the challenge to the Pennsylvania Supreme Court's ruling, at which point Alito's order became moot.

from voting, many of whom were believed to be likely to support Democrats at the polls. The South Carolina ruling in October likewise had a clear partisan valence, with three justices willing to disenfranchise voters who were, in the district court's view, more likely to be Democrats than Republicans.

Worse still, that partisan trend appeared to be the most consistent thread running through an otherwise inconsistent series of holdings in which the Court cited *Purcell*. A cynical observer could look at these rulings, all but one of which lacked a majority opinion, and see politics prevailing over principle. Given the internally contradictory nature of the Court's interventions and the lack of attempts by the justices in the majority to reconcile them (at least publicly), it would be hard to prove that cynicism unfounded. And therein lies the rub: even judges and justices acting in good faith can leave the impression that their decisions are motivated by bias or bad faith—which is why judicial ethics standards, even those few that apply to the Supreme Court itself, worry about both bias *and* the appearance thereof. When partisanship appears to be the best explanation for rulings that don't provide any alternative rationale, it is hard, if not impossible, to expect outside observers to assume that everything is aboveboard.[36]

Once again, though, if there was a silver lining in the 2020 election cases, it was how little new law they made. Borrowing yet another page from the death penalty cases, the Court's interventions (and noninterventions) in election-related disputes came either with no rationale or, as in the unsigned majority opinion in the April case from Wisconsin, with a concerted effort to express no view on the merits. Rather, the Court was preserving what it viewed as the appropriate status quo and leaving some of the more challenging legal questions raised by the COVID-related changes to voting rules for a later date, if ever. But that, too, was soon to change. Within fifteen months, the court would begin using the shadow docket much as it had in the religious liberty cases—to make new law that would affect not just a single election in a single state, but dozens of elections nationwide.

Every ten years, the Constitution requires that seats in the US House of Representatives be reapportioned among the states according to their population as measured in the most recent Census. The forty-four states with more than one representative in Congress use that Census data to redraw their House districts, in addition to redrawing state and local legislative districts. Because technology has made it easier for policymakers to use block-by-block (and, sometimes, house-by-house) data about party membership and other demographic features in drawing district lines, partisan gerrymandering—that is, drawing the lines in a way that will tend to favor a preferred political party—has become a dominant feature of contemporary redistricting.[37]

In 2019, the Supreme Court ruled by a 5–4 vote that federal courts couldn't hear challenges to partisan gerrymandering, because such disputes raised "political questions" to be resolved, somehow, by the very political branches that provoked them, rather than legal questions to be resolved by the courts. (Never mind that incumbents in Congress have very little incentive to pursue reforms that would make their seats less secure.) But redistricting can still be challenged in federal court on the ground that it disenfranchises voters based on race. Some states have also authorized their own courts to hear partisan gerrymandering claims under the state constitution. And because the maps are usually drawn right before (and, sometimes, during) the first post-Census election cycle, redistricting cases can provide regular fodder for the shadow docket.[38]

When Alabama redrew its seven US House districts following the 2020 Census, the map included only one district where Black voters would form a majority, even though 27 percent of the state's total population in the 2020 Census identified as Black. On November 4, 2021—the same day the map was signed into law by Governor Kay Ivey—a group of plaintiffs brought suit, arguing that the state had impermissibly engaged in "vote dilution" in violation of the Voting Rights Act. The suit was assigned to a special three-judge district court that featured two Trump-appointed district judges and the Clinton-appointed Eleventh Circuit judge Stanley Marcus.

On January 24, 2022, the three judges unanimously sided with the challengers. After a seven-day hearing featuring live testimony from seventeen witnesses, the court concluded that the plaintiffs had made out their case for a violation of the Voting Rights Act under a 1986 Supreme Court ruling known as *Thornburg* v. *Gingles*—and that Alabama should have drawn a second "majority-minority" district. Noting that there was still time for the state to try again before the map needed to be finalized for the 2022 primary and general elections (it had taken less than a week to draw the unlawful map), the court ordered Alabama to redraw its map to include a second "majority-minority" district. That district would almost certainly create a second Democratic seat within Alabama's 6–1 Republican House delegation.[39]

Because the ruling came from a three-judge district court, it could be appealed directly to the Supreme Court. Alabama took that path, and it also asked the Court to stay the district court's injunction pending that appeal, to allow the unlawful map to be used for the 2022 midterms. On February 7, the Court agreed. There was no majority opinion, but a concurring opinion by Justice Kavanaugh, joined by Justice Alito, rested heavily on *Purcell*. Now promoting the *Purcell* principle to "a *bedrock* tenet of election law" (emphasis mine), Kavanaugh wrote that, "when an election is close at hand, the rules of the road must be clear and settled." Thus, even though the district court injunction had specifically left it to the state to redraw its map in time for the 2022 midterm cycle (and had concluded that there was plenty of time for the state to comply), Kavanaugh complained that the district court was "swoop[ing] in and re-do[ing]" Alabama's laws "in the period close to an election."[40]

There's just one problem with Kavanaugh's *Purcell* analysis: It makes no sense. The district court decision (which Kavanaugh referred to as a "late-breaking injunction") came on January 24, more than nine months before the 2022 congressional election. And even if the Alabama primary was the relevant deadline, that election wasn't until May 24, still four months away. Moreover, the challengers in the Alabama case had filed suit on the very day that the map had been adopted—the earliest possible moment for such legal action under the Supreme Court's own precedents. Thus, Kavanaugh's *Purcell* analysis effectively suggested that there was nothing the district court could have done to stop Alabama from using an unlawful map for at least one election cycle. Like the principle of tort law that "every dog gets one free bite,"* every state would get one free election cycle using unlawful district maps every ten years. That's quite a shift compared to the VRA's preclearance regime (under which the maps presumably would never have been approved by the Justice Department), all the more so given that it came through a shadow docket ruling with no majority opinion.[41]

Perhaps in an attempt to buttress the unpersuasive *Purcell* analysis, Kavanaugh's concurrence also took a shot at the merits of the plaintiffs' claims, suggesting that it was not as clear as the district court had said that Alabama's proposed map violated the Voting Rights Act as interpreted in *Gingles*. In a footnote, he even alluded to the ordinary standard for a stay, writing that "even under the ordinary stay standard outside the

* In most states, the owner of a domestic pet can be held liable for injuries the pet causes to others only if the pet has a "propensity" to engage in harmful behavior. The idea that "every dog gets one free bite" colloquializes the propensity requirement; it's impossible to establish that most pets have a propensity for harmful behavior based on their first attack.

election context, the State has at least a fair prospect of success on appeal—as do the plaintiffs, for that matter." This formulation absolved the state of its burden to meet any of the other traditional requirements for a stay, focusing on just one of the four traditional factors. That omission is critical because, if the *plaintiffs* had a fair prospect of success, the significant risk that the new map violated their rights under the Voting Rights Act, together with the harm of using such a map, ought to have weighed conclusively against a stay (considerations that, again, fall out under *Purcell*).[42]

This last point appears to have provoked Chief Justice Roberts, who had written the Court's 2013 opinion in *Shelby County v. Holder* that weakened the Voting Rights Act, into writing his own dissent. As he explained, although he agreed that the Court should take up the merits of whether Alabama's map violated the Voting Rights Act, "the analysis below seems correct as *Gingles* is presently applied, and in my view the District Court's analysis should therefore control the upcoming election." In other words, because the district court correctly applied the law on the books, no emergency relief was warranted, even if, thanks to the conservative majority, that law was soon going to change. Roberts might well have been sympathetic to the rest of the conservatives' desire to narrow *Gingles*; he just wasn't willing to do so on the shadow docket.[43]

But the harsher words came, once again, from Justice Kagan. Writing for herself and Justices Breyer and Sotomayor, the Court's fiercest critic of the shadow docket again criticized not just the substance of the majority's ruling, but the way that it was reached. "There may—or may not—be a basis for revising our VRA precedent in light of the modern districting technology that Alabama's application highlights," Kagan wrote. "But such a change can properly happen only after full briefing and argument—not based on the scanty review this Court gives matters on its shadow docket." Indeed, "the District Court here did everything right under the law existing today. Staying its decision forces Black Alabamians to suffer what under that law is clear vote dilution."[44]

After explaining at some length why the district court's factual and legal conclusions were correct under current law, why *Purcell* could not possibly apply given the timelines under consideration, and why any delay in the litigation was the state's fault, not the plaintiffs', Kagan closed with another shot at the shadow docket: "Today's decision is one more in a disconcertingly long line of cases in which this Court uses its shadow docket to signal or make changes in the law," she wrote, "without anything approaching full briefing and argument." By staying the district court's ruling based upon a hypothetical future change in the meaning of the VRA, the majority's decision, she added, "does a disservice to our own appellate processes, which serve both to constrain and to legitimate the Court's authority. It does a disservice to the District Court, which meticulously applied this Court's longstanding voting-rights precedent. And most of all, it does a disservice to Black Alabamians who under that precedent have had their electoral power diminished—in violation of a law this Court once knew to buttress all of American democracy."[45]

Kagan's return to a direct and explicit criticism of the shadow docket, a theme she had first sounded in her September 2021 dissent from the Court's refusal to intervene in the Texas abortion case, provoked a new response from Kavanaugh. In his words, Kagan's "catchy but worn-out rhetoric about the 'shadow docket' is . . . off target": "The stay will allow this Court to decide the merits in an orderly fashion—after full briefing, oral argument, and our usual extensive internal deliberations—and ensure that we do not have to decide the merits on the emergency docket. To reiterate: The Court's stay order is not a decision on the merits."[46]

Just as in the Texas case, though, Kavanaugh's insistence that the Court's emergency order was not a decision on the merits rang more than a little hollow, and not just because he said it thrice. Not only was the *result* of the ruling that Alabama could use its putatively unlawful map in the 2022 midterm elections, but that ruling was also understood by other district courts to require the same practical result. Ten days after the Supreme Court's Alabama ruling, for instance, a Georgia district court refused to enjoin Georgia's redistricting *despite* finding the exact same violation—that Georgia had failed to create enough majority-minority districts in its post-2020 redistricting (a conclusion that should have required Georgia to create another likely safe seat for Democrats in the state's House delegation). Even worse, in Georgia, Governor Kemp had deliberately waited a month to sign the new maps into law—delay that could be explained only as an effort to frustrate preelection judicial review. The problem, the district court explained, was the Supreme Court's unexplained Alabama ruling, of which "it would be unwise, irresponsible, and against common sense for this Court not to take note."[47]

Thus, whether or not the majority in the Alabama dispute had formally made new law, its ruling had the effect of making new law by prompting other courts to allow multiple states to use congressional district maps for the 2022 election cycle that violated the Supreme Court's governing interpretation of the Voting Rights Act. As if *Purcell* wasn't problematic enough already, now its (deeply contestable) invocation in Alabama was producing substantive downstream consequences elsewhere. Any doubt on that score was eliminated in June 2022, when the Court likewise put new congressional maps in Louisiana back into effect after the district court and the Fifth Circuit had explained at great length why they should be blocked notwithstanding the Alabama ruling. The district court wrote 152 pages. The Fifth Circuit wrote 33. The Supreme Court wrote nothing.[48]

But the Court went still one step further in March 2022, in the same place its current spate of election-related rulings had started in April 2020—Wisconsin. In Wisconsin, the Democratic governor had vetoed the proposed state legislative redistricting maps adopted by the Republican-controlled state legislature. Both the legislature and the governor then turned to the Wisconsin Supreme Court, which solicited map proposals from the legislature, the governor, and various groups of voters. By a 4–3 vote, the state's highest court adopted the governor's proposal, which would have created a new majority-minority Black district in Milwaukee, a move the governor defended as being necessary to satisfy the Voting Rights Act.[49]

The state legislature, joined by a group of voters, then asked the US Supreme Court to stay the Wisconsin Supreme Court's decision—or, in the alternative, to grant certiorari and agree to resolve on the merits whether the governor's map, which intentionally drew a race-based distinction by creating a new majority-minority district, constituted impermissible racial discrimination under the federal Constitution. On March 23, 2022, the justices opted for a truncated version of the latter. In an unsigned opinion, the Court granted certiorari and, in the same order, summarily reversed the Wisconsin Supreme Court. As the Court tersely explained, the adoption of a majority-minority district, even for a state legislature, required the relevant state actor (whether the governor or the state supreme court) to show that such a district was *required* by the Voting Rights Act, and not just consistent with that statute. Because the Wisconsin Supreme Court had not actually conducted that analysis, its decision had to be wiped away.[50]

In her dissent, Justice Sotomayor captured the problem with the majority's analysis well: It was true that the Supreme Court had long allowed voters to contest redistricting maps that drew majority-minority districts on the grounds that they weren't required by the VRA. If a majority-minority district wasn't required by the VRA, it could be challenged as unconstitutional racial discrimination under the Equal Protection Clause. Here, though, the decision being appealed was not the type of lawsuit in which those claims are typically brought—that is, a suit challenging the maps that a state has adopted. Rather, this litigation came one crucial step earlier—from a state judicial proceeding in which the maps were first proposed and adopted. There was no precedent recognizing that judicial decisions adopting redistricting maps could themselves be challenged on such grounds, and for good reason: The question before the Wisconsin Supreme Court was not whether the maps it ended up choosing were required by the VRA, or whether they violated the Constitution; it was simply which of the various maps under consideration it should adopt as a matter of *state* law. There was no reason under the US Supreme Court's existing precedents for the Wisconsin Supreme Court to push its analysis any further at this juncture, so summarily reversing it for *not* going further was a bit rich.[51]

Indeed, it would have been easy enough, as Justice Sotomayor suggested in her dissent, for the Court to wait. As she wrote, "This Court's intervention today is not only extraordinary but also unnecessary. The Wisconsin Supreme Court rightly preserved the possibility that an appropriate plaintiff could bring an equal protection or VRA challenge in the proper forum." Moreover, such a suit could have been brought immediately. So why did the Court rush? The majority opinion didn't offer any explanation, but the answer may well have been *Purcell*. With Wisconsin's primary set for August 9, 2022, even if "an appropriate plaintiff" brought a new lawsuit challenging the state legislative maps adopted by the Wisconsin Supreme Court, such a suit would almost certainly end up in federal court—and a ruling would not be likely until within four months of the primary (just as in the Alabama cases). At that point, if the Court was even remotely faithful in its purported application of *Purcell*, injunctive relief would not be appropriate, so the (Democratic) governor's maps would be used for at least one cycle. In other words, rather than live with the consequences of *Purcell*, the Court jumped in prematurely in what at least appeared to be an attempt to avoid those consequences—another shadow docket innovation in a case with an unavoidably partisan (and pro-Republican) valence.[52]

~

The 2020 election cases reinforced many of the long-standing critiques of *Purcell*. But the 2022 redistricting cases took them to a new level, dovetailing with, and reinforcing, the emerging, broader critiques of the shadow docket. Not only was the Court intervening selectively and inconsistently when it came to lower-court injunctions of changes to state election rules, but it was increasingly doing so in a way that, as in the Alabama cases, made new law; and, as in the Wisconsin cases, had it waited for a more appropriate vehicle, it otherwise might not have been able to do before the 2022 election cycle. In other words, by the spring of 2022, the Court's use of the shadow docket in election cases had come to bear all the troubling hallmarks of the shadow docket that it had borne in the Trump administration and religious liberty cases we've already encountered. It's not just that the Court was issuing more shadow docket rulings with greater real-world impacts; it's that these rulings were increasingly producing effects in other legal decisions across the country, and that the Court's use of the shadow docket, rather than the merits docket, for those purposes increasingly appeared to be deliberate. And to an even greater extent than in those other categories of cases, the election cases appeared to be almost homogeneously partisan, with conservative justices voting in favor of whatever position supported the political power of Republicans; Democratic justices voting against it; and only Chief Justice Roberts, in a handful of the cases, publicly crossing over.

In that respect, the election cases—a body of law that started on the shadow docket, is shaped by a major shadow docket ruling (*Purcell*), and largely resides on the shadow docket—illustrate the depths to which the Supreme Court's use of unsigned, unexplained orders has truly sunk. By insisting on a subjective, manipulable standard to govern election cases in an "overdetermined and undertheorized" 2006 ruling that was itself on the shadow docket, the Court has enabled itself to accomplish far more change through far less writing than any number of unexplained, in-chambers orders by Justice Black ever could have. And by applying that standard inconsistently, and in a way that outwardly favors Republicans far more often than it does Democrats, the justices have only emboldened criticisms that the Court is carrying out a partisan political agenda rather than a neutral judicial one. More than any other subset of the Court's decision-making, it's the election cases that best vindicate Justice Kagan's charge in the Texas abortion case—that "every day," the Court's shadow docket behavior "becomes more unreasoned, inconsistent, and impossible to defend."[53]

# CHAPTER 7

# "READ THE OPINION"

## HOW THE COURT'S ABUSE OF THE SHADOW DOCKET UNDERMINES ITS LEGITIMACY

Even compared to the election cases, no shadow docket decision brought more public attention to the Court's growing reliance on unsigned, unexplained orders, or provoked more public outrage, than the single long paragraph that the Supreme Court handed down at 11:58 p.m. on September 1, 2021. In *Whole Woman's Health* v. *Jackson*, the Court, by a 5–4 vote, refused to block "SB8," or the Texas Heartbeat Act, a state law banning virtually all abortions after the sixth week of pregnancy, which had gone into effect twenty-three hours earlier, at midnight central time. Indeed, almost ten months before the justices would use the merits docket to controversially repudiate the constitutional right to a previability abortion that the Court had recognized in *Roe* v. *Wade* and reaffirmed in *Planned Parenthood* v. *Casey*, five of the conservative justices used the shadow docket to make it nearly impossible to get an abortion in the nation's second-largest state.[1]

As Justice Kagan argued in her brief but forceful dissent, the decision both embodied and crystallized the growing critiques of the shadow docket. Moreover, the public backlash that the ruling provoked helped to spur the first public defenses of the Court's changing behavior. It may also have precipitated a handful of subtle but significant changes in how the justices handled high-profile emergency applications during the Court's October 2021 Term. The problem, as it turned out, was that the Court's direct and indirect responses in many ways only reinforced the central critique—that the Court was not just *using* the shadow docket with greater frequency, but that it was abusing it, as well. And those abuses, as they have added up, have raised serious questions about the Court's broader institutional legitimacy—where it comes from, why it matters, and how it erodes. The harder question is how those abuses can and should be reined in. But that conversation is only possible once there's at least some consensus as to the full dimensions of the problem.[2]

After Justice Kavanaugh was confirmed to succeed Justice Kennedy in 2018, Republican-controlled state legislatures across the country passed a series of new laws to tighten existing restrictions on abortions. Some laws imposed new logistical or medical burdens on patients and doctors before abortions could be performed. Others banned most (or all) abortions after the fifteenth week of pregnancy, which was as much as nine weeks earlier than what had previously been the constitutional line, the "viability" standard articulated in *Roe* and endorsed in *Casey*. ("Viability" is generally understood as the point past which a typical fetus can survive outside of the womb.) These new state laws all appeared to be predicated on the assumption, which turned out to be correct, that there was no longer a majority on the Supreme Court willing to defend *Roe* and

*Casey*. As recently as 2016, Kennedy had been the swing vote in a 5–3 ruling (after Justice Scalia's death) striking down a series of onerous Texas requirements for abortion procedures, joining a majority opinion by Justice Breyer that had embraced a broad reading of *Roe* and *Casey*. But with Kavanaugh replacing Kennedy in 2018, there now appeared to be five votes unsympathetic to a constitutional right to abortion.

That impression was only enhanced by two different events in 2020. First, on June 29, Chief Justice Roberts provided the key fifth vote in favor of striking down Louisiana abortion restrictions modeled on the Texas restrictions that the Court had invalidated in 2016, but wrote a separate opinion embracing a far narrower scope for abortion protections than what the Court had articulated in the 2016 ruling (a ruling from which he had dissented). Second, and far more importantly, when Justice Ginsburg died on September 18, even Roberts's narrower view was no longer the median vote. With Justice Barrett's confirmation six weeks later, there now appeared to be not just five justices hostile to *Roe* and *Casey*, but six.[3]

Even against that backdrop, the restriction Texas enacted in 2021 was extreme. Most directly, SB8 banned virtually all abortions after the sixth week of pregnancy (a point at which many do not even know that they're pregnant), in flagrant violation of *Roe* and *Casey*. Under those rulings, states were prohibited from imposing an "undue burden" on the right of a pregnant person to obtain a previability abortion. Categorically *banning* abortions after the sixth week quite obviously fails that test. But SB8 was especially pernicious because it included a series of procedural tricks and traps that were designed to make its patently unconstitutional six-week ban exceedingly difficult to challenge in court.

Usually, when a state passed a new abortion restriction, the restriction would be immediately challenged in court by abortion providers in a suit against the chief state officer in charge of enforcing the restriction—typically, the state's attorney general. If the suit succeeded, the providers would obtain an injunction—a court order barring that state officer from enforcing the unconstitutional abortion restriction going forward. Defiance of that injunction would subject the officer to escalating sanctions, including fines and possibly even imprisonment. As a practical matter, then, all enforcement of the abortion restriction would be blocked, because, presumably, those state officers with authority to enforce the unconstitutional state law would all be subject to the court order enjoining it. When a news story reports that a court has "struck down" an unconstitutional law, this is usually what has happened; such a ruling does not literally erase the offending statute from the books, but it makes it practically impossible for the unconstitutional law to be enforced by anyone who would otherwise have the authority to do so.[4]

To frustrate that traditional path to judicial review, SB8 cut the state out of the loop, expressly denying to the attorney general or other state executive officials the power to enforce the six-week ban. Instead of having SB8 enforced by state executive officials, Texas authorized enforcement suits brought by private parties, allowing any person to sue an abortion provider alleging a violation of SB8, whether or not they had any connection to a specific abortion procedure. Public discussions of this approach centered on the problematic precedent of creating private "bounty hunters," who stood to recover at least $10,000 if they were successful. But the real point of the private enforcement model was to frustrate pre-enforcement suits by providers; unlike the attorney general, it's hard to sue a single private citizen, let alone thousands of them, to challenge what they might do in the future. Complicating matters further, SB8 barred abortion providers from recovering the costs of litigation even in cases they won.[5]

Tying these threads together, by absolving the state of any enforcement responsibility, SB8 made it difficult for providers to sue anyone to prevent the law from going into effect; after all, even if the providers successfully obtained an injunction against one potential plaintiff, that wouldn't prevent another one from suing to enforce the law. And the number of potential plaintiffs was, in theory, limitless. Of course, as the law's sponsors were quick to point out, providers could still invoke *Roe* and *Casey* as a defense if anyone ever sued them for performing an abortion after the sixth week of pregnancy. But because SB8 authorized any private party to sue, it opened the door to a potentially endless flood of such lawsuits against abortion providers for each abortion they performed. The providers might "win" each case, but unlike in almost any other context, winning the first case would not stop the second from being brought; winning the second would not stop the third; and so on. And because SB8 prevented the providers from recovering their costs or attorney's fees, they could win *every* case and still end up going out of business; each little "victory" would end up only costing them more. If SB8 went into effect, then, the only course of action reasonably available to abortion providers across the state would be to shut down.[6]

In an attempt to short-circuit this scheme and avoid having to cease operations, a group of Texas abortion providers brought suit before SB8 went into effect, naming eight defendants—seven state officials and one private citizen who had already threatened to sue the providers. In addition to suing the attorney general and four state health officials as defendants, the suit also named a state court judge and a state court clerk (on behalf of all state court judges and clerks). The providers' theory was that, even if SB8 had disclaimed any role for state executive officers in enforcing SB8, Texas's courts still had to play a role; SB8 enforcement suits had to be placed on the courts' dockets by clerks and heard by judges. (This was the very theory on which civil rights groups had challenged racially restrictive housing covenants—barring the white purchaser of a home from subsequently selling it to buyers who were Black—in the 1940s.) If the providers could obtain an injunction barring judicial officials from either docketing or hearing claims under SB8, they wouldn't have to worry about the potentially ruinous litigation costs they would otherwise face from continuing to perform constitutionally protected abortions after the sixth week of pregnancy.[7]

On August 25, one week before the law was set to go into effect, Austin-based federal district judge Robert Pitman denied the eight defendants' motion to dismiss the case, rejecting their claim that they were all immune from such a lawsuit. Judge Pitman scheduled a preliminary injunction hearing for Monday, August 30—timed to allow him, if necessary, to block SB8 from going into effect before it was scheduled to do so (at 12:00 a.m. on Wednesday, September 1). But before that hearing ever happened, the defendants convinced the Fifth Circuit (the New Orleans–based federal appeals court with jurisdiction over Louisiana, Mississippi, and Texas) to issue an extraordinary "administrative" stay of all proceedings in the district court, even though no injunction had yet been issued.* Although the Fifth Circuit ordered briefing on the stay to be completed by 9:00 a.m. on Tuesday, August 31 (presumably so it could conclusively rule on the stay by the end of that day), it did not rule on the application until ten days later, on Friday, September 10. Instead, it was from the Fifth Circuit's preliminary, administrative stay that the providers sought emergency relief in the Supreme Court on Monday, August 30. Specifically, the providers asked Justice Alito as circuit justice (and, through him, the full Court) either to vacate the Fifth Circuit's administrative stay or, as in the religious liberty cases, to issue an emergency writ of injunction directly against the eight named defendants, blocking the enforcement of SB8 pending further litigation.[8]

The first thing that ought to be said about the Supreme Court's ruling is that it did not come in time to prevent SB8

* An "administrative" stay is a temporary pause meant to give the appellate court time to consider whether to issue a "regular" stay, that is, a stay that will remain in force for the duration of the appeal.

from going into effect. Exactly eleven days earlier, Justice Alito had issued an administrative stay to temporarily prevent a different Texas district court's injunction against a Biden administration immigration policy from going into effect until the full Court could rule on the Justice Department's application for a stay pending appeal. Even though the full Court eventually rejected that application four days later, Justice Alito, as circuit justice for the Fifth Circuit, still froze the status quo long enough for the full Court to decide what it wanted to do before the district court's injunction would have gone into effect. No such interim relief was issued in the SB8 case. Instead, midnight on September 1 came and went with no order from the Court, and the most aggressive abortion restrictions since 1973 when *Roe* was decided went into effect across Texas. By the next morning, legal abortions in Texas had ground to a halt.[9]

It was only just before midnight the *next* day—at 11:58 p.m. EDT on Wednesday, September 1—that the Supreme Court handed down its ruling. In a single, unsigned paragraph, a 5–4 majority declined to provide either form of emergency relief that had been sought by the providers:

> [The] application . . . presents complex and novel antecedent procedural questions on which [the providers] have not carried their burden. For example, federal courts enjoy the power to enjoin individuals tasked with enforcing laws, not the laws themselves. And it is unclear whether the named defendants in this lawsuit can or will seek to enforce the Texas law against the applicants in a manner that might permit our intervention. The State has represented that neither it nor its executive employees possess the authority to enforce the Texas law either directly or indirectly. Nor is it clear whether, under existing precedent, this Court can issue an injunction against state judges asked to decide a lawsuit under Texas's law. Finally, the sole private-citizen respondent before us has filed an affidavit stating that he has no present intention to enforce the law.[10]

In other words, the order justified the Court's refusal to intervene by invoking three variations on the same procedural uncertainty: whether any of the eight named defendants could properly be the subject of the injunction that the providers were seeking. Critically, the Court wouldn't have had to answer that question to provide the *lesser* relief the providers sought—to lift the Fifth Circuit's administrative stay and leave it to the district court to decide whether to block SB8. But the majority had nothing to say about that distinction, or why the providers couldn't meet that lower bar. Instead, the majority went out of its way to "stress that we do not purport to resolve definitively any jurisdictional or substantive claim in the applicants' lawsuit. In particular, this order is not based on any conclusion about the constitutionality of Texas's law, and in no way limits other procedurally proper challenges to the Texas law, including in Texas state courts." The Court thus denied emergency relief without resolving any question of law, concluding that it was not sufficiently clear that the providers would ultimately win to justify preventing SB8 from going into effect—not because SB8 was constitutional, but because there might not be anyone the providers could sue to block it.[11]

Each of the four dissenting justices wrote a brief opinion. Justices Breyer and Sotomayor, in particular, focused on the merits, stressing the undeniable hardships that allowing SB8 to go into effect would put on Texans seeking to vindicate their constitutional right to a previability abortion. As Justice Sotomayor put it, "the Court's order is stunning. Presented with an application to enjoin a flagrantly unconstitutional law engineered to prohibit women from exercising their constitutional rights and evade judicial scrutiny, a majority of justices have opted to bury their heads in the sand."[12]

Chief Justice Roberts, whose skepticism of the Court's jurisprudence protecting the right to previability abortion was a matter of record, used his dissent to underscore that "the consequences of approving the state action [in insulating the six-week ban from judicial review], both in this particular case and as a model for action in other areas, counsel at least preliminary judicial consideration before the program devised by the State takes effect." Although Roberts's tone was moderate, his belief that the Court was bound to intervene in the SB8 case, when he had opposed similar emergency intervention in many religious liberty cases, is revealing. For Roberts, SB8 was an affront to the role of the courts even more than it was an aggressive abortion restriction, and the former trumped the latter.[13]

But it was Justice Kagan's dissent that most directly contrasted the Court's nonintervention in the SB8 case with its prior shadow docket rulings in the religious liberty cases challenging COVID restrictions. Leading with the practical consequences of the Court's decision, under which "Texas law prohibits abortions for the vast majority of women who seek them," Kagan sharply criticized not just the ends, but the means by which the majority had imposed those consequences. Her two-paragraph dissent castigated the majority for "barely bother[ing] to explain its conclusion—that a challenge to an obviously unconstitutional abortion regulation backed by a wholly unprecedented enforcement scheme is unlikely to prevail."[14]

Perhaps things would've been different if the *Whole Woman's Health* ruling had been further removed from the religious liberty cases. Instead, it came from the exact same 5–4 majority that had granted emergency relief in *Roman Catholic Diocese* (the New York religious liberty case from just before Thanksgiving 2020) and *Tandon* (the April 2021 case striking down California's restrictions on in-home gatherings). In both of those cases, as we've already seen, the five justices who now claimed to have their hands tied had ignored procedural roadblocks in order to vindicate claims of religious liberty.

Not only that, but when the Court eventually did decide the procedural questions in *Whole Woman's Health* three months later, the justices would hold, by an 8–1 vote, that the providers were allowed to proceed, at least temporarily, against at least four of the named defendants—the four state licensing officials.* In other words, four of the five justices who refused to intervene on September 1 ended up changing their minds and siding with the providers on part of the answer to the very procedural question that, in their view, had previously justified not intervening.[15]

More fundamentally, the same five justices who saw mootness as little more than a speed bump in *Roman Catholic Diocese* and who ignored a fatal procedural obstacle in *Tandon* relied upon unanswered procedural questions, not settled procedural obstacles, to justify their nonintervention to block enforcement of SB8. Put another way, in the earlier cases, the Court reached the merits even though it lacked the power to do so. Now, it declined to reach the merits solely because it *might* lack the power to do so. And, unlike *Tandon*, in which the Court jumped through procedural hoops to issue an emergency injunction based upon a *new* interpretation of the Constitution, the same justices refused to do so in *Whole Woman's Health* to protect a right that—at that point, anyway—was not just clearly established, but that SB8 unquestionably violated.

Indeed, even if those unsettled procedural questions were enough to militate against an emergency injunction (unlike in *Roman Catholic Diocese* or *Tandon*), it is worth reiterating that the providers had also asked the Supreme Court for the lesser relief of simply vacating the Fifth Circuit's stay. That more modest relief could have been based almost entirely on the harm the providers would have incurred from having SB8 remain in effect, much as Chief Justice Roberts appeared to suggest in his dissent. After all, as we've seen, the standard for granting or vacating a stay focuses on balancing the likelihood of success on the merits with the equities more generally, including which outcome would cause more harm—allowing the

* On remand, the Fifth Circuit ended up ruling that those defendants could *not* be sued, after the Texas Supreme Court clarified their limited ability to take any disciplinary actions against doctors who violated SB8.

law to go into effect, or blocking it pending appeal. And in the SB8 case, those equities overwhelmingly tilted in favor of the providers. But the majority never separately considered the providers' alternative request, or the lower standard that it should have applied in assessing it.[16]

By September 2021, the unexplained inconsistency of the majority's shadow docket behavior was nothing new. What *was* new about the SB8 ruling was that it made enormous waves publicly. The decision dominated newspaper headlines the following day, and a flood of critical editorials and op-eds quickly followed. But this time, picking up on Justice Kagan's dissent, the stories focused not just on the substance of the Court's shadow docket ruling, but also on the context in which it was handed down. For the first time, the justices' procedural behavior was a main character in the story, alongside (rather than overshadowed by) the bottom line of the Court's ruling. A subsequent study by the *Chicago Policy Review* found that the term "shadow docket" went through something of a renaissance in the days and weeks after September 1, appearing in more than twenty pieces in the *New York Times*, the *Washington Post*, the *Chicago Tribune*, and the *Wall Street Journal* in the six weeks between September 2 and October 15. By contrast, the term had appeared in fewer than fifteen pieces in those same publications in the first eight months of 2021, and fewer still during all of 2020. Apparently, it was bad enough that the Court had effectively ended abortion in Texas; but it was incomprehensible that it had done so via one technical and largely inscrutable paragraph that refused to specifically resolve anything.[17]

Perhaps the sharpest public critique came from the journalist Adam Serwer. Writing in *The Atlantic*, Serwer placed the SB8 ruling within the broader context of the Court's shadow docket rulings over the previous four years. In a piece titled "Five Justices Did This Because They Could," he wrote, "The shadow docket has begun to look less like a place for emergency cases than one where the Republican-appointed justices can implement their preferred policies without having to go through the tedious formalities of following legal procedure, developing arguments consistent with precedent, or withstanding public scrutiny." Thus, he explained, by allowing SB8 to go into effect, "five conservative justices told Republican-controlled states they could disregard *Roe* while insisting that wasn't what they were doing at all." As Serwer's piece underscored, to a far greater extent than prior shadow docket rulings, the real-world effect of the SB8 case was apparent for all to see. The impact the ruling would have, in Texas and eventually beyond Texas, helped to attract attention to the rise of the shadow docket itself, to the thin explanation the majority had provided, and to Justice Kagan's cutting charge of inconsistency.[18]

The public backlash also provoked the first sustained public defenses of the Court's changing behavior, beginning during the last week of September. On Wednesday, September 29, at the Senate Judiciary Committee's first-ever hearing on the shadow docket, Senate Republicans repeatedly defended the Court's behavior (and criticized the Democrats for making an issue out of it). Three days later, the editorial board of the *Wall Street Journal* published a piece titled "The 'Shadow Docket' Diversion," sounding similar themes. But the most sustained defense came in between those two, in a speech by Justice Alito at the Notre Dame Law School on Thursday, September 30. Titled "The Emergency Docket," Alito's speech, of which there is no public recording or transcript, offered four principal defenses of the Court's shadow docket behavior over the preceding months and years.[19]

First, Justice Alito argued that nothing meaningful had changed. Though he acknowledged that the Court was granting emergency relief more often than it had in prior years, he suggested that the uptick in volume was simply because the Court was receiving more requests for it to do so. Alito's factual claim was wrong; the Court was not receiving more total applications for emergency relief. But even if it had been correct, his conclusion wouldn't have followed. Just because more parties are seeking emergency relief doesn't mean the lower courts are handing down a higher number of rulings *warranting* such relief. And even if lower courts were handing down more rulings that justified emergency intervention from the justices, that fact would seem to speak to a different problem: a rather significant disconnect between the justices and the lower courts. Even assuming that such a disconnect existed, one might expect the Court to publicly identify that problem and seek to correct it, whether in its formal opinions or in speeches like Alito's. And yet, no such disconnect was ever identified.[20]

Second, describing and directly responding to Serwer's critique, Justice Alito argued that the Court's emergency orders weren't merits rulings in either form or function. Again, though, focusing on the terminology denigrates the substance of the objection. Although the SB8 decision was not a "merits ruling," that made little difference to the millions of Texans who, in an instant, could not obtain a constitutionally protected abortion anywhere in the state. In that respect, it is impossible to deny that the Court's nonintervention produced a major substantive effect—it had sanctioned the virtual abolition of abortion across all of Texas. And while the Court's ruling in the SB8 case had not changed the rules for when government officials could be sued, its April 2021 shadow docket ruling in *Tandon* unquestionably had changed other rules, enshrining a new, substantive principle of Free Exercise Clause jurisprudence. The SB8 ruling may have changed the law only on the ground in Texas, but *Tandon* changed the meaning of the Constitution everywhere. Suggesting that these weren't "merits" rulings may thus have had the superficial veneer of descriptive accuracy. But it missed the extent to which these orders would have the same practical, and, in many cases, legal, effects as the work of the Court's merits docket.

Third, and relatedly, Justice Alito insisted, twice, that these rulings were not precedential. Here, it's impossible to square

Alito's speech with the Court's own formal decision-making, especially in the religious liberty cases. Consider again the justices' February 2021 order in *Gateway City Church* v. *Newsom*, where, in granting injunctive relief against California COVID restrictions, the majority wrote that "the Ninth Circuit's failure to grant relief was erroneous" because "this outcome is clearly dictated by this Court's decision" in *South Bay II*, an earlier shadow docket order with no majority opinion. *Gateway City Church*, as we've seen, was hardly alone in this regard. Against that backdrop, Justice Alito's insistence that these orders weren't precedential was simply belied by the record—a record replete with rulings in which he joined. Only by looking at the shadow docket holistically does that incongruity become clear.[21]

Finally, Justice Alito attacked critics of the shadow docket for complaining about the lack of transparency surrounding shadow docket rulings. Among other things, Alito explained that the filings and orders in these cases were available on the Supreme Court's website for all to see, and that, when rulings came late at night, that was only because the justices were working to beat a midnight deadline. Leaving aside the fact that the SB8 ruling came twenty-three hours after the relevant deadline, not two minutes before it (to say nothing of *Roman Catholic Diocese* coming down four minutes before midnight the night before Thanksgiving), the idea that there's nothing wrong with the shadow docket because any member of the public can find the relevant filings and orders is, again, knocking down a straw man. The problem is not that these rulings are literally inaccessible; it's that they are practically inaccessible. That a one-paragraph order is publicly posted to a website doesn't change the fact that the means by which it was produced, the order itself, and the order's impact are all but impossible for the overwhelming majority of would-be readers to follow.[22]

In addition to defending the Court, Alito attacked the shadow docket's critics, including me (whom he called out by name), for weaponizing the term itself as part of a broader agenda to delegitimize the Court. "Recently," Alito argued, "the catchy and sinister term 'shadow docket' has been used to portray the Court as having been captured by a dangerous cabal that resorts to sneaky and improper methods to get its ways. This portrayal feeds unprecedented efforts to intimidate the Court or damage it as an independent institution." The previous day, Senator John Cornyn of Texas, the Republican Whip, had sounded a strikingly similar theme at the Senate Judiciary Committee's shadow docket hearing, saying, "It's clear that this [hearing] is a part of a concerted effort to intimidate and bully the members of the Supreme Court."[23]

Of course, the real issue is not the term that we use to describe the uptick in inconsistent, unsigned, and unexplained decisions that are affecting more and more Americans; it's the uptick itself. And I've tried my best in the preceding pages to marshal the evidence supporting both the descriptive conclusion that there has been a massive uptick of these rulings, in both degree and kind, and the normative conclusion that these developments are deeply problematic. Readers can and should judge that evidence for themselves. But if the portrayal to this point is a fair one, then fighting over what to *call* the phenomenon is little more than a distraction. (Nor is Alito's effort to rebrand the topic as the Court's "emergency docket" persuasive; as we've seen, the Court hands down plenty of unsigned, unexplained orders with substantive effects outside of the context of applications for emergency relief, most notably grants or denials of certiorari.)

Whatever the phenomenon is named, the claim that those trying to document and criticize it are seeking to "damage" the Court's independence confuses the symptom for the disease. I don't doubt that there are many whose views put them at odds with a majority of the current justices for whom weakening and delegitimizing the Court are, indeed, goals. For my part, though, I see (and intend) these critiques in exactly the opposite direction—as an effort to persuade the Court, or at least those who follow it, that it is the justices' shadow docket behavior itself that is damaging the Court and contributing to public erosion in its perceived legitimacy. Even if an illegitimate Court might reap short-term benefits for a particular set of partisan preferences (preferences that, in all candor, are not my own), it's a terrible long-term development for a constitutional system that depends upon an independent, legitimate judiciary to protect minority rights from the tyranny of the majority.[24]

To be sure, the source of the Court's legitimacy is a long-debated and oft-contested topic. Constitutional law scholar Alexander Bickel called the problem "the countermajoritarian difficulty," by which he meant the paradox of judicial review in a democracy—of having unelected, unaccountable judges with the power to override democratic majorities. But perhaps the most sustained reflection that the Court itself has ever undertaken comes from the joint "plurality"* opinion by Justices O'Connor, Kennedy, and Souter in *Planned Parenthood* v. *Casey*: "As Americans of each succeeding generation are rightly told, the Court cannot buy support for its decisions by spending money and, except to a minor degree, it cannot independently coerce obedience to its decrees." Instead, they wrote, the Court's power "lies in its legitimacy, a product of substance and perception that shows itself in the people's acceptance of the Judiciary as fit to determine what the Nation's law means and to declare what it demands."[25]

We follow the Supreme Court, in other words, not because we agree with all (or even most) of its decisions, but because we accept that the justices are exercising judicial, rather than political, power. That acceptance, in turn, is inextricably linked

* When the Supreme Court decides a merits case but there is no rationale in which a majority of the justices agree, the "plurality" opinion is the opinion that speaks for the most number of justices who support the result that a majority of the Court has reached—whether affirming, reversing, or vacating the decision below, or dismissing the appeal.

to the rationales the Court provides for its rulings. O'Connor, Kennedy, and Souter put it this way:

> The Court must take care to speak and act in ways that allow people to accept its decisions on the terms the Court claims for them, as grounded truly in principle, not as compromises with social and political pressures having, as such, no bearing on the principled choices that the Court is obliged to make. Thus, the Court's legitimacy depends on making legally principled decisions under circumstances in which their principled character is sufficiently plausible to be accepted by the Nation.

They concluded, "Our contemporary understanding is such that a decision without principled justification would be no judicial act at all."[26]

Justice Barrett sounded a similar theme in an April 2022 speech at the Ronald Reagan Presidential Library. Nodding toward the Court's impending decisions on a number of divisive topics, including abortion, gun control, and affirmative action, she implored Americans to "read the opinion," and digest the Court's reasoning for themselves, before making judgments about whether the Court was acting politically. "Does [the decision] read like something that was purely results driven and designed to impose the policy preferences of the majority," she asked, "or does this read like it actually is an honest effort and persuasive effort, even if one you ultimately don't agree with, to determine what the Constitution and precedent requires?"[27]

It's the right question to ask, but what if there's no opinion to read? As we've seen, the shadow docket is replete with "decision[s] without principled justification." When those decisions don't produce substantive effects, the absence of a principled justification seems immaterial: no one loses sleep over the Court's refusal to explain why a party received more time to file a brief; no lower court or policymaker is left to wonder what to do in the next case. When those decisions do produce substantive effects, however, the absence of a principled justification becomes a much more serious problem. And in the shadow docket context, specifically, the fact that so many of the decisions producing substantive effects break down along ideological, if not strictly partisan, lines only compounds the problem, for it bolsters a narrative that the only principle explaining the justices' votes in these cases is their own political preferences. Remember that, outside of death penalty cases, it used to be unusual for shadow docket orders to divide the justices at all, let alone along consistent, ideological lines. Lately, however, such divisions have become a matter of course.

Even if the three-justice formulation in *Casey* doesn't fully encapsulate the source of the Court's legitimacy, it ought to be beyond dispute that the Court's legitimacy is defined far more by its actions than by the charges of its critics. In that respect, it's bad enough that the rise of the shadow docket has brought with it the numerous pathologies that have been documented in these pages; but it's far worse for the justices to publicly insist that none of this is, in fact, happening. And Justice Alito is hardly alone. As we've seen, in his February 2022 concurrence in the Alabama redistricting cases, Justice Kavanaugh (joined by Alito) complained about the "catchy but worn-out rhetoric about the 'shadow docket,'" as if the problem were the term, rather than the increasingly alarming shift in the Court's practices that it describes.[28]

The other charge Alito leveled in his Notre Dame speech, echoing numerous other conservative defenders of the Court's contemporary use of the shadow docket, is that critics just don't like the results—that those who worry about the growing trend of inconsistent, unexplained rulings affecting ever more people are in fact just progressives arguing in bad faith, framing their opposition to the substance of the new conservative majority's rulings in procedural terms. As the *Wall Street Journal*'s editorial board put it two days later, "The Supreme Court has moved in a conservative direction, so Democrats and the legal establishment have ramped up the volume on their criticism."[29]

The simplest response to that claim is that not all critics of the shadow docket are progressives. A noted conservative lawyer, Donald Ayer, who held the number-two post at the Justice Department under President George H. W. Bush, wrote in the *New York Times* in October 2021 that "what is new is the court's frequency and brashness in achieving these radical outcomes, and its willingness to do so often without an honest explanation and acknowledgement of what is actually going on." For Ayer, even if the Court is ending up in what he believes to be the right place, the way it's getting there is still a problem. And William Baude, the Chicago law professor who first described this body of Supreme Court work as the "shadow docket," and who has continued to express concerns about at least some of the Court's shadow docket behavior, is a former clerk for Chief Justice Roberts and a highly regarded conservative constitutional scholar. And then, of course, there's Roberts himself, who has demonstrated increasing skepticism about the Court's use of the shadow docket even (if not especially) to produce bottom lines he would support, and has supported, on the merits docket.[30]

But leaving aside the lazy attempt to paint shadow docket critiques in purely partisan colors, what this response truly shows is that those offering it don't actually understand the criticisms to which they are responding. The problem is not the shadow docket itself; every appellate court needs some mechanism for resolving both routine case-management issues and emergency applications. And it ought to follow that at least *some* emergency applications will justify intervention. Nor is it the volume of shadow docket rulings in the abstract. Nor is it that the justices are granting emergency relief more often; or that they are more divided when they are doing it; or even that they are deciding significant questions that impact millions of people through these emergency applications. It's that all of this is happening through rulings that are unsigned and unexplained (or, at least, insufficiently explained); that those rulings are objectively inconsistent in how they apply the same procedural standards—in ways that certainly appear to favor Republican policies (or litigants) over Democratic ones; and that Alito (apparently) aside, the justices themselves are now insisting that at least some of these inconsistent and insufficiently explained rulings have precedential effects. In other words, it's all of this *together.* If critics were just unhappy with the results in these cases, it certainly would be odd for them to be encouraging the justices to provide more persuasive (or, at least, lengthier) rationales to support them. And if no such rationales exist, that is a damning indictment of the Court's behavior all its own.[31]

Consider two different shadow docket orders in cases involving the Biden administration. In the first, decided in August 2021, the Court (over three public dissents) put back into effect a lower-court injunction against the Centers for Disease Control and Prevention's (CDC's) COVID-related eviction moratorium, effectively ending the policy. In a succinct, eight-page opinion, the majority identified the correct standard for the relief the applicants were seeking (vacating a lower-court stay); carefully applied each prong of the standard; and explained why, in their view, the moratorium exceeded the authority that Congress had given the CDC to respond to a public health emergency. Although my own view on whether the CDC had statutory authority for the moratorium is more in line with the analysis in Justice Breyer's dissent (joined by Justices Sotomayor and Kagan), I thought then (and still think) that, as shadow docket rulings go, this one was by the book, at least procedurally.[32]

Contrast that ruling with a March 2022 order in which, over three public dissents, the Court partially blocked a lower-court injunction that had required the US Navy to deploy twenty-six Navy SEALs who refused, on religious grounds, to comply with the Navy's COVID vaccine mandate. Justice Alito wrote a lengthy dissent (joined by Justice Gorsuch), and Justice Thomas separately noted his dissent. Meanwhile, there was no analysis by the majority, just a short, solo concurrence by Justice Kavanaugh. The SEALs case raises an important and somewhat tricky legal question about the relationship between the Religious Freedom Restoration Act (RFRA) and the deference that courts usually give to military decision-making even where that decision-making interferes with religious exercise. And yet, the majority's order provided no guidance about how that question was resolved in that case, or how it ought to be resolved going forward. Although my own view is that the Court came to the right conclusion, granting emergency relief with no explanation when the dissenting justices have offered an alternative (and unrebutted) rationale reflects much of what is wrong with the shadow docket; it's not the shadow docket itself, but how the Court is increasingly misusing it.[33]

More fundamentally, the response that "you just don't like the results" bespeaks surprising (and callous) disregard for the related notions that procedural regularity and principled justifications are a central part of what makes the Supreme Court a court, rather than just another font of partisan political power. Indeed, that shadow docket critics' concerns are not shared by many who think that the Court is reaching the correct bottom-line results in these cases speaks as much to their true motivations as it does to those of the critics. We ought to be able to agree that, between a lengthy, principled analysis that reaches a result we dislike and a one-line order that has the exact same immediate and precedential effect, the former is infinitely preferable for advancing the rule of law. Even Justice Alito, in a merits docket dissent in June 2022, criticized the Court's resolution of "difficult . . . questions on which . . . we have received only hurried briefing and no argument." Or, as Justice Robert Jackson bluntly put it for the Court seventy years ago, "Procedural fairness and regularity are of the indispensable essence of liberty. . . . Indeed, if put to the choice, one might well prefer to live under Soviet substantive law applied in good faith by our common-law procedures than under our substantive law enforced by Soviet procedural practices." And yet, here we are.[34]

Justice Alito's and Justice Kavanaugh's public dismissiveness notwithstanding, the Court appears to be taking at least some of these critiques to heart. Closer inspection reveals a series of subtle but significant alterations to the justices' behavior starting not long after the SB8 ruling. For instance, just one week after turning away the Texas abortion providers' application for emergency relief, the Court granted a stay of execution to John Ramirez—a Texas death-row inmate who had argued that he had a right to have a religious officiant pray aloud and touch him while he was in the execution chamber. Rather than resolving the underlying dispute on the shadow docket (as the Court had in 2019, in the cases about whether other death-row inmates could have officiants practicing *their* religion in the execution chamber), the Court treated the stay application as a petition for certiorari, granted it, and expedited full, plenary review of the underlying legal question on its merits docket. The justices heard oral argument in *Ramirez* v. *Collier* on November 9, 2021, and handed down an 8–1 merits ruling in Ramirez's favor on March 24, 2022. (Ramirez was eventually executed, with a religious officiant close at hand, in October 2022.)[35]

Similarly, even after refusing to grant emergency relief in the SB8 case, the Court moved with remarkable dispatch to provide plenary consideration of the merits of that dispute as well. On October 22, 2021, the Court granted petitions for certiorari before judgment (leapfrogging the court of appeals) in a pair of challenges to SB8—the providers' original suit at issue in the September 1 order and a separate suit by the federal government. The same order scheduled oral argument for just ten days later. It was the quickest turnaround from a grant of certiorari to oral argument since *Bush* v. *Gore* in December 2000. As in *Ramirez*, the Court handed its merits rulings down quickly in the SB8 cases, issuing the final decisions on December 10.

Those rulings allowed the providers to proceed against four state licensing officials, at least for the moment, while dismissing the federal government's appeal without resolving it.[36]

In the SB8 cases and *Ramirez*, the Court hustled disputes onto the merits docket to avoid having to grapple with complicated legal questions on the shadow docket. But a less noticed shadow docket order from late October also appeared to presage potential moderation in the Court's approach. In *Does 1–3* v. *Mills*, the Court denied a request for an emergency injunction against Maine's vaccination mandate for health-care workers pending appeal. Although Justices Thomas, Alito, and Gorsuch publicly dissented, as we already saw, Justice Barrett—joined by Justice Kavanaugh—penned a one-paragraph concurrence. As she explained, when asked to grant emergency relief, she viewed the task not only as an assessment of whether the applicant had met the conventional criteria, but "also a discretionary judgment about whether the Court *should* grant review in the case" (emphasis mine).[37]

"Were the standard otherwise," the Court's junior-most justice wrote, "applicants could use the emergency docket to force the Court to give a merits preview in cases that it would be unlikely to take—and to do so on a short fuse without benefit of full briefing and oral argument." In other words, Justices Barrett and Kavanaugh, whose votes were typically dispositive in any closely divided shadow docket ruling, seemed to be signaling that they would not automatically grant emergency relief just because they thought the party seeking it was right. Perhaps they were also acknowledging, in the same vein, that the Court had gone a bit too far in prior cases. Indeed, there would be a number of shadow docket rulings over the rest of the October 2021 Term in which Justices Thomas, Alito, and Gorsuch publicly dissented—but Justices Kavanaugh and Barrett didn't. It's hard to view such a shift as a coincidence.[38]

Even in their most mundane behavior, the justices started to show increasing awareness of the growth of the shadow docket.

In March 2022, for instance, the Court proposed a series of changes to its procedural rules, one of which was specifically directed at *amicus curiae* (friend-of-the-Court) briefs supporting or opposing emergency applications. Before March 2022, the Court's rules said nothing at all about such briefs. The proposed amendment stressed that such briefs were "disfavored," but also set out the circumstances (and timing) in which they would be considered.[39]

But perhaps the best illustration of both the Court's apparent reaction to these criticisms and its concomitant unwillingness to take them seriously are a pair of cases involving Biden administration COVID vaccination mandates. The first involved a series of challenges to the mandate imposed by the Center for Medicare and Medicaid Services (CMS) for all health professionals in facilities receiving federal Medicare or Medicaid funds. The second involved an even larger series of challenges to a rule promulgated by the Occupational Safety and Health Administration (OSHA), which would have mandated that virtually all large employers across the country impose a vaccination-or-testing requirement for their employees.

The CMS mandate was subject to separate nationwide injunctions by two different district courts. The OSHA mandate was initially blocked by the Fifth Circuit, but then unblocked when all of the challenges to it were consolidated in the Sixth Circuit (the Cincinnati-based appeals court covering Kentucky, Michigan, Ohio, and Tennessee). The Biden administration asked the Supreme Court to unblock the CMS mandate, and an array of red states and private groups asked the Court to block the OSHA mandate. On December 22, 2021, the Court did something it hadn't done in a half-century: it agreed to hold oral arguments on an emergency application—setting both sets of applications for one hour hearings on January 7, 2022. Six days after those arguments, on January 13, the justices granted both sets of applications—issuing unsigned majority opinions that unfroze the CMS mandate (over the public dissents of

Justices Thomas, Alito, Gorsuch, and Barrett); and that froze the OSHA mandate (over the public dissents of Justices Breyer, Sotomayor, and Kagan).[40]

And yet, even as the handling of the cases spoke to greater awareness on the Court's part of the need for more transparency in especially significant shadow docket cases, the substance of the OSHA ruling, in particular, only reinforced the claim that the justices were abusing the shadow docket to hand down what are merits rulings in all but name. In the very last section of the unsigned majority opinion blocking the OSHA rule, the Court identified the competing equities—summarizing the economic harm that those challenging OSHA's rule claimed they would suffer if the rule went into effect, on one hand, and the deaths and hospitalizations that the government claimed the rule would help to prevent, on the other. But then, the Court concluded that "it is not our role to weigh such tradeoffs. In our system of government, that is the responsibility of those chosen by the people through democratic processes."[41]

In fact, when parties ask the Supreme Court for emergency relief, "weigh[ing] such tradeoffs" is—or, at least, historically has been—the justices' *exact* role. That kind of balancing of the equities is precisely what separates emergency relief from the merits, distinguishing between who should ultimately prevail and what the status quo ought to be while the ultimate resolution is pursued. And so even as the Court seemed to be nodding toward some of the critiques of the shadow docket, by holding argument and allowing for broader consideration of the emergency applications in the federal vaccine mandate cases, the ultimate analysis the justices provided only reinforced what is perhaps the dominant shadow docket critique—that the Court no longer sees any distinction between what it's supposed to be doing on the shadow docket and what it's supposed to be doing on the merits docket. This pattern was arguably already clear from the shadow docket rulings in the Trump administration and COVID cases, but here was the majority finally saying the quiet part out loud.

Just like in the Alabama redistricting cases six weeks later, and just like in the religious liberty cases the previous year, the shadow docket had become a truncated means of achieving the desired merits result faster, with less transparency, and with less scrutiny than the merits docket—and with complete disregard for the additional procedural and prudential considerations that had historically factored into whether or not to grant emergency relief. Indeed, Justice Kagan made this point expressly in April 2022 in dissenting from another unexplained stay, this time of a lower-court ruling that had blocked a Trump-era rule under which it had become easier for energy plants to dump pollutants into navigable waterways. Because the states and energy companies seeking a stay had made no serious showing that the ruling they were seeking to block was causing them ongoing (let alone "irreparable") harm, the ruling could be seen only as turning entirely on the majority's view of the merits. As Kagan wrote, "That renders the Court's emergency docket not for emergencies at all."[42]

Ultimately, if the justices' reactions during the October 2021 Term are any indication, wholesale reform of the shadow docket is not likely to come from within, at least barring some fundamental shift in either the views of multiple justices or the center of gravity on the Court. The easiest and best solution for the Court's problematic behavior would simply be for the justices to change their ways. It ought to be beyond dispute, for instance, that the Court should provide a rationale anytime it grants emergency relief—analysis that identifies the correct standard for such relief and applies that standard to the case at issue, as in the CDC eviction moratorium case. And yet, just when it looked like the Court was trying to tread more carefully, it handed down a slew of unexplained rulings granting emergency relief, including the Alabama redistricting decision in February 2022; the Wisconsin redistricting decision and Navy SEALs rulings in March 2022; the Clean Water Act decision in April 2022; the Texas social media decision in May

2022; the Louisiana redistricting decision in June 2022; and the unexplained lifting of lower-court rulings that had blocked an Alabama execution in September 2022. That these rulings came down amid mounting public criticism of the shadow docket seems to drive home the unlikelihood of a more significant internal course correction.

If change won't come from within, then the focus must shift to Congress—which, regardless of what the justices do, can and should play far more of a role in this story. After all, as we saw earlier, throughout the Court's first two hundred years, Congress was regularly and repeatedly involved in regulating the Supreme Court's jurisdiction, including in response to concerns raised by the justices or others about the state and shape of the Court's docket.

Article III of the US Constitution draws a sharp distinction between the Supreme Court's "original" jurisdiction (cases that start and end in front of the highest court in the land) and its appellate jurisdiction. In cases that originate in lower state and federal courts, "the Supreme Court shall have appellate jurisdiction, both as to law and fact, with such exceptions, and under such regulations as the Congress shall make." Although scholars continue to debate whether, by dint of this text, Congress has total control over the justices' appellate docket, all agree that it at least has significant control over that body of Supreme Court work—including over virtually every facet of the shadow docket. (In one especially notorious Reconstruction-era example, Congress took away the Supreme Court's power to decide a specific appeal *after* the case had already been argued—and the justices ruled that Congress's transparent ploy was valid.)[43]

Insofar as the rise of the shadow docket is, then, a response to pressures from elsewhere, one response would be for Congress to attempt to reduce those pressures. In capital cases, for instance, Congress could provide for expedited, mandatory merits appeals of execution protocols (and automatic stays of execution) once an execution date is set to avoid the need for eleventh-hour emergency appeals. In cases in which plaintiffs have sought nationwide relief against the federal government, Congress could provide for expedited, mandatory merits appeals of lower-court orders granting such relief to the Supreme Court—to make it easier for the justices to affirm or reject the injunction on the merits sooner rather than later. And, in general, if the justices are intervening more often at earlier stages in litigation because of a view that certain types of cases are taking too long to reach them, Congress can (and should) respond by enabling more expeditious plenary review. These reforms would not be taking away the Court's power; they would be redistributing it away from the shadow docket and toward the merits docket in response to publicly articulated—and objective—concerns. As we saw earlier, generations of statutory reforms to the Supreme Court's docket were motivated at least in part by the justices' own views—and complaints—about their existing jurisdiction. Having the Court involved in articulating what the justices view as contemporary problems with their case load and possible reforms would necessarily be consistent with that practice.[44]

Congress also has the unquestioned power to prescribe the standards that the justices follow in granting emergency relief. Although the Court has, as we've seen, defied those standards in many of its recent shadow docket rulings, perhaps a legislative reaffirmation would exert pressure on the justices to hew closer to them. And although Congress would come closer to constitutional limits if it ordered the Court to publicly disclose the vote counts on its orders or to provide a rationale anytime it grants an application for emergency relief, Congress could certainly encourage the justices to adopt those and similar norms going forward. Likewise, Congress could push the Court to return to the historical model for shadow docket decision-making more generally, with the default of having emergency applications resolved by circuit justices, on the narrowest possible grounds, and with an understanding that those orders have no effect beyond the immediate dispute in which they were issued.

This is not meant to be an exhaustive list of policy initiatives, but merely an observation about the myriad avenues available to the political branches if they chose to prioritize shadow docket reform. More generally, it is also a reminder that Congress historically has played far more of an active and important role in regulating and circumscribing the Court's docket than it is currently playing, and that it may be high time for the political branches to return to that fray.[45]

~

On December 8, 2021, the Presidential Commission on the Supreme Court of the United States submitted its final report to President Biden. The commission had been formed in response to a campaign pledge by then-candidate Biden in the run-up to the 2020 election, one that allowed him to avoid taking a position on high-profile reform proposals such as adding seats to the Court. In its work, the commission made headlines mostly by not making headlines. It steered clear of endorsing any significant structural reforms, such as adding seats to the Court, subjecting the justices to term limits, and so on. But even on more technical topics, including the shadow docket, the commission's final report offered little more than a disappointing, milquetoast assessment. The Court "may well benefit," the report meekly suggested, "from continuing to adjust its explanatory practices in important cases, with an eye toward providing insight into its reasoning, reinforcing procedural consistency, and avoiding any possible appearance of arbitrariness or bias."[46]

As with much of the commission's report, it's hard to disagree that the Court "may well benefit" from such adjustments. The harder question is what everyone else should do if and when the Court declines that invitation. But even if reasonable minds might disagree over the specific shape of the reforms Congress can and should pursue, it ought not to be controversial to observe that, since 1988 (if not before), Congress has done far too little to assert its institutional authority over the Supreme Court. For the better part of the Court's first two centuries, it was engaged in an ongoing, dynamic, interbranch conversation over how the justices went about discharging their duties. Parroting James Madison's hope, in *Federalist* No. 51, that "ambition must be made to counteract ambition," the institutions pushed against each other's boundaries—a robust system of checks and balances that prevented the courts from getting too out of kilter from the political branches, and vice versa. Congress used its power over the Court's jurisdiction; over its budget; and even over the justices' travel as subtle but serious sources of leverage over the Supreme Court as an institution. And, in reverse, the justices used their judicial power to keep Congress in check.

But that conversation has basically ground to a halt. Other than a few context-specific statutes, Congress has not touched the Supreme Court's jurisdiction since 1988. It hasn't so much as considered using its power over the Court's budget as a means of enticing, and then coercing, the justices into adjusting any of their behavior more broadly. And the result has been a Court seemingly untroubled by even the specter of legislative oversight or intervention. In his 2021 Year-End Report on the Federal Judiciary, Chief Justice Roberts took a not-so-subtle shot at proposals for legislative reforms to the Court, writing, "The Judiciary's power to manage its internal affairs insulates courts from inappropriate political influence and is crucial to preserving public trust in its work as a separate and coequal branch of government." But political influence is not necessarily inappropriate "to preserving public trust" in the Supreme Court; indeed, for much of the Court's history, it was essential. Meanwhile, with multiple justices who have faced accusations of sexual assault or harassment; with growing ethical questions about Justice Thomas's wife, Ginni Thomas, becoming involved in efforts to overturn the results of the 2020 presidential election; and with the Court's woefully inadequate compliance with its annual financial disclosure requirement, the chief justice's breezy faith in "the Judiciary's power to manage its internal affairs" seems increasingly misplaced. And that's *without* taking the shadow docket into account. With the shadow docket, it's even more evident that the time has come (if it has not long-since passed) for the legislature to become more involved.

Reasonable minds may disagree as to which reforms are the most desirous; the more important point is that any effort on Congress's part to reassert itself in ongoing discussions about the work of the Supreme Court can, in the long term, only be a good thing. Throughout the nation's first two centuries, such an interbranch dialogue was a healthy and recurring feature of our constitutional system, even when it seemed, at least in the short term, that one party was seeking to maximize its power or limit the power of the other. There's no reason why that can't be true again: the separation of powers ought not to depend upon the separation of parties. And if the justices' recent behavior is a symptom of nothing else, it is, at bottom, emblematic of a Court that is entirely unafraid of its shadow—or of even the specter of legislative intervention. Whatever one's views of what that means in the short-term, it has ominous implications for checks and balances going forward.

## CONCLUSION

# BRINGING THE SUPREME COURT OUT OF THE SHADOWS

The Supreme Court Building's architect, Cass Gilbert, envisioned the building's main plaza as its aesthetic centerpiece. Today, the iconic plaza is depicted in countless photographs and illustrations, including on the cover of this book. As lawyer (and architect) Paul Byard described it, Gilbert's design "emphasizes the processional progress toward justice reenacted daily in [the Court's] premises." The procession culminates at the Court's massive bronze front doors, which stand seventeen feet high and weigh thirteen tons. Each door includes four panels featuring bas-relief sculptures that chronologically depict, in the Court's own words, "significant events in the evolution of justice in the Western tradition." The last of those is Chief Justice John Marshall's 1803 decision in *Marbury* v. *Madison*, which cemented the Supreme Court's power to invalidate unconstitutional laws—and, with that power, its status as an equal branch of the federal government. To reach those doors, visitors ascend forty-four marble steps flanked by a pair of massive James Earle Fraser sculptures, titled *Contemplation of Justice* and *Authority of Law*. Eight pairs of columns, under the inscription "Equal Justice Under Law," dominate the front portico. As Justice Stephen Breyer put it, "This Court's main entrance and front steps are not only a means to, but also a metaphor for, access to the Court itself."[1]

In the past, visitors passed under that inscription and through those grand columns to enter the building. In 2010, however, the Court permanently closed its front doors. Those attending oral arguments could still exit the building and descend via the front steps, but anyone wishing to enter the building had to do so through one of two side doors at plaza level. The move was justified as a post–September 11 security measure, but its symbolic significance was not lost, at least not on all of the justices. In a highly unusual "statement" published in the Court's official *Journal*, Justice Breyer, joined by Justice Ginsburg, expressed the hope that the Court might one day reconsider. "In making this decision," Breyer wrote, "it is important not to undervalue the symbolic and historical importance of allowing visitors to enter the Court after walking up Gilbert's famed front steps."[2]

Fast-forward to the October 2021 Term, during which the Court did not even take the bench when it handed down its fifty-eight signed decisions in argued cases. Although the COVID pandemic had forced the justices to take all of their business online from March 2020 through the summer of 2021, they returned to the courtroom to hear oral arguments in person beginning in October 2021. The argument sessions were closed to the public, but they were very much open to the advocates, the parties, and the press. And as had been true since the Court first started hearing cases remotely in May 2020, anyone else who wished to follow along could do so through live-streamed audio. Even with the Court hearing arguments in person, though, merits decisions continued to come down exclusively through PDFs posted to the Supreme Court's website.[3]

Among other things, the remote hand-downs made it impossible for the justices to read their dissents from the bench, an option historically available to them when they wanted to underscore an especially profound or bitter disagreement. For instance, in a 2007 case decided shortly after Justice Alito's confirmation, replacing the more moderate O'Connor, a 5–4 majority blocked public high schools from taking race into account in school-choice tiebreakers. In dissenting from the bench, Justice Breyer took a shot at his conservative colleagues and the sharp rightward turn they had taken: "It is not often in the law that so few have quickly changed so much." Yet this widely quoted line did not actually appear in Breyer's written dissent; he said it, with more than a little emotion, from the bench. As much as Breyer intended that line for his colleagues and the bar, his audience, as Harvard law professor Lani Guinier has explained, was really the public.[4]

There would be no similar oral punctuation mark in June 2022, even as the Court radically expanded the Second Amendment; eviscerated the constitutional right to abortions; constrained Congress's ability to delegate authority to executive branch agencies in a dispute over climate-change regulations; and expanded the Constitution's protection for religious practice. Just like the closing of the front doors in 2010, this change in procedure impacted the public, which was deprived of yet another symbolic yet significant measure of access to the Court, even if the public didn't realize it. The symbolism around the Court for the public it is intended to serve deteriorated further after a draft of the majority opinion in *Dobbs* v. *Jackson Women's Health Organization* was leaked, provoking widespread protests, and the Court erected massive, unscalable security fences around the entire plaza. Though the fences may have been necessary for security, they further reinforced the image of a cloistered, inaccessible institution. The justices were now acting behind doors that were literally and figuratively closed.

Regardless of whether these developments are properly understood as part of the shadow docket, they are unquestionably of a piece with it, for they each reflect significant shifts in how the Supreme Court does its job in a way that its merits decisions do not illuminate. And they also help to place the shadow docket developments we've already encountered into a broader context: The Supreme Court has become increasingly isolated from the public over the past decade in lots of ways both big and small—and that trend is continuing even now. Some of the changes, such as closing the front doors and cordoning off the Court's plaza after the *Dobbs* leak, surely stem at least in part from legitimate safety concerns. And those concerns were only made more immediate when a suspect was arrested outside of Justice Kavanaugh's house in June 2022 and indicted on charges of attempting to kidnap or murder him. But as Justice Breyer pointed out in 2010, the countervailing interest in a publicly accessible institution ought not to be so quickly dismissed.

In the same vein, more and more in recent years, the justices have declined to publicly announce their outside speaking appearances or to make copies of their remarks publicly available. On the Supreme Court's website, there's a section dedicated to listing, and providing copies of, the justices' public speeches. But as of October 2022, the most recent entry was for a speech given three years earlier, on August 26, 2019—by the late Justice Ginsburg. (The justices have given dozens—if not hundreds—of speeches since then, many of which have no public recording or transcript.) The rise of the shadow docket is not just about the Supreme Court amassing power through unsigned and unexplained rulings; it is about the Supreme Court as an institution, and the justices as individuals, conducting ever more of the Court's business in the literal and metaphorical darkness—in ways that are knowingly, if not intentionally, in tension with what ought to be unobjectionable principles of transparency.

By some appearances, the contemporary Court might even be said to see the public less as its audience than as its enemy—a nuisance to be kept away from the justices as much while they're working as while they're not. Chief Justice Taft would often walk the four miles from his Woodley Park home in Northwest DC to the Supreme Court's 1920s-era headquarters at the Capitol, giving his name to the bridge that carries Connecticut Avenue over Rock Creek Park. Along the way, he would regularly interact with well-wishers—and the occasional critic. Those days are, quite obviously, long behind us.[5]

In that respect, among others, the rise of the shadow docket has both occurred alongside and mirrored the ever-sharpening polarization and toxification of American politics. As the political center has hollowed out in favor of two dominant parties pushing increasingly toward their flanks, we have likewise seen a rise in polarized feeling about the courts, if not polarization of the courts themselves, through ever more politically aggressive judicial appointments. And the hollowing out of America's political center has come at roughly the same time as the hollowing out of the Supreme Court's center. When Justice O'Connor announced her retirement in July 2005, Justice Scalia wrote to her that she had been "the forger of the social bond that [had] kept the Court together" between its increasingly divergent ideological blocs. And he wondered, "Who will take that role when you are gone?" Almost two decades later, that question remains unanswered.[6]

Especially since the retirement of Justice Kennedy in the summer of 2018, the Court has come to resemble the country—two deeply entrenched groups, each having a hard time seeing the arguments and principles that define the other side or even accepting that those arguments are made in good faith. As we look back on the sharply divisive merits rulings the Court has handed down over the five years following his retirement, it's easy to see the wisdom in something my friend and former dean Ward Farnsworth wrote two decades ago, that "those who accuse the majority of having partisan *motives* underestimate the good faith of the justices; but those who acquit the Court of partisan *behavior* may overestimate the utility of good faith as a constraint on wishful thinking."[7]

It's hard to divorce the Court's recent shadow docket behavior from the state of the country's partisan divide. The Court itself is more polarized in these cases. It may also be responding, at least in part, to the polarization of lower-court judges, many of whom are handing down decisions pushing ever further to the flanks of the ideological spectrum—and issuing relief more likely to trigger immediate requests for appellate, if not Supreme Court, intervention. Meanwhile, the public and academic perception of the propriety (or impropriety) of what the Court is doing on the shadow docket has thus far broken down largely along the conventional party lines. It would be easy enough, then, to chalk the shadow docket up to being just another battlefield in a long line of them in the same war: an interesting one, to be sure, but one that offers no lessons beyond those we could have learned from studying the Court's more visible merits decisions.

But then there's John Roberts.

Hostile to abortion, administrative agencies, affirmative action, campaign finance reform, constitutional protections for LGBTQ+ individuals, voting rights, and lots of things in between, Roberts is a dyed-in-the-wool conservative and a product of the Washington right-wing legal establishment. No one could fairly call him a centrist or a moderate. And yet, when it comes to the shadow docket, his votes have been the canary in the coal mine. As the rest of the Court's conservatives have come to increasingly abuse the shadow docket, Roberts has been (to extend the metaphor) the *rara avis*—often standing on procedural principles that cut against his preferred substantive bottom line. In that respect, it's fitting to end the story of the shadow docket with the seventeenth chief justice of the United States. The principal objection to the current Court's abuse of the shadow docket is that the justices are acting in a way that is antithetical to the long-term interests of the Supreme Court as a body, and thus, to our constitutional system writ large. However powerful that viewpoint is when it comes from those who also oppose the bottom line the Court is reaching in these cases, it's simply devastating coming from a justice who does not.

Roberts was never supposed to become chief justice. When President George W. Bush nominated him to the Supreme Court on July 29, 2005, it was to succeed Justice O'Connor, who had announced four weeks earlier that she planned to retire upon the confirmation of her successor. In early September, though, just days before Roberts's Senate confirmation hearing was set to begin, Chief Justice William Rehnquist, for whom Roberts had clerked during the October 1980 Term, died of complications from thyroid cancer. President Bush quickly withdrew Roberts's nomination for O'Connor's seat and nominated him instead for the Court's center chair. On September 29, 2005, the Senate voted 78–22 to confirm him. Much like John Marshall, who became chief justice only after John Jay declined to accept President John Adams's nomination in 1801, or Earl Warren, who became chief justice in 1953 only because then presidential candidate Dwight Eisenhower had promised him the next open spot on the Court in exchange for his delegates at the 1952 Republican National Convention, Roberts ended up in the Court's most important seat almost by accident.[8]

Historical fortuities notwithstanding, most discussions of periods in the Supreme Court's history nevertheless use the tenure of its chief justices as both a descriptive convention and a temporal dividing line. The "Warren Court" refers not just to the Supreme Court under the tenure of Chief Justice Earl Warren (from 1953 to 1969), but to a particularly robust era of decisions recognizing civil rights and criminal procedure protections. The "Marshall Court" likewise refers not just to the Supreme Court from 1801 to 1835, but to the remarkably consistent, nationalizing decisions handed down under the leadership (and almost always from the pen) of Chief Justice John

Marshall. In those examples, and others, the chief justice looms as the dominant figure of the era, even if other justices were even more directly associated with the Court's key decisions—such as Justice Antonin Scalia during the "Rehnquist Court" (1986 to 2005).

For Roberts's first fourteen terms, the "Roberts" Court was a deeply unsatisfying description of the Supreme Court. From 2005 to 2018, the Court went not as Roberts wanted it to, but as Justice Kennedy did. Once Kennedy retired, that changed overnight. Within months, Roberts became the force behind the throne in addition to the figurehead of the Court—not only because of his center seat, but because he became the median vote in virtually every case with a partisan or ideological valence. During the Court's October 2018 Term, for instance, Roberts wrote for different 5–4 majorities in the two biggest merits cases, joining the other conservatives in *Rucho* v. *Common Cause* (which held that federal courts couldn't hear lawsuits challenging partisan gerrymandering), and joining the liberals in *Department of Commerce* v. *New York* (which held that the Trump administration could not put a citizenship question on the 2020 Census).[9]

Roberts's central role in the next term, starting in October 2019, was even more remarkable. He was in the majority in fifty-one of the Court's fifty-three merits decisions, including eleven of the twelve rulings that were 5–4. Although he wrote only seven of the fifty-three majority opinions, four of those were 5–4 decisions, including two of the term's biggest—rulings arising out of congressional and grand jury subpoenas for President Trump's financial records. And his only concurring opinion of the term—in a challenge to abortion restrictions in Louisiana—was effectively speaking on behalf of the Court, since he provided the critical fifth vote to strike down the Louisiana law.

As we've seen, Roberts was also the decisive fifth vote in a host of shadow docket rulings from October 2019 through

September 2020, joining the conservatives in clearing the way for the first federal executions in seventeen years and in refusing to extend the mail-in ballot deadline for Wisconsin's spring election; joining the liberals in refusing to block California's and Nevada's COVID-based restrictions on religious gatherings; and so on. It's difficult to find another term in the Court's modern history in which a single justice, let alone the chief justice, played such a pivotal procedural and substantive role in such a high percentage of the Court's work. The "Roberts Court" had finally arrived. And as if all of that weren't enough, in the middle of the October 2019 Term Roberts also presided over the third presidential impeachment trial in US history (the first of President Trump's two trials).[10]

Of course, the Court's center of gravity shifted even further to the right when Justice Barrett replaced Justice Ginsburg in October 2020. But that shift did not immediately marginalize the chief justice in merits cases. During the October 2020 Term, for instance, Roberts dissented from only four merits decisions, and none in which the Court split along strict ideological lines. In all, Roberts was in the majority in 93 percent of the Court's merits decisions—and, once again, he wrote for the majority in four of the most significant decisions of the term. The October 2021 Term told a similar story: Roberts was in the majority in 95 percent of the Court's merits decisions (his highest total since joining the Court), and he wrote only two dissenting opinions. Even though he broke from the conservatives as to whether to overrule *Roe*, he still joined them in voting to uphold Mississippi's fifteen-week abortion ban. Driving the point home, numerous media summaries of the Court's overall output during the October 2021 Term focused on the "rise of the 6–3 Court."[11]

As we first saw in the context of religious liberty cases, though, the shadow docket tells a completely different story. Almost immediately after Justice Barrett's confirmation, Roberts started joining the three remaining Democratic appointees—Justices

Breyer, Sotomayor, and Kagan—in a slew of shadow docket dissents. Indeed, by April 2022, Roberts had publicly dissented from nine different 5–4 rulings since October 2020. Seven of those nine had come on the shadow docket. And in all seven of those cases (along with one of the two merits rulings—the Texas abortion case in December 2021), he joined Breyer, Sotomayor, and Kagan. Right-wing commentators, still bitter over Roberts's 2012 vote with the liberals to uphold the Affordable Care Act, portrayed his votes in these cases as further proof of his lack of a true conservative backbone. But something else was afoot.[12]

Roberts's objections in those cases, as we have seen, were invariably procedural. When he wrote separately, he was careful to express either no opinion on the merits or sympathy for the position seemingly (or overtly) taken by the majority. Recall the Alabama redistricting cases, for instance, in which he specifically endorsed the idea that the Court should revisit the test for vote-dilution claims under section 2 of the Voting Rights Act. His problem, each time, was not with the bottom line the other conservative justices reached, but rather that they had reached that result through the shadow docket rather than the merits docket.

In his dissent from the 2020 Thanksgiving-eve ruling in *Roman Catholic Diocese*, blocking New York's COVID-based restrictions on religious gatherings, Roberts agreed that "the challenged restrictions raise serious concerns under the Constitution," but concluded that granting an injunction wasn't warranted because there was "simply no need to do so." In his September 2021 dissent from the Court's refusal to block Texas's six-week abortion ban, he explained that the defendants "may be correct" that they could not ultimately be sued by abortion providers, but that "the consequences of approving the state action, both in this particular case and as a model for action in other areas, counsel at least preliminary judicial consideration before the program devised by the State takes effect." And in the February 2022 Alabama redistricting cases, he dissented, he said, "because . . . the District Court properly applied existing law in an extensive opinion with no apparent errors for our correction," even though he agreed that the existing law warranted reconsideration. In the Texas and Alabama cases, Justice Kagan had specifically called out the conservative majority for abusing the shadow docket. Roberts had hewed to narrower grounds in his separate dissenting opinions.[13]

But it was in an otherwise technical case about the Clean Water Act in April 2022 where Roberts may finally have crossed the Rubicon. The issue in *Louisiana* v. *American Rivers* was a Trump-era regulation that made it easier for energy providers to pollute rivers and other navigable waterways. A federal district judge in San Francisco blocked the Trump rule in October 2021, holding that there was significant reason to believe that the rule was inconsistent with the Clean Water Act and had been promulgated in violation of the Administrative Procedure Act. The district court refused to stay its ruling, and the Ninth Circuit likewise left the ruling in place in February 2022. After waiting over one month to ask the Supreme Court for a stay, a group of red states and private businesses asked the justices to put the Trump rule back into effect in March 2022. Shortly after 9:00 a.m. on April 6, the Court acquiesced, staying the district court's injunction with no majority rationale or separate concurring opinions. (The unusual early-morning ruling was perhaps a tacit response to objections that too many shadow docket rulings were coming late at night.)[14]

Justice Kagan wrote on behalf of the dissenters. This time, though, that cohort included the chief justice. In her short but scathing opinion, Kagan noted how patently inappropriate a stay was under the Court's traditional factors, mostly because the applicants had provided no evidence of any harm resulting from the district court's injunction (which, by that point, had been in effect for five months), let alone irreparable harm. "By nonetheless granting relief," Kagan wrote, the Court "signals its view of the merits, even though the applicants have failed to make the irreparable harm showing we have traditionally required. That renders the Court's emergency docket not for emergencies at all. The docket becomes only another place for merits determinations—except made without full briefing and argument." It certainly wasn't the first time that Kagan had leveled this charge. But it was the first time that Roberts joined her in leveling it.[15]

By publicly endorsing the charge that the other conservative justices were short-circuiting ordinary procedures to reach their desired results without sufficient explanation, Roberts thus provided perhaps the strongest evidence to date that objections to those shortcuts are not bad-faith arguments by disappointed progressives (as Justice Alito had insinuated in his September 2021 speech at Notre Dame), but valid critiques of an institutional change already underway. As much as anyone, Chief Justice Roberts understands the dangers of the Court being perceived as serving partisan political—rather than judicial—ends.[16]

That doesn't necessarily mean that Roberts's votes in these cases (and his endorsement of Kagan's dissent in the *American Rivers* case) were altruistic. After all, a desire to preserve the Court's legitimacy in the long run can stem just as much from motives that are ignoble (a Court perceived as legitimate is essential to implementing a justice's ideological agenda) as from motives that are noble (the Court's legitimacy is an end unto itself). Nor, it should be said, is Roberts's record perfect. But the upshot is still the same: The one justice who appears to be voting against his short-term policy preferences on the shadow docket is doing so to express his disapproval of the shortcuts that the conservative majority is taking—*because they are shortcuts*. Beyond writing the dissenting opinion in *American Rivers* himself, it was as significant a signal as Roberts could have sent—at least to that point in the evolution (and devolution) of the shadow docket.

But perhaps the most revealing takeaway from the April 2022 ruling in the Clean Water Act case was not the chief justice's endorsement of Kagan's dissent, but how the media covered it.

Virtually every mainstream media outlet had in either its headline or lede the fact that Roberts had, for the first time, spoken out against the shadow docket. In some cases, it took several paragraphs to find out what the underlying dispute was even about. It would have been impossible for anyone following media coverage of the decision to miss that it was a shadow docket ruling, or that it was significant that Roberts had joined the dissenters in criticizing the process by which the ruling was reached. The shadow docket, as such, was finally receiving mainstream media attention.[17]

The point is not that each shadow docket order is as important as each merits ruling; it's that any story of the Supreme Court that doesn't include the shadow docket is a story that's looking at an increasingly skewed and incomplete portion of the Court's work. The justices look far more sharply partisan on the shadow docket than on the merits docket, yet those numbers are rarely included in end-of-term tallies. Similarly, the Court looks far more political when one accounts for what it is actually deciding—recognizing that these are cases in which the justices are choosing to grant certiorari, rather than disputes that have been foisted upon them. And the notion that the justices are simply calling balls and strikes is increasingly difficult to reconcile with the Court's institutional behavior—and the justices' individual behavior—in contexts outside the written pages of its merits decisions. After all, when Justice Barrett suggested, as she did in an April 2022 speech at the Ronald Reagan Presidential Library, that members of the public who were worried that the Court was acting politically should just "read the opinion," it's essential context to point out that, just two days later, she joined a 5–4 shadow docket ruling with no opinion for the public to read. It's all part of the story—or, at least, it should be.[18]

That story is not just increasingly important; it's also increasingly alarming. Reasonable minds may differ about just how concerning the rise of the shadow docket is. What can no longer be denied is that it's a development that warrants our attention. Wholly apart from the direct impact of specific decisions, these rulings in the aggregate affect how lower courts, policymakers, and lawyers follow the Court. They affect how we teach—and should teach—law school students about the Court. And they affect how we as members of the general public ought to think about and understand the Court. We have agreed to give unelected, unaccountable judges with life tenure enormous power over our daily lives—on the assumption that they will act *as judges* in wielding it. The more rulings the Court hands down with major, substantive effects but without explanation, the less the terms of that constitutional arrangement are being honored.

What's more, all of this is true not in spite of the inscrutability of so much of the Court's shadow docket output, but because of it. After all, lawyers shouldn't have a monopoly on understanding the full contours of the Supreme Court's decision-making: the Court's rulings affect all Americans, not just those admitted to the bar, and the Court's legitimacy depends on how its efforts are perceived by the public, not just by the putative experts. As one especially prominent case in point, when Chief Justice Warren wrote the landmark 1954 opinion in *Brown* v. *Board of Education*, holding that racially segregated public schools were inherently (and constitutionally) unequal, his goal was not only for the Court to be unanimous, but for its reasoning to be read by the public. The entire decision was only eleven pages long, and it was written, deliberately, in conversational language rather than legal jargon. In light of that history, the April 2022 Clean Water Act ruling may well have been an inflection point not just for Chief Justice Roberts's public views of the shadow docket, but also, perhaps because of that shift, for how the media *covers* the shadow docket—and, in turn, how the public understands it.[19]

This last point is the critical one. The story of the shadow docket is a specific and technical account of a series of legal doctrines and judicial decisions, but it's also a broader narrative about the importance of involving and investing the public in understanding the technicalities of legal process itself. For all of the time and attention we devote to talking about constitutional rights in the United States, we devote embarrassingly little time and attention to how those rights are—and are not—enforced, and by and against whom. In an era dominated by clickbait, it may be no surprise that a case about the First Amendment rights of a cheerleader who cursed out a coach on Snapchat draws more attention than a case about whether Congress can authorize citizens to sue credit reporting agencies who misreport their personal information. Both were merits decisions that the Supreme Court handed down over a three-day span in June 2021. But the latter has far more significance for our constitutional system, since it's about what Congress can (or, as a 5–4 majority ruled in *TransUnion LLC* v. *Ramirez*, cannot) do in all cases, not what a school district can't do in one.[20]

Indeed, part of the public backlash to the Supreme Court's refusal to block Texas's six-week abortion ban in September 2021 stemmed from the surprise that such an important constitutional right could be effectively frustrated without being formally overruled. Lawyers encounter that reality—that many rights don't have remedies—all too often; the public does not. But, as the SB8 case and so many of the other rulings surveyed in the preceding pages drive home, the means by which legal claims are or are not vindicated in American courts are usually just as important as, if not more important than, the claims themselves. Too often, lawyers act as if (and assume that) those process-oriented questions are uninteresting—or incomprehensible—to lay audiences. To the contrary, in many ways, the shadow docket tells an even more interesting story about the Supreme Court as an institution than the merits docket does—and a far more complete one, as well.

Now, more than ever, it might seem especially odd to situate the shadow docket at the center of a narrative about the Supreme Court. After all, to a greater extent than has been true in generations, the merits docket is providing plenty of fodder all by itself. The October 2021 Term alone gave us massively important—and controversial—merits rulings on abortion, climate change, guns, *Miranda* warnings, religious liberty, and plenty of other things besides. And the October 2022 Term is set to follow suit, with high-profile cases on everything from affirmative action to voting rights to whether website designers have to serve same-sex couples to how elections are conducted. In that respect, drawing more attention to the shadow docket at this precise moment in the Court's history may well come across to some as akin to criticizing the design of the deck chairs on the *Titanic*.

But what happens on the merits docket is only possible *because* of the evolution of the shadow docket—especially the power the justices have claimed to decide not only which cases they'll resolve, but which questions they'll resolve within those cases. That is to say, the merits docket exists in the shadows of the shadow docket, not the other way around. The shadow docket's role in helping to create the conditions for the contemporary merits docket would be reason enough to elevate the place of the shadow docket in our understanding of the Supreme Court. And yet, the rise of the shadow docket is not just an indirect contributor to eroding public confidence in the Court; it is, as we have seen, a *direct* contributor as well. Some of that is surely because the shadow docket is a softer target for the Court's (growing) body of critics than the merits docket; it's harder to defend decisions that don't defend themselves. But some of that is also because, on the justices' own terms, much of what the Court is doing on the shadow docket necessarily lacks the legitimacy of what it's doing on the merits docket—where even those decisions we might disagree with are based upon principled justifications, even ones of varying degrees of persuasiveness.

Simply put, Supreme Court decisions are not legitimate or illegitimate because they are right or wrong; their legitimacy flows from the more amorphous but no less important belief that they represent exercises of judicial, rather than political, power. This insight is equal parts crucial and elusive: The Court can't enforce its own decisions. Instead, it depends upon popular support to compel obedience even (if not especially) to unpopular rulings. Thus, its power depends to a large degree upon the public's willingness to accept its decrees—to quote from *Planned Parenthood* v. *Casey* again, its legitimacy is based in "the people's acceptance of the Judiciary as fit to determine what the Nation's law means and to declare what it demands." If that legitimacy turns upon the Court's ability to explain itself, then the rise of the shadow docket is anathema to that understanding. The people can hardly be expected to acquiesce in decisions that they can't possibly be expected to understand. And if the Court's legitimacy turns on something else, it sure would behoove the justices to say so. Either way, the better the public understands the inextricable link between the rise of the shadow docket and the decline of public confidence in the Court, the more ominous the implications of the Court staying this course become—not just for the justices, but for the country.

As we've seen, Justice Alito's September 2021 speech at Notre Dame Law School accused the shadow docket's critics of trying to intimidate the Court and undermine its legitimacy in the eyes of the public. I can't speak for others, but I've been critical of the Court's shadow docket behavior—and I wrote this book—not because I want to delegitimize the Court, but because I fear that the Court is delegitimizing itself, and that not enough people—the justices included—are caring. From my perspective, at least, it is vital that the Court as an institution and the justices as individuals take more of an interest in ending, or at least ameliorating, the legitimacy crisis that the justices' own actions have precipitated. A necessary first step is to call out that crisis for what it is—and acknowledge how it came about.

My personal policy preferences are radically at odds with the substantive and methodological aspirations of the current majority on the Court. I disagree with many—if not most—of their decisions in ideologically charged cases. And I worry about the amount of power the justices have claimed over matters that, from the late 1930s until recently, have been left to the elected branches of government. To that end, a Court that is losing its legitimacy, and thus its moral authority, and that holds increasingly less sway over our most contentious social debates, might seem, at first blush, like a good thing—and a better path to victories in the near and medium term for the policies and principles that I support. For all of the power that the Court has amassed, it still has no army to enforce its dictates. If we reach a point at which a sufficiently large part of the country decides to stop abiding by the Court's decisions, there's not much that the justices, by themselves, can do to stop them.

Even though the demise of the Supreme Court might produce short-term outcomes that some view as salutary, I firmly believe that our constitutional republic *needs* a legitimate Supreme Court, even one staffed by a majority of justices with whom many of us routinely disagree. No less so than when this country was founded, and perhaps far more so with the proliferation of partisan gerrymandering, tyrannies of the elected majority remain a very real threat. The whole point of having an independent, unelected judiciary was to stand as a bulwark against the mob: to enforce the Constitution at the expense of democratic (or not-so-democratic) majorities in those infrequent but important moments when it becomes desperately necessary to do so.

We will never all agree on which moments (and which of the Constitution's provisions) justify such countermajoritarian judicial intervention. But I'm fervently of the view that when they come, we need not just a Supreme Court in name, but a Supreme Court in reality—a tribunal that is legitimate, and that is *perceived* as legitimate by a sufficiently large body of citizens.

A toothless Court would lack the ability to stand up for our rights, whether the unchecked tyrannical majorities have Democratic leaders or Republican ones. Its decisions would simply be ignored or dismissed as partisan claptrap that should not be understood to bind the other side. When the Supreme Court in 1832 invalidated Georgia's seizure of large swaths of Cherokee territory, President Andrew Jackson is reported to have responded, "John Marshall has made his decision, now let him enforce it." Imagine if that became the standard reaction to controversial Supreme Court decisions, rather than the exception that has long proved the rule—such as when President Eisenhower sent the 101st Airborne into Little Rock, Arkansas, in 1957 to help enforce *Brown* v. *Board of Education*.[21]

After all, it is no exaggeration to say that in the months and years to come, as courts become the battlefield for fights over voter suppression laws, election integrity disputes, and perhaps even the legitimacy of future election results, democracy itself may depend upon a Supreme Court widely perceived to be legitimate. While the alternative to a legitimate court may be satisfying in the short term, it will end poorly, not just for the justices, but for all of us. That is why it is incumbent upon the Supreme Court to bring more and more of its work out of the shadows—and upon all of us to understand the increasingly grave implications for our Republic if and when it does not.

# ACKNOWLEDGMENTS

This book began as nothing more than a series of tweets. I've always been both professionally and personally interested in some of the more arcane areas of the Supreme Court's practice, but it wasn't until the fall of 2017—after the June 2017 travel ban ruling and a series of subsequent Supreme Court orders over that summer—that I started to see the germ of a more focused study of the Court's evolving behavior through unsigned orders. From the beginning, I was spurred on to write a book by my former dean at the University of Texas School of Law, Ward Farnsworth. Ward was convinced that translating technical, procedural concepts into accessible prose was a worthwhile endeavor, and, just as importantly, one I was capable of pursuing. This book would never have happened without Ward's support and encouragement, for which I remain deeply grateful.

I'm also grateful to Julia Solomon-Strauss and her colleagues on Volume 133 of the *Harvard Law Review*, whose invitation to write about the solicitor general and the shadow docket for the *Review*'s flagship annual Supreme Court issue in 2019 (from which Chapter 4 of this book is derived) inspired a lot of what followed, pushing me to take a broader view of the Court's growing use of emergency orders. Ditto Amy Howe, Edith Roberts, James Romsomer, and the folks at *SCOTUSblog*, who invited me to write about the shadow docket on multiple occasions starting in 2017; and Mark Joseph Stern and the team at

Slate, who have likewise been interested in popular writing on the shadow docket since before it was a thing.

This project really started to build steam once my superstar sister-in-law, Doree Shafrir, introduced me to her (and now my) agent, Alia Hanna Habib. From the beginning, Alia understood what I hoped to accomplish through this book, and her timely feedback on various iterations of the proposal, her guidance about the publishing process, and the efforts that she and her team (especially Sophie Pugh-Sellers) made behind the scenes at the Gernert Company were instrumental in getting this book off the ground. At the other end of the publishing spectrum, I'm also grateful to Emma Berry and her colleagues at Basic Books. Emma repeatedly helped to translate my complicated ("chewy") legally infused writing into more accessible prose and to tighten the numerous overlapping and interlacing stories that the book tries to tell, and the project is only the better for her Herculean efforts in those regards (and innumerable others). I'm not sure anyone else has had to listen to me talk about this book, specifically—or the shadow docket, in general—more than Emma, and this book wouldn't be the same without her. Thanks as well to Katie Carruthers-Busser and my superlative copy editor, Kathy Streckfus, for all of the really good and hard work that no one else got to see in turning the idiosyncratic style of my manuscript into a readable book; and to Jessica Breen, Meghan Brophy, and Liz Wetzel for their tireless efforts in helping to figure out how to make the book as impactful as possible.

The title of this book isn't mine; it's Will Baude's. I'm grateful to Will not only for so graciously allowing me to appropriate it, but also for being the first to realize that one of the ways to draw increasing public attention to the more technical work of the Supreme Court is to give it a catchy name. Will's contributions go beyond nomenclature, though: his 2015 article in the *New York University Journal of Law and Liberty*, and his subsequent popular writing on several features of the shadow docket, helped to define a field that I still feel like I'm just visiting.

I also owe deep thanks to a number of faculty colleagues both at the University of Texas and at other law schools for their generosity in answering my questions, giving me advice, and, in some cases, reviewing drafts of particular sections in areas of their expertise. I was fortunate to be able to present aspects of this project to faculty workshops at UT (for which I'm grateful to Jennifer Laurin), at Stanford Law School (for which I'm grateful to Bernie Meyler), at the St. Louis University School of Law (for which I'm grateful to Sam Jordan), and at the William and Mary School of Law (for which I'm grateful to Alli Larsen and Aaron-Andrew Bruhl). Thanks especially to Lisa Bressman, Wilfred Codrington III, Ross Davies, Lisa Eskow, Eric Freedman, Barry Friedman, Abbe Gluck, Jack Goldsmith, Ed Hartnett, Rick Hasen, Ben Johnson, Lee Kovarsky, Marty Lederman, Jim Liebman, Leah Litman, Michael McConnell, Jim Oleske, H. W. Perry, Judith Resnik, Jane Schacter, Liz Sepper, Brad Snyder, Jordan Steiker, Nick Stephanopoulos, Michael Sturley, Mark Tushnet, Adam Winkler, and Steve Yelderman.

This book has also benefited directly and indirectly from the feedback and writings of many savvy and sophisticated friends and colleagues in the professional media. Between them, Joan Biskupic, Linda Greenhouse, and Dahlia Lithwick have not only been fantastic sounding boards but also models for how to write about the Court with clarity and élan, traits that I have done my best to emulate here. Thanks also to Ariane de Vogue, CNN's Supreme Court reporter, a name far more people would know if she wasn't as selfless as she is an accomplished journalist and Court watcher. I'm also grateful to Burt Neuborne and Norm Siegel, who both generously agreed to recount their first-person experiences working on the 1973 Cambodia bombing case. And Adam Feldman and Isaac Green have both been unduly generous in sharing and discussing their own research with me to help me see other pieces of the puzzle.

I've been lucky enough to get to teach a pair of upper-level research seminars on the topic of the book at the University of Texas School of Law. I'm grateful to students in my Spring 2021 seminar for helping me to think through what the book should cover (and why), and to students in my Fall 2022 seminar for helping to test-drive the result. Thank you, Justin Atkinson, Laura Beth Bienhoff, Leah Butterfield, Rob Castañeda, Madison Chilton, Wes Dodson, Niko Fotinos, Alex Gaudio, Kelly Katherine Howe, Henry Humphreys, Aaron Lozano, Ryland Maksoud, Hannah Masraff, Stewart McDonald, Emily Meier, Julie Molina, Jonathan Molinar, Jason Onyediri, Lulú Ortiz, Will Pratt, Sean Reilly, Camille Richieri, Sydney Salters, Melody Shaff, Layton Sussman, Ben Whitehead, Taylor Wilson, and Anastasia Zaluckyj. And special thanks to Taitum Aland, Olivia Horton, Katherine Rossmiller, and Chelsea Sincox for our informal Fall 2022 reading group.

Speaking of students, I've been blessed, throughout my career, to have a cadre of dedicated, hardworking, and exceptionally bright research assistants. Three, in particular, were instrumental in bringing this book to fruition: Rachael Jensen, from the University of Texas School of Law Class of 2020, and Bonnie Devany and Christina Peterman, from UT's Class of 2022. Rachael was there for—and helped to shape—a lot of the early thinking; Bonnie and Christina helped turn that thinking into substance. I've also been incredibly lucky to have the support and skills of Matt Steinke, Joe Noel, and the other reference librarians in the Tarlton Law Library at the University of Texas—for whom no ask is too obscure (and I tried). Ditto my faculty assistant, Marsha Moyer, who regularly reminds me which things matter and which things don't.

This may seem cheesy, but I'm also grateful to you, the reader. One of the theses that I set out to prove in this book is that a popular audience would be interested in a book about the more technical sides of the Supreme Court's workload. Whether or not you've made it to this part of the acknowledgments (please do send me a note if so), the mere fact that you've opened these pages have hopefully proved the point. Along those lines, two of my most regular and supportive nonlawyer readers have been my parents, Bruce and Fredda Vladeck, whose comments on draft chapters have pushed me to make the substance and style of the book more accessible to everyone.

In addition to my wife and daughters (more on them in a moment), I dedicated this book to Nasser Hussain—my mentor and college thesis adviser, who left this world in November 2015 at the tragic young age of fifty. Although Nasser would "tsk" me for saying it, he ranks right behind my parents in shaping the course of my life—from when I met him as an overeager eighteen-year-old Amherst College first-year student in his Spring 1998 "Law and Historical Trauma" class to when he helped me to see that law school was my calling as an only-slightly-less-overeager senior. Nasser taught me how to write, but he also taught me how to think—how to see the interwoven nature of law and the society it both structures and responds to. It's not just that I never would have gone to law school but for Nasser; I would never have thought to look at the world the way that I now do—or to devote a career to trying to help others do the same. Nasser also taught me that the politics of memory can be very fickle—all the more reason to remind people of him, and of my unredeemable debt to him, as often as I can.

Last, but certainly not least, I'm grateful to my best friend and better half, Karen, for always putting up with me—but especially when I was manically (if not maniacally) trying to finish the manuscript for this book. Having a partner who knows when it's time for support versus time for mockery (and vice versa) is something I wouldn't trade even for a Mets World Series title. Having a partner who is as excited about your work as you are is truly priceless. And I'm also grateful to—and for—our daughters, Madeleine and Sydney, who may be too young to understand what's in these pages (and too cool to care), but who make everything worth it.

# NOTES

## Preface

1. David B. Rivkin Jr. and James Taranto, "The Weekend Interview with Samuel Alito: The Supreme Court's Plain-Spoken Defender," *Wall Street Journal*, July 29, 2023, A11.

2. William Baude, "Foreword: The Supreme Court's Shadow Docket," *New York University Journal of Law and Liberty* 9 (2015): 1–63. Baude was not the first to use the term "shadow docket" to refer to the more obscure side of an appellate court's practice (nor did he claim to be). Texas appellate lawyer Pamela Baron started referring to some of the work of the Texas Supreme Court as a "shadow docket" as far back as the mid-2000s. But Baude originated usage of the term as a reference to the US Supreme Court, specifically.

3. The September 2021 ruling is *Whole Woman's Health* v. *Jackson*, 141 S. Ct. 2494 (2021) (mem.). The Court overruled *Roe* in *Dobbs* v. *Jackson Women's Health Organization*, 597 U.S. 215 (2022).

4. The one merits ruling is *Trump* v. *Hawaii*, 138 S. Ct. 2392 (2018). On the Trump immigration rulings more generally, see Stephen I. Vladeck, "The Supreme Court, 2018 Term—Essay, The Solicitor General and the Shadow Docket," *Harvard Law Review* 133 (Nov. 2019): 123–63 [hereafter "Vladeck Essay"].

5. The February 2022 ruling is *Merrill* v. *Milligan*, 142 S. Ct. 879 (2022) (mem.). The June 2023 ruling is *Allen* v. *Milligan*, 599 U.S. 1 (2023). On the electoral ramifications of the former, see Michael Wines, "Maps in Four States Were Ruled Illegal Gerrymanders. They're Being Used Anyway," *New York Times*, Aug. 9, 2022, A16.

6. Barrett's speech was delivered at the Ronald Reagan Presidential Library. There is no publicly available transcript or recording of the remarks, but they were widely reported. The decision two days later was *Louisiana* v. *American Rivers*, 142 S. Ct. 1347 (2022) (mem.).

7. *Whole Woman's Health*, 141 S. Ct. at 2500 (Kagan, J., dissenting).

## Introduction: The Shadow Docket

1. Burt Neuborne, "I Fought the Imperial Presidency, and the Imperial Presidency Won," American Civil Liberties Union, Sept. 27, 2019,

https://www.aclu.org/issues/national-security/i-fought-imperial-presidency-and-imperial-presidency-won; James F. Simon, *Independent Journey: The Life of William O. Douglas* (New York: Harper and Row, 1980), 414–16.

2. The legislative and political machinations are comprehensively laid out in John Hart Ely, *War and Responsibility: Constitutional Lessons of Vietnam and Its Aftermath* (Princeton, NJ: Princeton University Press, 1993), 32–46.

3. See Joel K. Goldstein, "Assuming Responsibility: Thomas F. Eagleton, the Senate and the Bombing of Cambodia," *Saint Louis University Law Journal* 52, no. 151 (2007): 166, https://papers.ssrn.com/sol3/papers.cfm?abstract_id=3297634; "Bombing Compromise Stalls Suit," *ACLU News* 38, no. 6 (July 1973) (image and transcript available at California Historical Society Digital Library, https://digitallibrary.californiahistoricalsociety.org/object/16141).

4. *Holtzman* v. *Schlesinger*, 361 F. Supp. 553 (E.D.N.Y. 1973).

5. Ibid.

6. The procedural history is set out in the Second Circuit's (belated) reversal of Judge Judd's injunction. *Holtzman* v. *Schlesinger*, 484 F.2d 1307, 1308 (2d Cir. 1973).

7. *Holtzman* v. *Schlesinger*, 414 U.S. 1304, 1315 (Circuit Justice Marshall, 1973).

8. Neuborne, op. cit.

9. Rodric B. Schoen, "A Strange Silence: Vietnam and the Supreme Court," *Washburn Law Journal* 33 (1994): 275–322.

10. *Gilligan* v. *Morgan*, 413 U.S. 1, 12 (1973).

11. Daniel M. Gonen, "Judging in Chambers: The Powers of a Single Justice of the Supreme Court," *University of Cincinnati Law Review* 76 (2008): 1159–1231.

12. The earlier order is in *Dexter* v. *Schrunk*, 400 U.S. 1207 (Circuit Justice Douglas, 1970). For the far more colorful story behind it, see Gonen, op. cit., 1160. The specific details of Norman Siegel's encounter with Justice Douglas are from my telephone interview with him, conducted on November 5, 2020.

13. *Holtzman* v. *Schlesinger*, 414 U.S. 1316, 1320 (Circuit Justice Douglas, 1973).

14. Eugene R. Fidell, "Why Did the Cambodia Bombing Continue?," *Green Bag*, 2nd ser., 13 (Spring 2010): 321–26.

15. *Schlesinger* v. *Holtzman*, 414 U.S. 1321, 1321–22 (Circuit Justice Marshall, 1973). As Gonen recounts, it was not unheard of for justices acting in chambers (by themselves) to informally consult their colleagues in especially noteworthy or controversial cases. Gonen, op. cit., 1174–75. In 1962, for instance, Justice Hugo Black, in an in-chambers opinion vacating stays issued by a lower court, had noted that he had "submitted" the matter "to each of my Brethren," and that he was "authorized" to state that they agreed. *Meredith* v. *Fair*, 83 S. Ct. 10, 11 (Circuit Justice Black, 1962). What made *Holtzman* seemingly unique was that two of the justices had already (publicly) divided, so that Marshall's "informal" consultation was, in effect if not in form, a vote of a majority of the full Court to side with one of them.

16. For a more complete account of the *Rosenberg* litigation, see Brad Snyder, "Taking Great Cases: Lessons from the *Rosenberg* Case," *Vanderbilt Law Review* 63 (2010): 885–956.

17. *Schlesinger*, 414 U.S. at 1322–26 (Douglas, J., dissenting).

18. "Cambodia Town Hit in U.S. Error; 25 to 65 Killed," *New York Times*, Aug. 7, 1973, 1. For the later estimate of fatalities, see, for example, Donald Kirk, "Cambodia 1973: Year of the 'Bomb Halt,'" *Asian Survey* 14, no. 1 (January 1, 1974): 100.

19. Stephen M. Shapiro, Kenneth S. Geller, Timothy S. Bishop, Edward A. Hartnett, and Dan Himmelfarb, *Supreme Court Practice*, 11th ed. (Arlington, VA: Bloomberg Law, 2019), §§ 1.2(F), 1.3.

20. The ACA ruling is *National Federation of Independent Business* v. *Sebelius*, 567 U.S. 519 (2012). The marriage ruling is *Obergefell* v. *Hodges*, 576 U.S. 644 (2015). The abortion ruling is *Dobbs* v. *Jackson Health Services Organization*, 142 S. Ct. 2228 (2022).

21. The data are summarized in Testimony of Stephen I. Vladeck, "Texas's Unconstitutional Abortion Ban and the Role of the Shadow Docket: Hearing Before the S. Comm. on the Judiciary," Sept. 29, 2021, https://www.judiciary.senate.gov/imo/media/doc/Vladeck%20testimony1.pdf [hereafter "Vladeck SJC Testimony"].

22. *Singleton* v. *Merrill*, No. 2:21-cv-1291, 2022 WL 265001 (N.D. Ala. Jan. 24, 2022) (three-judge court); *Caster* v. *Merrill*, No. 2:21-cv-1536, 2022 WL 264819 (N.D. Ala. Jan. 24, 2022).

23. *Merrill* v. *Milligan*, 142 S. Ct. 879, 879 (2022) (mem.).

24. Ibid., 882–83 (Roberts, C.J., dissenting). The 2013 ruling is *Shelby County* v. *Holder*, 570 U.S. 529 (2013).

25. *Merrill*, op. cit., 883, 889 (Kagan, J., dissenting).

26. *Alpha Phi Alpha Fraternity* v. *Raffensperger*, No. 1:21-cv-5337, 2022 WL 633312 (N.D. Ga. Feb. 28, 2022).

27. *Ardoin* v. *Robinson*, 142 S. Ct. 2892 (2022) (mem.). For the *Times* study, see Michael Wines, "Maps in Four States Were Ruled Illegal Gerrymanders. They're Being Used Anyway," *New York Times*, Aug. 9, 2022, A16.

28. Vladeck SJC Testimony, op. cit.

29. Vladeck Essay, op. cit.

30. *National Federation of Independent Business* v. *Department of Labor*, 142 S. Ct. 661 (2022) (per curiam); *Whole Woman's Health* v. *Jackson*, 141 S. Ct. 2494.

31. Stephen I. Vladeck, "The Most-Favored Right: COVID, the Supreme Court, and the (New) Free Exercise Clause," *New York University Journal of Law and Liberty* 15 (2022): 699–750.

32. *Zivotofsky ex rel. Zivotofsky* v. *Clinton*, 566 U.S. 189, 201 (2012) (quoting *Adarand Constructors* v. *Mineta*, 534 U.S. 103, 110 (2001) (per curiam)). The Jackson quote is from *Brown* v. *Allen*, 344 U.S. 443, 540 (1953) (Jackson, J., concurring in the result).

33. Vladeck SJC Testimony, op. cit.

34. *Does 1–3* v. *Mills*, 142 S. Ct. 17, 18 (2021) (Barrett, J., concurring).

35. For an example in which there was clearly a "stealth" dissent, see *Arthur* v. *Dunn*, 137 S. Ct. 14 (2016) (mem.). There, the Court (with eight justices) granted a stay of execution over only two public dissents, but Chief Justice Roberts wrote to note that he was providing a *fifth* vote for a stay. Ibid., 15. In other words, the vote was 5–3, even though only Justices Thomas and Alito publicly dissented.

36. Vladeck SJC Testimony, op. cit.

37. Steve Vladeck (@steve_vladeck), Twitter (Sept. 2, 2021), https://twitter.com/steve_vladeck/status/1433284987806261250.

38. *Planned Parenthood of Southeastern Pennsylvania* v. *Casey*, 505 U.S. 833, 866 (1992) (plurality opinion).

39. If the decision comes with an opinion of the Court, it is posted under the "Opinions" page. If there is no opinion of the Court, but there are concurring and/or dissenting opinions, it is posted under the "Opinions Relating to Orders" page. If there is no opinion at all, it is posted under the "Orders" page. And if the ruling is by a circuit justice, in chambers, it will appear on the "In-Chambers Opinions" page if there is a separate writing; on the "Orders" page if there is no separate writing but relief is granted; or on the docket page for that case if there is no separate writing and no relief is provided. What's more, someone looking for one of these rulings will never know in advance where to look first.

40. Unlike virtually every other state and federal court, the Supreme Court does not time-stamp its decisions, even those that produce immediate effects. Where specific times are mentioned, they reflect the time stamps on emails from the Court circulating the ruling to its press corps. Those emails are never later than, and are often a few minutes ahead of, the public posting of the decision to the Court's website.

41. The July 14 ruling was in *Barr* v. *Lee*, 140 S. Ct. 2590 (2020) (per curiam). The July 16 ruling was in *Barr* v. *Purkey*, 140 S. Ct. 2594 (2020) (mem.). And the Thanksgiving-eve rulings were in *Roman Catholic Diocese of Brooklyn* v. *Cuomo*, 141 S. Ct. 63 (2020) (per curiam), and *Agudath Israel of America* v. *Cuomo*, 141 S. Ct. 889 (2020) (mem.).

## Chapter 1. The Rise of Certiorari

1. Taft's biographers, especially those who devoted more than just passing attention to his judicial aspirations and his tenure as chief justice, are unanimous on this point. Jonathan Lurie, *The Chief Justiceship of William Howard Taft, 1921–1930* (Columbia, SC: Columbia University Press, 2019); Henry F. Pringle, *The Life and Times of William Howard Taft*, vol. 2 (New York: Farrar and Reinhart, 1939); Jeffrey Rosen, *William Howard Taft* (New York: Times Books, 2018); Robert Post, "The Incomparable Chief Justiceship of William Howard Taft," *Michigan State Law Review* (2020): 1–187.

2. Lurie, op. cit., 4–5; Pringle, op. cit., 956–59.

3. *Myers* v. *United States*, 272 U.S. 52 (1926). In holding that the Constitution required that the president have the ability to remove "principal officers" in the executive branch at will, *Myers* necessarily (and explicitly) called into question the constitutionality of the 1867 Tenure of Office Act—which

had required Senate approval before the president could remove any executive officer confirmed by the Senate, and the violation of which had formed the putative basis for Andrew Johnson's impeachment.

4. Post, op. cit.

5. Ben Johnson, "A Brief History of Certiorari, Error, and Appeal," Volokh Conspiracy, Reason, May 10, 2022, https://reason.com/volokh/2022/05/10/a-brief-history-of-certiorari-error-and-appeal.

6. The most comprehensive modern study of the Judges' Bill is Edward A. Hartnett, "Questioning Certiorari: Some Reflections Seventy-Five Years After the Judges' Bill," *Columbia Law Review* 100 (Nov. 2000): 1643–1738. No less significant was the contemporaneous account in Felix Frankfurter and James M. Landis, *The Business of the Supreme Court: A Study in the Federal Judicial System* (New York: Macmillan, 1928). In many respects, Frankfurter and Landis's monograph was prompted *by* the lobbying for and enactment of the Judges' Bill.

7. Taft's motivations may not have been purely institutional. As Post wrote, "Taft was in the paradoxical position of urging progressive reform of the judiciary so as to pre-empt what he candidly term[ed] . . . the growing progressive disposition to try experiments." Robert Post, "Taft and the Administration of Justice," *Green Bag*, 2nd ser., 2 (Spring 1999): 311, 312.

8. Kevin O'Kelly, "The Very First Days of the Supreme Court," *Experience* (American Bar Association) (Winter 2006): 6–10.

9. Richard H. Fallon Jr., John E. Manning, Daniel J. Meltzer, and David L. Shapiro, *Hart and Wechsler's The Federal Courts and the Federal System*, 7th ed. (St. Paul, MN: Foundation Press, 2015), 1–20.

10. Ibid.

11. Ibid.

12. Alexander Hamilton, "Number 78," in *The Federalist Papers* (New York: Mentor Books, 1961), 465.

13. Judiciary Act of 1789, ch. 20, 1 Stat. 73.

14. Julius Goebel Jr., *History of the Supreme Court of the United States: Antecedents and Beginnings to 1801* (New York: Macmillan, 1971), 552–661.

15. Fallon, op. cit., 26–27. On the "rump Court," see Ross Davies, "The Other Supreme Court," *Journal of Supreme Court History* 31 (2006): 221–34.

16. Fallon, op. cit., 24–26.

17. Ibid.

18. *Cohens* v. *Virginia*, 19 U.S. (6 Wheat.) 264, 404 (1821).

19. Fallon, op. cit., 26–28.

20. For the cases cited, see *Dred Scott* v. *Sandford*, 60 U.S. (19 How.) 393 (1857); *McCulloch* v. *Maryland*, 17 U.S. (4 Wheat.) 316 (1819); *Martin* v. *Hunter's Lessee*, 14 U.S. (1 Wheat.) 304 (1816); *Marbury* v. *Madison*, 5 U.S. (1 Cranch) 137 (1803).

21. Jerry L. Mashaw, "Federal Administration and Administrative Law in the Gilded Age," *Yale Law Journal* 119 (May 2010): 1362, 1368–72.

22. David P. Currie, "The Civil War Congress," *University of Chicago Law Review* 73 (Summer/Fall 1993): 1131–1226. For the "New Deal" line, see

Roger Lowenstein, *Ways and Means: Lincoln and His Cabinet and the Financing of the Civil War* (New York: Penguin, 2022), 314.

23. Fallon, op. cit., 28–30. The quote is from *Steffel* v. *Thompson*, 415 U.S. 452, 464 (1974).

24. Frankfurter and Landis, op. cit., 56–102.

25. Ibid., 103–45.

26. *Ex parte Lau Ow Bew*, 141 U.S. 583, 589 (1891); Hartnett, op. cit., 1652–57.

27. Ibid., 1657–60.

28. Jonathan Sternberg, "Deciding Not to Decide: The Judiciary Act of 1925 and the Discretionary Court," *Journal of Supreme Court History* 33 (March 2008): 1, 7. The baseball ruling is *Federal Baseball Club of Baltimore* v. *National League*, 259 U.S. 200 (1922).

29. Hartnett, op. cit., 1661.

30. On Taft's efforts prior to joining the Court, see Post, op. cit., 70–76; Hartnett, op. cit., 1660–61.

31. Ibid.

32. Post, op. cit., 78n236.

33. Hartnett, op. cit., 1662–72.

34. Ibid.

35. Ibid., 1673–75.

36. Ibid., 1675–1704.

37. Ibid., 1704n364.

38. Sup. Ct. R. 10.

39. *Olmstead* v. *United States*, 276 U.S. 609 (1928) (mem.).

40. *Olmstead* v. *United States*, 277 U.S. 438 (1928).

41. Benjamin B. Johnson, "The Origins of Supreme Court Question Selection," *Columbia Law Review* 122 (2022): 839.

42. Hartnett, op. cit., 1707. For an example of the Supreme Court rewriting a question presented, see *New York State Rifle and Pistol Association* v. *Corlett*, 141 S. Ct. 2566 (2021) (mem.). ("Petition for writ of certiorari to the US Court of Appeals for the Second Circuit granted limited to the following question: Whether the State's denial of petitioners' applications for concealed-carry licenses for self-defense violated the Second Amendment.")

43. Henry Monaghan, "On Avoiding Avoidance, Agenda Control, and Related Matters," *Columbia Law Review* 112 (2012): 665–730.

44. Harold B. Wiley, "Jurisdictional Statements on Appeals to the U.S. Supreme Court," *ABA Journal* 31 (May 1945): 239. The Frankfurter opinion is *Maryland* v. *Baltimore Radio Show*, 338 U.S. 912, 917–20 (1950) (Frankfurter, J., respecting denial of certiorari).

45. Herbert Wechsler, "The Appellate Jurisdiction of the Supreme Court: Reflections on the Law and the Logistics of Direct Review," *Washington and Lee Law Review* 34 (Fall 1977): 1043, 1061.

46. Hartnett, op. cit., 1709n392, and sources cited therein.

47. Ibid. For the Clark quote, see Richard Delgado, "*Naim* v. *Naim*," *Nevada Law Journal* 12 (Summer 2012): 525, 526.

48. For the Minnesota case, see *Baker* v. *Nelson*, 409 U.S. 810, 810 (1972) (mem.).

49. *United States* v. *Carolene Products Company*, 304 U.S. 144, 153n4 (1938).

50. Hartnett, op. cit., 1730–33. For an example of a justice soliciting a future cert. petition, see *Avery* v. *United States*, 140 S. Ct. 1080, 1081 (2020) (Kavanaugh, J., respecting the denial of certiorari) ("In a future case, I would grant certiorari to resolve the circuit split on this question of federal law.").

51. Gerald M. Gunther, "The Subtle Vices of the 'Passive Virtues'—A Comment on Principle and Expediency in Judicial Review," *Columbia Law Review* 64 (Jan. 1964): 1, 3.

52. Alexander M. Bickel, *The Least Dangerous Branch: The Supreme Court at the Bar of Politics* (New Haven, CT: Yale University Press, 1962).

53. Stephen I. Vladeck, "War and Justiciability," *Columbia Law Review Sidebar* 111 (Oct. 20, 2011): 122–40.

54. Doris Marie Provine, *Case Selection in the United States Supreme Court* (Chicago: University of Chicago Press, 1980), 43–44.

55. *Ohio* v. *Wyandotte Chemicals Corporation*, 401 U.S. 493 (1971).

56. Fallon, op. cit., 273–75.

57. *Texas* v. *Pennsylvania*, 141 S. Ct. 1230 (2020) (mem.). Two justices—Thomas and Alito—specifically noted that, in their view, the Court had no discretion not to hear Texas's suit, without regard to its merits. Ibid., 1230 (statement of Alito, J.). This was not a new position; both had consistently taken that view in prior cases as well. *Arizona* v. *California*, 140 S. Ct. 684, 685 (2020) (Thomas, J., dissenting); *Nebraska* v. *Colorado*, 577 U.S. 1211, 1211–14 (2016) (Thomas, J., dissenting).

58. Erwin N. Griswold, "Rationing Justice—The Supreme Court's Caseload and What the Court Does Not Do," *Cornell Law Review* 60 (March 1975): 335, 340; Bennett Boskey and Eugene Gressman, "The Supreme Court Bids Farewell to Mandatory Appeals," *Federal Rules Decisions* 121 (1988): 81.

59. Act of June 27, 1988, Pub. L. No. 100-352, 102 Stat. 662.

60. For term-over-term data, see the "Statistics" page maintained by *SCOTUSblog*, https://www.scotusblog.com/statistics.

61. Stephen I. Vladeck, "AEDPA, *Saucier*, and the Stronger Case for Rights-First Constitutional Adjudication," *Seattle University Law Review* 32 (Spring 2009): 595–616.

62. Hartnett, op. cit., 1731.

## Chapter 2. Substance in Procedure

1. *Obergefell* v. *Hodges*, 576 U.S. 644 (2015).

2. For a comprehensive list of when and how same-sex marriage was legalized in each state, see Appendix 1 in William N. Eskridge Jr. and Christopher R. Riano, *Marriage Equality: From Outlaws to In-Laws* (New Haven, CT: Yale University Press, 2020), 755–74.

3. *Varnum* v. *Brien*, 763 N.W.2d 862 (Iowa 2009).

4. *Goodridge* v. *Department of Public Health*, 798 N.E.2d 941 (Mass. 2003).

5. "The Supreme Court, 2014 Term—The Statistics," *Harvard Law Review* 129 (2015): 381, 389 Table II(B).

6. *Maryland* v. *Baltimore Radio Show*, 338 U.S. 912, 917–20 (1950) (statement of Frankfurter, J.); *Halprin* v. *Davis*, 140 S. Ct. 1200, 1202 (2020) (statement of Sotomayor, J.) (citing Frankfurter's opinion for the proposition that "this Court's denial of certiorari does not prevent Halprin from seeking direct review from a constitutional ruling by the Texas courts. Nor does it preclude Halprin from seeking an original writ of habeas corpus under this Court's Rule 20").

7. H. W. Perry, *Deciding to Decide: Agenda Setting in the United States Supreme Court* (Cambridge, MA: Harvard University Press, 1991).

8. In *Sekhar* v. *United States*, 570 U.S. 729 (2013), the Court held that attempting to compel a person to recommend that his employer approve an investment does not constitute the "obtaining of property from another" under the federal anti-extortion criminal statute.

9. Pub. L. No. 104-199, 110 Stat. 2419 (1996).

10. *United States* v. *Windsor*, 570 U.S. 744 (2013).

11. Ibid., 775.

12. Fast readers would have been tipped off about the bottom line in the forthcoming ruling in *Perry* by citations to it in Chief Justice Roberts's and Justice Alito's dissenting opinions in *Windsor.*

13. See *In re Marriage Cases*, 183 P.3d 384 (Cal. 2008). Proposition 8 was enacted as Article I, § 7.5 of the California Constitution.

14. See *Perry* v. *Schwarzenegger*, 704 F. Supp. 2d 921 (N.D. Cal. 2010), *aff'd sub nom. Perry* v. *Brown*, 671 F.3d 1052 (9th Cir. 2012).

15. *Hollingsworth* v. *Perry*, 570 U.S. 693, 704–14 (2013).

16. Eskridge and Riano, op. cit., 535.

17. *Perry*, 570 U.S. at 715–28 (Kennedy, J., dissenting).

18. Eskridge and Riano, op. cit., 755–74.

19. Ibid., 776 (Roberts, C.J., dissenting) ("While I disagree with the result to which the majority's analysis leads it in this case, I think it more important to point out that its analysis leads no further. The Court does not have before it, and the logic of its opinion does not decide, the distinct question whether the States, in the exercise of their 'historic and essential authority to define the marital relation,' may continue to utilize the traditional definition of marriage" (citation omitted).).

20. *Kitchen* v. *Herbert*, 961 F. Supp. 2d 1181 (D. Utah 2013).

21. Chris Geidner, "Cert. Denied, Stays Denied, Marriage Equality Advanced: How the Supreme Court Used Nonprecedential Orders to Diminish the Drama of the Marriage Equality Decision," *Ohio State Law Journal Furthermore* 76 (2015): 161, 162–63.

22. *Kitchen* v. *Herbert*, No. 2:13-cv-217, 2013 WL 6834634, at *3 (D. Utah Dec. 23, 2013); *Herbert* v. *Kitchen*, 571 U.S. 1116 (2014) (mem.). For the total number of marriages performed during those two weeks, see Eskridge and Riano, op. cit., 562.

23. Eskridge and Riano, op. cit., 563.

24. Ibid.

25. Geidner, op. cit., 163–64. For the rulings themselves, see *Baskin* v. *Bogan*, 766 F.3d 648 (7th Cir. 2014); *Bostic* v. *Schaefer*, 760 F.3d 352 (7th Cir. 2014); and *Kitchen* v. *Herbert*, 755 F.3d 1193 (10th Cir. 2014).

26. Eskridge and Riano, op. cit., 577.

27. Ibid.

28. Geidner, op. cit., 164–65.

29. Ibid. For the Supreme Court's order, see *Otter* v. *Latta*, 574 U.S. 929 (2014) (mem.).

30. *Armstrong* v. *Brenner*, 574 U.S. 1068 (2014) (mem.); Geidner, op. cit., 168.

31. Eskridge and Riano, op. cit., 578.

32. *DeBoer* v. *Snyder*, 772 F.3d 388, 402 (6th Cir. 2014).

33. Sup. Ct. R. 10(a).

34. *Obergefell* v. *Hodges*, 574 U.S. 1118 (2015) (mem.). When the Supreme Court consolidates multiple cases, it typically gives the consolidated cases the name of the one with the lowest docket number—reflecting which one was first placed on the docket. As Eskridge and Riano noted, the lawyers in the Ohio case won the race to the Court—filing first thing in the morning on the same day as two of the other three petitions. Eskridge and Riano, op. cit., 593.

35. *Searcy* v. *Strange*, 81 F. Supp. 3d 1285 (S.D. Ala.), *stay denied*, 574 U.S. 1145 (2015).

36. *Strange*, op. cit., 1145 (Thomas, J., dissenting).

37. Geidner, op. cit., 171–72.

38. Eskridge and Riano, op. cit., 576–77.

39. Perry, op. cit., 33.

40. Ibid.

41. Ibid.

42. There are documented instances of horse-trading in merits cases. For one especially prominent example, see Joan Biskupic, *The Chief: The Life and Turbulent Times of Chief Justice John Roberts* (New York: Basic Books, 2019), 234–42. According to Biskupic, in the first Affordable Care Act case, *National Federation of Independent Business* v. *Sebelius*, 567 U.S. 519 (2012), Chief Justice Roberts agreed to uphold the statute's "individual mandate" in exchange for Justices Breyer and Kagan agreeing to strike down the statute's expansion of Medicaid—so that neither holding would divide the Court along strictly partisan lines.

43. Perry, op. cit., 199–207.

44. Alex Kozinski and James Burnham, "I Say Dissental, You Say Concurral," *Yale Law Journal Forum* 121 (April 2012): 601–27.

45. *Ricci* v. *DeStefano*, 557 U.S. 557 (2009).

46. For one specialized federal appeals court—the Court of Appeals for the Armed Forces (CAAF), which hears appeals of convictions by military courts-martial—the Supreme Court's jurisdiction *turns* on whether the court of appeals chose to hear the service member's appeal in the first place. See 28

U.S.C. § 1259(3). Thus, CAAF can frustrate Supreme Court review simply by denying review of its own.

47. Except in capital cases (in which responses are mandatory), the Supreme Court's rules specifically permit waivers of responses to cert. petitions. S. Ct. R. 15.5.

48. For a helpful summary (and illustrative example), see Scott L. Nelson, "Opposing Cert: A Practitioner's Guide," *Public Citizen*, n.d., https://www.citizen.org/wp-content/uploads/opposingcertguide-1.pdf.

49. Ibid.

50. *Pavan* v. *Smith*, 137 S. Ct. 2075 (2017) (per curiam).

51. *Wright* v. *Van Patten*, 552 U.S. 120 (2008) (per curiam).

52. William Baude, "Foreword: The Supreme Court's Shadow Docket," *New York University Journal of Law and Liberty* 9 (2015): 25–55.

53. One of many examples is *Hankston* v. *Texas*, 138 S. Ct. 2706 (2018) (mem.).

54. *Rasul* v. *Bush*, 542 U.S. 466 (2004); *Bush* v. *Gherebi*, 542 U.S. 952 (2004) (mem.).

55. For the Supreme Court order, see *Gherebi*, op. cit., 952. The Ninth Circuit ruling on remand is *Gherebi* v. *Bush*, 374 F.3d 727, 739 (9th Cir. 2004). And on the mischief caused by funneling every Guantánamo case into the DC federal courts, see Stephen I. Vladeck, "The D.C. Circuit After *Boumediene*," *Seton Hall Law Review* 41 (2011): 1451–90.

## Chapter 3. The Machinery of Death

1. *Ex parte Quirin*, 317 U.S. 1 (1942).

2. The story of the saboteurs' ill-fated mission, and the litigation it precipitated, has been well told. For examples, see Michael Dobbs, *Saboteurs: The Nazi Raid on America* (New York: Knopf, 2004); and Louis Fisher, *Nazi Saboteurs on Trial: A Military Tribunal and American Law* (Lawrence: University of Kansas Press, 2003).

3. *Ex parte Milligan*, 71 U.S. (4 Wall.) 2 (1866).

4. Carlos M. Vázquez, "'Not a Happy Precedent': The Story of *Ex parte Quirin*," in *Federal Courts Stories*, ed. Vicki C. Jackson and Judith Resnik (St. Paul, MN: Foundation Press, 2009), 218.

5. Frankfurter's "Soliloquy" is reprinted, and its background is recounted, in G. Edward White, "Felix Frankfurter's 'Soliloquy' in *Ex parte Quirin*," *Green Bag* 5 (Summer 2002): 423–40. More of the background, including why Frankfurter should have recused in *Quirin*, comes from Brad Snyder, *Democratic Justice: Felix Frankfurter, the Supreme Court, and the Making of the Liberal Establishment* (New York: W. W. Norton, 2022), 407–15.

6. The Scalia quote is from *Hamdi* v. *Rumsfeld*, 542 U.S. 507, 569 (2004) (Scalia, J., dissenting). For Frankfurter's continuing reflections, see White, op. cit., 436.

7. Snyder, op. cit.; *Rosenberg* v. *United States*, 346 U.S. 273 (1953).

8. *Waley* v. *Johnston*, 316 U.S. 101 (1942).

9. Act of Feb. 5, 1867, ch. 28, § 1, 14 Stat. 385, 386.

10. For the 1908 statute, see Act of March 10, 1908, ch. 76, 35 Stat. 40. The background to the 1908 act is recounted in the House Judiciary Committee's report accompanying the bill, H.R. Rep. No. 60-23 (1908).

11. The 1934 act had no similar explanatory report. Act of June 19, 1934, ch. 673, 45 Stat. 1177.

12. The 1942 ruling is *Scripps-Howard Radio* v. *FCC*, 316 U.S. 4, 17 (1942). For the modern standard, see *Hollingsworth* v. *Perry*, 558 U.S. 183, 190 (2010) (per curiam).

13. Snyder, op. cit.

14. Frank Felleman and John C. Wright Jr., Note, "The Powers of the Supreme Court Justice Acting in an Individual Capacity," *University of Pennsylvania Law Review* 119 (May 1964): 981, 1022, app. B. *Mapp* v. *Ohio*, 367 U.S. 643 (1961), applied the Fourth Amendment to the states. *Robinson* v. *California*, 370 U.S. 660 (1962), applied the Eighth Amendment to the states. And *Gideon* v. *Wainwright*, 372 U.S. 335 (1963), applied the right to court-appointed counsel to all state felony prosecutions (the Court had previously applied such a right to state *capital* prosecutions in *Powell* v. *Alabama*, 287 U.S. 45 (1932)).

15. The data comes from the so-called ESPY file, as maintained by the Death Penalty Information Center, https://files.deathpenaltyinfo.org/legacy/documents/ESPYyear.pdf. On LDF, race, and the death penalty, see Carol S. Steiker and Jordan M. Steiker, "The American Death Penalty and the (In)Visibility of Race," *University of Chicago Law Review* 82 (Winter 2015): 243.

16. *Furman* v. *Georgia*, 408 U.S. 238, 309–10 (1972) (Stewart, J., concurring).

17. There are several excellent, accessible accounts of the Court's internal dynamics between the decisions in *Furman* and the July 2 cases (*Gregg* v. *Georgia*, 428 U.S. 153 (1976)), and in the aftermath of the latter, derived heavily from Justice Blackmun's papers. The two on which I've relied the most here are Linda Greenhouse, *Becoming Justice Blackmun: Harry Blackmun's Supreme Court Journey* (New York: Henry Holt, 2005), 160–81; and Edward Lazarus, *Closed Chambers: The Rise, Fall, and Future of the Modern Supreme Court* (New York: Penguin, 1999), 86–165.

18. For a thorough breakdown of the different types of claims that can arise in death penalty litigation, and when they arise, see Lee Kovarsky, "Delay in the Shadow of Death," *New York University Law Review* 95 (Nov. 2020): 1319–85.

19. Carol S. Steiker and Jordan M. Steiker, *Courting Death: The Supreme Court and Capital Punishment* (Cambridge, MA: Belknap Press of Harvard University Press, 2016), 40.

20. Kovarsky, op. cit.

21. *Wainwright* v. *Sykes*, 433 U.S. 72 (1977).

22. *Estelle* v. *O'Bryan*, 459 U.S. 961 (1982) (mem.). O'Bryan eventually lost his appeals and was executed on March 31, 1984.

23. Greenhouse, op. cit., 161.

24. For more on Vasil's role, see Lazarus, op. cit., 120–22.

25. Daniel M. Gonen, "Judging in Chambers: The Powers of a Single Justice of the Supreme Court," *University of Cincinnati Law Review* 76 (2008): 1159–1231. For 1980 as the last in-chambers argument, see Stephen M. Shapiro, Kenneth S. Geller, Timothy S. Bishop, Edward A. Hartnett, and Dan Himmelfarb, *Supreme Court Practice*, 11th ed. (Arlington, VA: Bloomberg Law, 2019), § 17.2. The norm in capital cases prior to 1976 was for individual justices to resolve them in chambers. Felleman and Wright, op. cit., 1022, app. B.

26. James S. Liebman, Jeffrey Fagan, Valerie West, and Jonathan Lloyd, "Capital Attrition: Error Rates in Capital Cases, 1973–1995," *Texas Law Review* 78 (2000): 1839–65.

27. Kovarsky, op. cit.

28. Lazarus, op. cit., 150–52.

29. *Barefoot* v. *Estelle*, 463 U.S. 880 (1983).

30. Lazarus, op. cit., 152.

31. For an example, see *Wainwright* v. *Spenkelink*, 442 U.S. 901 (1979) (mem.), and Justice Rehnquist's solo dissent therein, ibid., 901–6 (Rehnquist, J., dissenting).

32. *Woodard* v. *Hutchins*, 464 U.S. 377 (1984) (per curiam). For Justice Brennan's dissent, see ibid., 382–83 (Brennan, J., dissenting). The justices' own cursory review is summarized in Justice Marshall's dissent, ibid, 384n2 (Marshall, J., dissenting).

33. Editorial, "Kill Him, 4-4," *New York Times*, Jan. 10, 1985, A22.

34. Greenhouse, op. cit., 165–74; Lazarus, op. cit., 160–65.

35. *Darden* v. *Wainwright*, 473 U.S. 928, 929 (1985) (Powell, J., concurring). For the earlier denial, see *Darden* v. *Wainwright*, 473 U.S. 927 (1985) (mem.).

36. The Court ruled against Darden on the merits in *Darden* v. *Wainwright*, 477 U.S. 168 (1986).

37. By the 1960s, several justices were of the view that the likelihood of granting certiorari was one of the factors to consider in whether to stay a lower court's judgment *in general*. But the notion that the likelihood of granting certiorari should be relevant to a stay of *execution* did not come into broad acceptance until after *Darden*.

38. Lazarus, op. cit., 505–9. The Ninth Circuit ruling came in *Fierro* v. *Gomez*, 77 F.3d 301, 309 (9th Cir. 1996), but was vacated by the Supreme Court after California amended its penal code to allow prisoners to *choose* between lethal injection and cyanide gas. *Gomez* v. *Fierro*, 519 U.S. 918 (1996) (mem.).

39. Adam Liptak, "Going to Court, But Not in Time to Live," *New York Times*, Oct. 8, 2007, A13.

40. Antiterrorism and Effective Death Penalty Act of 1996, Pub. L. No. 104-132, 110 Stat. 1214. For the current shortcomings of the "courtesy-fifth" regime, see Eric M. Freedman, "No Execution if Four Justices Object," *Hofstra Law Review* 43 (2015): 639–66.

41. *Felker* v. *Turpin*, 518 U.S. 651 (1996). For the obscurity of "original" habeas, see Stephen I. Vladeck, "The Supreme Court, Original Habeas, and

the Paradoxical Virtue of Obscurity," *Virginia Law Review In Brief* 97 (July 2011): 31–40.

42. *Dunn* v. *Ray*, 139 S. Ct. 661, 662 (2019) (Kagan, J., dissenting).

43. *Murphy* v. *Collier*, 139 S. Ct. 1475, 1476n* (2019) (Kavanaugh, J., concurring). On May 13—six weeks later—Justice Alito filed a dissenting opinion, prompting Kavanaugh (this time joined by Chief Justice Roberts) to file a second concurrence, again attempting to distinguish the cases. Ibid., 1476–77 (statement of Kavanaugh, J.).

44. *Bucklew* v. *Precythe*, 139 S. Ct. 1112, 1134 (2019).

45. Ibid., 1146 (Sotomayor, J., dissenting).

46. *Barr* v. *Lee*, 140 S. Ct. 2590 (2020) (per curiam).

47. The procedural history is recounted in Lee Kovarsky, "The Trump Executions," *Texas Law Review* 100 (2022): 621–81.

48. *Lee*, op. cit., 2591–92.

49. Kovarsky, op. cit., 678.

50. *Barr* v. *Purkey*, 140 S. Ct. 2594 (2020) (mem.).

51. William Baude, "Death and the Shadow Docket," Volokh Conspiracy, Reason, April 2, 2019, https://reason.com/volokh/2019/04/12/death-and-the-shadow-docket. The majority's emphasis on expedition produced downstream effects even when the justices *denied* emergency relief. In one challenge brought by four of the federal prisoners slated for execution objecting to how their death sentences had been imposed, the Court declined the federal government's application to stay a lower-court injunction, but emphasized that "we expect that the Court of Appeals will render its [merits] decision with appropriate dispatch." *Barr* v. *Roane*, 140 S. Ct. 353, 353 (2019) (mem.). When a divided DC Circuit panel sided with the federal government on remand, *In re Federal Bureau of Prisons' Execution Protocol Cases*, 955 F.3d 106 (D.C. Cir. 2020) (per curiam), the dissenting judge noted that he was *not* asking for the full court of appeals to review the decision—even though he likely had the votes to accomplish such rehearing—solely because of the Supreme Court's insistence on dispatch. *In re Federal Bureau of Prisons' Execution Protocol Cases*, No. 19-5322, order at 2 (D.C. Cir. May 15, 2020) (statement of Tatel, J.), https://www.cadc.uscourts.gov/internet/orders.nsf/4296E931F354517685258569005l5F5F/%24file/19-5322CCEN.pdf.

52. 18 U.S.C. § 3596(a) ("When the sentence is to be implemented, the Attorney General shall release the person sentenced to death to the custody of a United States marshal, who shall supervise implementation of the sentence in the manner prescribed by the law of the State in which the sentence is imposed. If the law of the State does not provide for implementation of a sentence of death, the court shall designate another State, the law of which does provide for the implementation of a sentence of death, and the sentence shall be implemented in the latter State in the manner prescribed by such law.").

53. *United States* v. *Higgs*, 141 S. Ct. 645 (2021) (mem.).

54. Steve Vladeck, "The Rise of Certiorari Before Judgment," *SCOTUSblog*, Jan. 25, 2022, https://www.scotusblog.com/2022/01/the-rise-of-certiorari-before-judgment.

55. Vladeck SJC Testimony, op. cit., 9.

56. *Higgs*, 141 S. Ct. at 645–47 (Breyer, J., dissenting); ibid., 647–52 (Sotomayor, J., dissenting).

57. *Hamm* v. *Miller*, No. 22A258, 2022 WL 4391940 (U.S. Sept. 22, 2022) (mem.).

58. Kovarsky, op. cit., 647.

59. Norman Mailer, "Until Dead: Thoughts on Capital Punishment," *Parade*, Feb. 6, 1981, 6.

60. Lincoln Caplan, *The Tenth Justice: The Solicitor General and the Rule of Law* (New York: Knopf, 1987).

## Chapter 4. The Tenth Justice

1. Exec. Order No. 13,769, 82 Fed. Reg. 8977 (Feb. 1, 2017).

2. Vladeck Essay, op. cit., 135.

3. *Washington* v. *Trump*, No. C17-0141, 2017 WL 462040, at *1 (W.D. Wash. Feb. 3, 2017).

4. *Washington* v. *Trump*, 847 F.3d 1151 (9th Cir. 2017).

5. Vladeck Essay, op. cit., 135. The order itself is Exec. Order No. 13,780, 82 Fed. Reg. 13,209 (March 9, 2017).

6. Steve Vladeck, "How the Acting Solicitor General (Sort of) Saved the Travel Ban," *SCOTUSblog*, July 12, 2017, https://www.scotusblog.com/2017/07/symposium-acting-solicitor-general-sort-saved-travel-ban.

7. Ibid.

8. *Maryland* v. *King*, 567 U.S. 1301, 1303 (Circuit Justice Roberts, 2012).

9. Vladeck Essay, op. cit., 132n60.

10. Ibid.

11. *Trump* v. *International Refugee Assistance Project*, 137 S. Ct. 2080 (2017) (per curiam). In a break from protocol, the Court handed down the ruling as if it had been an argued case rather than as an order—a move that, if nothing else, befuddled the Court's press corps.

12. Ibid., 2086.

13. Vladeck Essay, op. cit., 137–38.

14. Proclamation No. 9645, 82 Fed. Reg. 45,161 (Sept. 24, 2017). In light of the changes, the Supreme Court canceled the impending oral argument; vacated the lower-court decisions; and remanded with instructions to dismiss the cases as moot. *Trump* v. *Hawaii*, 138 S. Ct. 377, 377 (2017) (mem.); *Trump* v. *International Refugee Assistance Project*, 138 S. Ct. 353, 353 (2017) (mem.).

15. *Trump* v. *Hawaii*, 138 S. Ct. 2392 (2018).

16. Vladeck Essay, op. cit., 138.

17. Vladeck, "How the Solicitor General (Sort of) Saved the Travel Ban," op. cit.

18. Act of Sept. 24, 1789, ch. 20, § 35, 1 Stat. 73, 93 (codified as amended at 28 U.S.C. § 503).

19. How Congress structured the head positions in the three executive departments, in contrast, was a matter of extended debate, culminating in what's known as the "Decision of 1789," in which Congress did not specify

how those officers were to be removed—silence that has long been interpreted as recognition of the president's constitutional authority to fire those officials at will. For the background, see Saikrishna Prakash, "New Light on the Decision of 1789," *Cornell Law Review* 91 (July 2006): 1021–78. On the broader historical and political developments in President Washington's formation of his first Cabinet, see Lindsay M. Chervinsky, *The Cabinet: George Washington and the Creation of an American Institution* (Cambridge, MA: Belknap Press of Harvard University Press, 2020).

20. The early history of the position of attorney general, including the legislative debates leading to the 1789 act, is retold in Susan Low Bloch, "The Early Role of the Attorney General in Our Constitutional Scheme: In the Beginning There Was Pragmatism," *Duke Law Journal* (1989): 561–653.

21. Ibid., 571.

22. The origins of the position of solicitor general were recounted by then solicitor general Seth Waxman in a June 1, 1998, address to the Supreme Court Historical Society, "Presenting the Case of the United States as It Should Be: The Solicitor General in Historical Context." Text of the speech is available at US Department of Justice, https://www.justice.gov/osg/solicitor-general-historical-context.

23. Act of June 22, 1870, ch. 150, 16 Stat. 162, 162.

24. Rex E. Lee, "Lawyering for the Government: Politics, Polemics and Principle," *Ohio State Law Journal* 47 (1986): 595, 597.

25. There is a voluminous body of academic literature on the historical role of the solicitor general (from which most of these quotations were derived). The definitive popular treatment remains Lincoln Caplan, *The Tenth Justice: The Solicitor General and the Rule of Law* (New York: Knopf, 1987). The case from which Sobeloff effectively (but not formally) recused is *Peters* v. *Hobby*, 349 U.S. 331 (1955), in which a former federal employee challenged his removal and debarment from future federal employment by the Civil Service Commission's Loyalty Review Board.

26. Waxman, op. cit.

27. Vladeck Essay, op. cit.

28. Ibid.

29. Ibid. For data postdating the essay cited in the text accompanying the preceding endnotes, see Steve Vladeck (@steve_vladeck), Twitter (Jan. 20, 2021), https://twitter.com/steve_vladeck/status/1351927798882066436.

30. Vladeck Essay, op. cit., 138–39; Donald J. Trump (@realDonaldTrump), Twitter (July 26, 2017, 8:55:58 a.m. and 9:04:39 a.m. EST), archived at Trump Twitter Archive, https://www.thetrumparchive.com.

31. Ibid., 139–40.

32. Ibid., 140.

33. *Wolf* v. *Cook County, Illinois*, 140 S. Ct. 681 (2020) (mem.). The January ruling was *Department of Homeland Security* v. *New York*, 140 S. Ct. 599 (2020). For Justice Gorsuch's concurrence, see ibid., 599–601 (Gorsuch, J., concurring).

34. *East Bay Sanctuary Covenant* v. *Barr*, 385 F. Supp. 3d 922 (N.D. Cal. 2019).

35. *Barr* v. *East Bay Sanctuary Covenant*, 140 S. Ct. 3 (2019) (mem.); *East Bay Sanctuary Covenant* v. *Barr*, 934 F.3d 1026 (9th Cir. 2019).

36. *East Bay Sanctuary Covenant* v. *Garland*, 994 F.3d 962 (9th Cir. 2021).

37. *Wolf*, op. cit., 684 (Sotomayor, J., dissenting); *East Bay Sanctuary Covenant*, op. cit., 6 (Sotomayor, J., dissenting). Sotomayor's dissent in *East Bay* was also the first time the term "shadow docket" ever appeared in a Supreme Court decision—in a citation to my then forthcoming essay, "The Supreme Court, 2018 Term—Essay, The Solicitor General and the Shadow Docket," *Harvard Law Review* 133 (Nov. 2019) (Vladeck Essay).

38. On the unprecedented nature of the solicitor general's filing, see Marty Lederman, "The SG's Remarkable Cert. Petition in *Hargan* v. *Garza*, the 'Jane Doe' Abortion Case," *Balkinization*, Nov. 8, 2017, https://balkin.blogspot.com/2017/11/the-sgs-remarkable-cert-petition-in.html. On the legal ethics piece, see Marty Lederman and David Luban, "Who's on Ethical Thin Ice in the *Hargan* v. *Garza* Abortion Case?," *Balkinization*, Dec. 31, 2017, https://balkin.blogspot.com/2017/12/whos-on-ethical-thin-ice-in-hargan-v_31.html.

39. Vladeck Essay, op. cit., 150–51. In an unsigned summary ruling with no public dissents, the Court eventually granted the government's request to vacate the lower-court ruling on the ground that it was moot, but took no position on the solicitor general's request for sanctions. *Azar* v. *Garza*, 138 S. Ct. 1790 (2018) (per curiam).

40. *American College of Obstetricians and Gynecologists* v. *U.S. Food and Drug Administration*, 472 F. Supp. 3d 183, 189–97 (D. Md. 2020).

41. Ibid.

42. Ibid., 198–233.

43. *Food and Drug Administration* v. *American College of Obstetricians and Gynecologists*, 141 S. Ct. 10, 11 (2020) (mem.).

44. Ibid., 141 S. Ct. 578, 579 (2021) (Sotomayor, J., dissenting).

45. *Department of Homeland Security* v. *New York*, 140 S. Ct. 599, 600–1 (2020) (Gorsuch, J., concurring); *Trump* v. *Hawaii*, 138 S. Ct. at 2424–29 (Thomas, J., concurring).

46. The stay denials are *United States* v. *Texas*, No. 22A17, 2022 WL 2841804 (U.S. July 21, 2022) (mem.), and *Biden* v. *Texas*, 142 S. Ct. 926 (2021) (mem.). The merits decision in the latter case is *Biden* v. *Texas*, 142 S. Ct. 2528 (2022). Chief Justice Roberts and Justice Kavanaugh joined Justices Breyer, Sotomayor, and Kagan in the majority on the merits—even though at least one of them, and quite possibly both, had voted against a stay the previous August. And the vaccine mandate ruling is *Biden* v. *Missouri*, 142 S. Ct. 647 (2022) (per curiam).

47. Vladeck Essay, op. cit., 155–56.

48. *Trump* v. *Sierra Club*, 140 S. Ct. 1, 1–2 (2019) (Breyer, J., concurring in part and dissenting in part).

49. *Louisiana* v. *American Rivers*, 142 S. Ct. 1347, 1349 (2022) (Kagan, J., dissenting).

50. Steve Vladeck, "October Term 2020 and the Specter of (a Lot of) Mootness," *SCOTUSblog*, Sept. 28, 2020, https://www.scotusblog.com/2020/09/october-term-2020-and-the-specter-of-a-lot-of-mootness.

## Chapter 5. COVID and the Court

1. Carter G. Phillips, "A Snow Story," *Supreme Court Historical Society*, Feb. 12, 2021, https://supremecourthistory.org/a-snow-story-by-carter-g-phillips.

2. *Patent and Trademark Office* v. *Booking.com B.V.*, 140 S. Ct. 2298 (2020).

3. The Court also received a handful of emergency applications in cases by prisoners challenging the (deteriorating) health conditions in their detention facilities. The most contentious example is *Barnes* v. *Ahlman*, 140 S. Ct. 2620 (2020) (mem.), in which, by a 5–4 vote, the Court stayed an injunction requiring the Orange County Jail to implement a range of safety measures to protect inmates from the spread of COVID. For more on COVID-related prisoner litigation, see Brandon L. Garrett and Lee Kovarsky, "Viral Injustice," *California Law Review* 110 (Feb. 2022): 117–78. Suffice it to say, the Court's refusal to intervene in the prisoner cases only reinforces some of the broader themes of the majority's selective use of the shadow docket in recent years.

4. 28 U.S.C. § 1651(a) ("The Supreme Court and all courts established by Act of Congress may issue all writs necessary or appropriate in aid of their respective jurisdictions and agreeable to the usages and principles of law.").

5. *South Bay United Pentecostal Church* v. *Newsom*, 141 S. Ct. 716, 717 (2021) (Barrett, J., concurring); *Roman Catholic Diocese of Brooklyn* v. *Cuomo*, 141 S. Ct. 63 (2020) (per curiam).

6. *Employment Division* v. *Smith*, 494 U.S. 872, 888–89 (1990).

7. James M. Oleske Jr., "Free Exercise (Dis)Honesty," *Wisconsin Law Review* (2019): 689, 718–26.

8. Stephen I. Vladeck, "The Most-Favored Right: COVID, the Supreme Court, and the (New) Free Exercise Clause," *New York University Journal of Law and Liberty* 15 (2022): 699–750.

9. Lucien J. Dhooge, "The Impact of State Religious Freedom Restoration Acts: An Analysis of the Interpretive Case Law," *Wake Forest Law Review* 52 (2017): 585.

10. Douglas Laycock, "The Remnants of Free Exercise," *Supreme Court Review* (1990): 1.

11. *Fraternal Order of Police Newark Lodge No. 12* v. *City of Newark*, 170 F.3d 359, 365 (3d Cir. 1999).

12. For one such example, see *Trinity Lutheran Church of Columbia, Inc.* v. *Comer*, 137 S. Ct. 2012 (2017).

13. Petition for a Writ of Certiorari at i, *Fulton* v. *City of Philadelphia*, 140 S. Ct. 1104 (2020) (No. 19-123), 2019 WL 3380520. After granting certiorari on February 24, 2020, the Supreme Court scheduled *Fulton* for a November 4 argument on August 19. Docket, *Fulton* v. *City of Philadelphia*, No. 19-123, US Supreme Court, https://www.supremecourt.gov/docket/docketfiles/html/public/19-123.html. For the earlier opinion, see *Kennedy* v. *Bremerton School District*, 139 S. Ct. 634, 637 (2019) (Alito, J., respecting the denial of certiorari).

14. Emergency Application for Writ of Injunction, *South Bay United Pentecostal Church* v. *Newsom* ("*South Bay I*"), 140 S. Ct. 1613 (2020) (No. 19A1044), https://www.supremecourt.gov/DocketPDF/19/19A1044/144133/20200523140701636_Emergency%20Application%20for%20Writ%20of%20Injunction.pdf; Opposition of State Respondents, *South Bay I*, 140 S. Ct. 1613 (No. 19A1044), https://www.supremecourt.gov/DocketPDF/19/19A1044/144426/20200528194451283_South%20Bay%20Pentecostal%20Church%20v.%20Newsom%20-%20Opposition%20-%205.28.20%20-%20No%2019A1044.pdf.

15. *South Bay United Pentecostal Church* v. *Newsom*, No. 20-cv-865, 2020 WL 2814636 (S.D. Cal. May 15, 2020), *injunction denied*, 959 F.3d 938 (9th Cir. 2020).

16. *Ohio Citizens for Responsible Energy, Inc.* v. *Nuclear Regulatory Commission*, 479 U.S. 1312, 1313 (Circuit Justice Scalia, 1986).

17. *Akina* v. *Hawaii*, 577 U.S. 1024 (2015) (mem.); *Zubik* v. *Burwell*, 576 U.S. 1049 (2015) (mem.); *Wheaton College* v. *Burwell*, 573 U.S. 958 (2014) (mem.); *Holt* v. *Hobbs*, 571 U.S. 1019 (2013) (mem.).

18. *South Bay United Pentecostal Church* v. *Newsom*, 140 S. Ct. 1613, 1613–14 (2020) (Roberts, C.J., concurring).

19. *Calvary Chapel Dayton Valley* v. *Sisolak*, No. 3:20-cv-303, 2020 WL 4260438 (D. Nev. June 11, 2020); *injunction denied*, No. 20-16169, 2020 WL 4274901 (9th Cir. July 2, 2020); *injunction denied*, 140 S. Ct. 2603 (2020) (mem.).

20. *Calvary Chapel*, 140 S. Ct. at 2609–15 (Kavanaugh, J., dissenting); ibid., 2603–4 (Alito, J., dissenting); ibid., 2609 (Gorsuch, J., dissenting).

21. *Roman Catholic Diocese of Brooklyn* v. *Cuomo*, 493 F. Supp. 3d 168, 171 (E.D.N.Y. 2020).

22. *Roman Catholic Diocese of Brooklyn* v. *Cuomo*, 980 F.3d 222, 228–31 (2d Cir. 2020) (Park, J., dissenting).

23. Emergency Application for Writ of Injunction, *Roman Catholic Diocese of Brooklyn* v. *Cuomo*, 141 S. Ct. 63 (2020) (per curiam) (No. 20A87), https://www.supremecourt.gov/DocketPDF/20/20A87/160205/20201109225714204_Diocese%20Application%20TO%20FILE.pdf; Opposition to Application for Writ of Injunction, *Roman Catholic Diocese*, 141 S. Ct. 63 (No. 20A87), https://www.supremecourt.gov/DocketPDF/20/20A87/161095/20201118134346148_20A87%20NY%20Opposition%20to%20Application%20for%20Injunction.pdf.

24. Letter of Respondent, *Roman Catholic Diocese*, 141 S. Ct. 63 (No. 20A87), https://www.supremecourt.gov/DocketPDF/20/20A87/161185/20201119123532129_20A87%20Letter.pdf; Reply Brief in Support of Emergency Application for Writ of Injunction, *Roman Catholic Diocese*, 141 S. Ct. 63 (No. 20A87), https://www.supremecourt.gov/DocketPDF/20/20A87/161295/20201119164437704_Diocese%20Reply%20TO%20FILE.pdf.

25. *Roman Catholic Diocese*, 141 S. Ct. 63.

26. Ibid., 66–69.

27. Ibid., 68. For the "certainly impending" analysis, see *Clapper* v. *Amnesty International USA*, 568 U.S. 398, 410–14 (2013).

28. *Roman Catholic Diocese*, 141 S. Ct. at 73 (Kavanaugh, J., concurring).

29. Ibid., 76–78 (Breyer, J., dissenting); ibid., 78–81 (Sotomayor, J., dissenting).

30. Ibid., 75 (Roberts, C.J., dissenting).

31. *Agudath Israel of America* v. *Cuomo*, 141 S. Ct. 889 (2020) (mem.).

32. *Harvest Rock Church, Inc.* v. *Newsom*, 141 S. Ct. 889 (2020) (mem.).

33. *Lunding* v. *New York Tax Appeals Tribunal*, 522 U.S. 287, 307 (1998).

34. *Robinson* v. *Murphy*, 141 S. Ct. 972 (2020) (mem.); *High Plains Harvest Church* v. *Polis*, 141 S. Ct. 527 (2020) (mem.).

35. *High Plains Harvest Church*, 141 S. Ct. at 527 (Kagan, J., dissenting).

36. *South Bay United Pentecostal Church* v. *Newsom*, 508 F. Supp. 3d 756 (S.D. Cal. 2020).

37. *South Bay United Pentecostal Church* v. *Newsom*, 985 F.3d 1128 (9th Cir. 2021); *Harvest Rock Church, Inc.* v. *Newsom*, 985 F.3d 771 (9th Cir. 2021) (mem.).

38. *South Bay United Pentecostal Church* v. *Newsom* ("*South Bay II*"), 141 S. Ct. 716 (2021) (mem.); *Harvest Rock Church, Inc.* v. *Newsom*, 141 S. Ct. 1289 (2021) (mem.).

39. *South Bay II*, 141 S. Ct. at 717 (Barrett, J., concurring).

40. *United States Fish and Wildlife Service* v. *Sierra Club, Inc.*, 141 S. Ct. 777 (2021).

41. *South Bay II*, 141 S. Ct. at 717 (Barrett, J., concurring); ibid., 717–20 (statement of Gorsuch, J.).

42. Ibid., 721 (Kagan, J., dissenting).

43. Ibid., 722–23.

44. Ibid., 723.

45. *Gish* v. *Newsom*, 141 S. Ct. 1290 (2021) (mem.).

46. *Gateway City Church* v. *Newsom*, 141 S. Ct. 1460, 1460 (2021) (mem.). For the Ninth Circuit's ruling, see *Gateway City Church* v. *Newsom*, No. 21-15189, 2021 WL 781981 (9th Cir. Feb. 12, 2021) (mem.).

47. *Tandon* v. *Newsom* 992 F.3d 916, 920 (9th Cir. 2021) (mem.).

48. *Tandon* v. *Newsom*, 141 S. Ct. 1294, 1296 (2021) (per curiam).

49. Jim Oleske, "Tandon Steals Fulton's Thunder: The Most Important Free Exercise Decision Since 1990," *SCOTUSblog*, April 15, 2021, https://www.scotusblog.com/2021/04/tandon-steals-fultons-thunder-the-most-important-free-exercise-decision-since-1990.

50. *Tandon*, 141 S. Ct. at 1297–98.

51. Ibid., 1298 (Kagan, J., dissenting).

52. Stephen I. Vladeck, "The Supreme Court Is Making New Law in the Shadows," *New York Times*, April 15, 2021, https://www.nytimes.com/2021/04/15/opinion/supreme-court-religion-orders.html.

53. *South Bay United Pentecostal Church* v. *Newsom*, 141 S. Ct. 2563, 2563 (2021) (mem.); *Calvary Chapel Dayton Valley* v. *Sisolak*, 141 S. Ct. 1285 (2021) (mem.).

54. *Dr. A.* v. *Hochul*, 142 S. Ct. 2569, 2571 (2022) (Thomas, J., dissenting from the denial of certiorari).

55. *Whole Woman's Health* v. *Jackson*, 141 S. Ct. 2494 (2021) (mem.). The one non-religious-liberty grant of emergency injunctive relief was *Chrysafis* v. *Marks*, 141 S. Ct. 2482 (2021) (mem.), in which the Court blocked New York's COVID-related eviction moratorium.

56. *Does 1–3* v. *Mills*, 142 S. Ct. 17, 18 (2021) (Barrett, J., concurring).

57. *Dr. A* v. *Hochul*, 142 S. Ct. 552, 555 (2021) (Gorsuch, J., dissenting) (citation omitted); *Roman Catholic Diocese of Brooklyn* v. *Cuomo*, 141 S. Ct. 63, 69 (2020) (Gorsuch, J., concurring); *Calvary Chapel Dayton Valley* v. *Sisolak*, 140 S. Ct. 2603, 2605 (2020) (Alito, J., dissenting); ibid., 2614 (Kavanaugh, J., dissenting).

58. *Trump* v. *Hawaii*, 138 S. Ct. 2392, 2418 (2018).

59. Lindsay F. Wiley and Stephen I. Vladeck, "Coronavirus, Civil Liberties, and the Courts: The Case Against 'Suspending' Judicial Review," *Harvard Law Review Forum* 133 (2020): 179, 189 & n63.

60. The dissent in the Texas case is *NetChoice* v. *Paxton*, 142 S. Ct. 1715, 1718 (2022) (Alito, J., dissenting). The dissent in the New York case is *Yeshiva University* v. *YU Pride Alliance*, No. 22A184, 2022 WL 4232541, at *1–3 (U.S. Sept. 14, 2022) (Alito, J., dissenting).

61. *Whole Woman's Health* v. *Jackson*, 141 S. Ct. 2494, 2500 (2021) (Kagan, J., dissenting).

## Chapter 6. The "*Purcell* Principle"

1. The 1948 Texas primary is the dominant subject of Robert Caro, *The Years of Lyndon Johnson: Means of Ascent* (New York: Knopf, 1990). The political and legal aftermath of the runoff are exhaustively recounted ibid., 308–84.

2. Ibid., 313–17. For more on Stevenson, see Robert Caro, "My Search for Coke Stevenson," *New York Times Book Review*, Feb. 3, 1991, 1.

3. Caro, *Means of Ascent*, op. cit., 328–29.

4. John Q. Barrett, "'Landslide Lyndon' in the Supreme Court (1948)," Jackson List, Nov. 3, 2008, https://thejacksonlist.com/wp-content/uploads/2014/02/20081103-Jackson-List-LBJ-v.-Stevenson.pdf.

5. The post-runoff litigation is comprehensively recounted in Josiah M. Daniel III, "*LBJ v. Coke Stevenson*: Lawyering for Control of the Disputed Texas Democratic Party Senatorial Primary Election of 1948," *Review of Litigation* 31 (Winter 2012): 1–70.

6. Caro, *Means of Ascent*, op. cit., 332.

7. Ibid., 373–84; Edward B. Foley, *Ballot Battles: The History of Disputed Elections in the United States* (New York: Oxford University Press, 2006), 206–16.

8. Barrett, op. cit., 4–6. Barrett's essay reproduces the order Justice Black signed on Wednesday, September 29. Ibid., 9. For the newspaper account of Black's oral ruling on Tuesday, see Lewis Wood, "Texas Ballot Writ Is Stayed by Black," *New York Times*, Sept. 29, 1948, 22. Neither of Black's in-chambers rulings is memorialized in any official Supreme Court source.

9. Barrett recounts what happened inside the Court. Barrett, op. cit., 5–7. The full Court's orders are reported as *Johnson* v. *Stevenson*, 335 U.S. 801 (1948) (mem.). The Johnson quote is in Roger K. Newman, *Hugo Black: A Biography* (New York: Pantheon, 1994), 376.

10. This principle of nonintervention can be traced to *Taylor* v. *Beckham*, 178 U.S. 548 (1900).

11. The 1941 ruling is *United States* v. *Classic*, 313 U.S. 299 (1941).

12. Congressional Research Service, "The Voting Rights Act of 1965: Background and Overview," July 20, 2015, https://crsreports.congress.gov/product/pdf/R/R43626/15.

13. *Gonzalez* v. *Arizona*, No. CV 06-1268-PHX, 2006 WL 3627297 (D. Ariz. Sept. 11, 2006). The Ninth Circuit's order is not reported, but it is discussed in that court's subsequent ruling. *Gonzalez* v. *Arizona*, 485 F.3d 1041, 1046 (9th Cir. 2007).

14. *Purcell* v. *Gonzalez*, 549 U.S. 1 (2006) (per curiam). For Hasen's critique, see Richard L. Hasen, "Reining in the *Purcell* Principle," *Florida State University Law Review* 43 (Winter 2016): 427–64.

15. Wilfred U. Codrington III, "*Purcell* in Pandemic," *New York University Law Review* 96 (Oct. 2021): 941–84.

16. The Alabama case is *Merrill* v. *Milligan*, 142 S. Ct. 879 (2022) (mem.).

17. Hasen, op. cit., 429–44.

18. Ibid.

19. Codrington, op. cit., 956–60.

20. Nicholas Stephanopoulos, "Freeing *Purcell* from the Shadows," *Take Care Blog*, Sept. 27, 2020, https://takecareblog.com/blog/freeing-purcell-from-the-shadows.

21. Daniel P. Tokaji, "Leave It to the Lower Courts: On Judicial Intervention in Election Administration," *Ohio State Law Journal* 68 (2007): 1065, 1087.

22. *Democratic National Committee* v. *Bostelmann*, 451 F. Supp. 3d 952 (W.D. Wis. 2020).

23. *Republican National Committee* v. *Democratic National Committee*, 140 S. Ct. 1205, 1207 (2020) (per curiam).

24. Ibid., 1209–11 (Ginsburg, J., dissenting).

25. *Jones* v. *DeSantis*, 462 F. Supp. 3d 1196 (N.D. Fla. 2020).

26. *McCoy* v. *Governor of Florida*, No. 20-12003, 2020 WL 4012843 (11th Cir. July 1, 2020) (en banc) (mem.).

27. *Raysor* v. *DeSantis*, 140 S. Ct. 2600, 2603 (2020) (Sotomayor, J., dissenting).

28. *Andino* v. *Middleton*, 141 S. Ct. 9, 10 (2020) (Kavanaugh, J., concurring).

29. Ibid., 10 (order).

30. Codrington, op. cit., 974 & n156.

31. *People First of Alabama* v. *Secretary of State for Alabama*, No. 20-13695-B, 2020 WL 6074333 (11th Cir. Oct. 13, 2020) (mem.).

32. *Merrill* v. *People First of Alabama*, 141 S. Ct. 25, 27 (2020) (Sotomayor, J., dissenting).

33. *Democratic National Committee* v. *Wisconsin State Legislature*, 141 S. Ct. 28, 28 (2020) (Roberts, C.J., concurring).

34. *Republican Party of Pennsylvania* v. *Boockvar*, 141 S. Ct. 643, 643 (2020) (mem.); *Scarnati* v. *Boockvar*, 141 S. Ct. 644, 644 (2020) (mem.). The March 2022 ruling is *Moore* v. *Harper*, 142 S. Ct. 1089 (2022) (mem.).

35. *Bush* v. *Gore*, 531 U.S. 98 (2000) (per curiam).

36. For a prominent example of such cynicism, see Linda Greenhouse, "The Supreme Court Fails Us," *New York Times*, April 9, 2020.

37. "The Impact of Partisan Gerrymandering," Center for American Progress, Oct. 1, 2019, https://www.americanprogress.org/article/impact-partisan-gerrymandering.

38. *Rucho* v. *Common Cause*, 139 S. Ct. 2484 (2019).

39. *Singleton* v. *Merrill*, No. 2:21-cv-1291, 2022 WL 265001 (N.D. Ala. Jan. 24, 2022) (per curiam) (three-judge court).

40. *Merrill* v. *Milligan*, 142 S. Ct. 879, 881 (2022) (Kavanaugh, J., concurring).

41. Mark Joseph Stern, "SCOTUS Just Blew Up the Voting Rights Act's Ban on Racial Gerrymandering," Slate, Feb. 7, 2022, https://slate.com/news-and-politics/2022/02/supreme-court-alabama-racial-gerrymander-roberts-kavanaugh.html.

42. *Merrill* v. *Milligan*, 142 S. Ct. at 881 & n2.

43. Ibid., 882–83 (Roberts, C.J., dissenting).

44. Ibid., 883 (Kagan, J., dissenting).

45. Ibid., 888–89.

46. Ibid., 879 (Kavanaugh, J., concurring).

47. *Alpha Phi Alpha Fraternity* v. *Raffensperger*, No. 1:21-CV-5337-SCJ, 2022 WL 633312, at *75 (N.D. Ga. Feb. 28, 2022).

48. *Ardoin* v. *Robinson*, 142 S. Ct. 2892 (2022) (mem.).

49. *Johnson* v. *Wisconsin Elections Commission*, 971 N.W.2d 402 (Wis. 2022).

50. *Wisconsin Legislature* v. *Wisconsin Elections Commission*, 142 S. Ct. 1245 (2022) (per curiam).

51. Ibid., 1251–53 (Sotomayor, J., dissenting).

52. Ibid., 1253.

53. *Whole Woman's Health* v. *Jackson*, 141 S. Ct. 2494, 2500 (2021) (Kagan, J., dissenting).

## Chapter 7. "Read the Opinion"

1. *Whole Woman's Health* v. *Jackson*, 141 S. Ct. 2494 (2021) (order).

2. Ibid., 2499–500 (Kagan., J, dissenting).

3. The 2016 ruling is *Whole Woman's Health* v. *Hellerstedt*, 579 U.S. 582 (2016). The 2020 ruling is *June Medical Services* v. *Russo*, 140 S. Ct. 2103 (2020). For Chief Justice Roberts's concurrence, see ibid., 2133–42 (Roberts, C.J., concurring in the judgment).

4. For the decisions, see *Roe* v. *Wade*, 410 U.S. 113 (1973), and *Planned Parenthood of Southeastern Pennsylvania* v. *Casey*, 505 U.S. 833 (1992).

5. Most of SB8 is codified at Texas Health and Safety Code §§ 171.201–212. For the full text of the bill, and how it amended existing law,

see LegiScan, https://legiscan.com/TX/text/SB8/id/2395961. For a discussion of its effects, see *Whole Woman's Health* v. *Jackson*, No. 1:21-cv-616-RP, 2021 WL 3821062, at *2 (W.D. Tex. Aug. 25, 2021).

6. Laurence H. Tribe and Stephen I. Vladeck, "The Texas Abortion Law Threatens Our Legal System," *New York Times*, July 22, 2021, A20.

7. The leading decision on racially restrictive covenants is *Shelley* v. *Kraemer*, 334 U.S. 1 (1948).

8. *Whole Woman's Health* v. *Jackson*, 13 F.4th 434 (5th Cir. 2021) (per curiam); *Whole Woman's Health*, No. 1:21-cv-616-RP, 2021 WL 3821062.

9. Adam Liptak, J. David Goodman, and Sabrina Tavernise, "Justices' Silence Lets Texas Halt Most Abortions," *New York Times*, Sept. 2, 2021, A1.

10. *Whole Woman's Health* v. *Jackson*, 141 S. Ct. 2494, 2495 (2021) (mem.).

11. Ibid.

12. Ibid., 2496–98 (Breyer, J., dissenting), 2498–99 (Sotomayor, J., dissenting).

13. Ibid., 2496 (Roberts, C.J., dissenting).

14. Ibid., 2500 (Kagan, J., dissenting).

15. *Whole Woman's Health* v. *Jackson*, 142 S. Ct. 522 (2022).

16. Steve Vladeck, "The Supreme Court Doesn't Just Abuse Its Shadow Docket. It Does So Inconsistently," *Washington Post*, Sept. 3, 2021.

17. Mike Bedell, "Public Perception May Curb Supreme Court's Shadow Docket," *Chicago Policy Review*, Dec. 23, 2021, https://chicagopolicyreview.org/2021/12/23/public-perception-may-curb-supreme-courts-shadow-docket.

18. Adam Serwer, "Five Justices Did This Because They Could," *The Atlantic*, Sept. 2, 2021, https://www.theatlantic.com/ideas/archive/2021/09/supreme-court-guts-roe-shadow-docket/619957.

19. Editorial, "The 'Shadow Docket' Diversion," *Wall Street Journal*, Oct. 2, 2021, A12.

20. Quotes and references from Alito's speech are from an unofficial transcript in my possession that was generated from the live-stream of the speech using Otter.ai.

21. *Gateway City Church* v. *Newsom*, 141 S. Ct. 1460 (2021) (mem.).

22. Even the claim about public accessibility is a bit misleading, as shadow docket orders can be posted, without any advance notice, to any one of four different pages on the Supreme Court's website.

23. "Texas's Unconstitutional Abortion Ban and the Role of the Shadow Docket," *Hearing Before the Senate Committee on the Judiciary*, 117th Cong., Sept. 29, 2021 (statement of Senator Cornyn).

24. Steve Vladeck, "Why Many of the Supreme Court's Critics Are Trying to Save the Court from Itself," Slate, Oct. 4, 2021, https://slate.com/news-and-politics/2021/10/the-supreme-court-is-nearing-a-legitimacy-crisis.html.

25. *Planned Parenthood of Southeastern Pennsylvania* v. *Casey*, 505 U.S. 833, 865 (1992) (joint opinion of O'Connor, Kennedy, and Souter, JJ.).

26. Ibid.

27. "With Divisive Supreme Court Rulings Coming, Barrett Says: 'Read the Opinion,'" Associated Press, April 5, 2022.

28. *Merrill* v. *Milligan*, 142 S. Ct. 879, 879 (2022) (Kavanaugh, J., concurring).

29. Editorial, *Wall Street Journal*, op. cit., A12.

30. Donald Ayer, "The Court Has Lost Its Way," *New York Times*, Oct. 6, 2021, A21; William Baude, "Death and the Shadow Docket," Volokh Conspiracy, Reason, April 12, 2019, https://reason.com/volokh/2019/04/12/death-and-the-shadow-docket.

31. Vladeck SJC Testimony, op. cit., 21.

32. *Alabama Association of Realtors* v. *United States Department of Health and Human Services*, 141 S. Ct. 2485 (2021) (per curiam).

33. *Austin* v. *U.S. Navy Seals 1–26*, 142 S. Ct. 1301 (2022) (mem.).

34. *Shaughnessy* v. *United States ex rel. Mezei*, 345 U.S. 206, 224 (1953). For the Alito dissent, see *Biden* v. *Texas*, 142 S. Ct. 2528, 2550 (2022) (Alito, J., dissenting).

35. *Ramirez* v. *Collier*, 142 S. Ct. 1264 (2022). The order granting a stay and certiorari is *Ramirez* v. *Collier*, 142 S. Ct. 50 (2021) (mem.).

36. *Whole Woman's Health* v. *Jackson*, 142 S. Ct. 522 (2021).

37. *Does 1–3* v. *Mills*, 142 S. Ct. 17, 18 (2021) (Barrett, J., concurring).

38. Ibid.

39. Proposed Revisions to Rules of the Supreme Court of the United States, March 2022, https://www.supremecourt.gov/filingandrules/2021_Proposed_Rules_Changes-March_2022-redline_strikeout_version.pdf.

40. *National Federation of Independent Business* v. *Department of Labor*, 142 S. Ct. 661 (2022) (per curiam); *Biden* v. *Missouri*, 142 S. Ct. 647 (2022) (per curiam). The last emergency application to be argued before the full Court appears to be *Morton* v. *A Quaker Action Group*, 402 U.S. 926 (1971) (mem.).

41. *National Federation of Independent Business*, 142 S. Ct. at 666.

42. *Louisiana* v. *American Rivers*, 142 S. Ct. 1347, 1349 (2022) (Kagan, J., dissenting).

43. U.S. Const. art. III, § 2, cl. 2. The Reconstruction-era ruling is *Ex parte McCardle*, 74 U.S. (7 Wall.) 506 (1869).

44. Stephen I. Vladeck, "Reforming the U.S. Supreme Court by Reforming Its Docket," *Journal of Parliamentary and Political Law* 16 (2022): 7; Daniel Epps and Ganesh Sitaraman, "The Future of Supreme Court Reform," *Harvard Law Review Forum* 134 (May 30, 2021): 398–414.

45. Vladeck SJC Testimony, op. cit., 31–34.

46. Presidential Commission on the Supreme Court of the United States, *Final Report* (Dec. 2021): 10, https://www.whitehouse.gov/wp-content/uploads/2021/12/SCOTUS-Report-Final-12.8.21-1.pdf.

## Conclusion: Bringing the Supreme Court Out of the Shadows

1. "Statement Concerning the Supreme Court's Front Entrance," *Supreme Court Journal*, October 2009 Term (May 3, 2010).

2. Ibid.

3. Amy Howe, "After 19 Months, Eight Justices Return to Courtroom," *SCOTUSblog*, Oct. 4, 2021, https://www.scotusblog.com/2021/10/after-19-months-eight-justices-return-to-the-courtroom.

4. Lani Guinier, "The Supreme Court, 2007 Term—Foreword: Demosprudence Through Dissent," *Harvard Law Review* 122 (Nov. 2008): 4–138.

5. Erick Trickey, "Chief Justice, Not President, Was William Howard Taft's Dream Job," *Smithsonian*, Dec. 5, 2016, https://www.smithsonianmag.com/history/chief-justice-not-president-was-william-howard-tafts-dream-job-180961279.

6. The exchange is recounted in Evan Thomas, *First: Sandra Day O'Connor—An Intimate Portrait of the First Woman Supreme Court Justice* (New York: Random House, 2019), 378.

7. Ward Farnsworth, "'To Do a Great Right, Do a Little Wrong': A User's Guide to Judicial Lawlessness," *Minnesota Law Review* 86 (2001): 227, 258–59.

8. Joan Biskupic, *The Chief: The Life and Turbulent Times of Chief Justice John Roberts* (New York: Basic Books, 2019), 141–60.

9. Lyle Denniston, "The 'Kennedy Court,' Only More So," *SCOTUSblog*, April 9, 2010, https://www.scotusblog.com/2010/04/the-kennedy-court-only-more-so. For the 2019 decisions, see *Department of Commerce* v. *New York*, 139 S. Ct. 2551 (2019); *Rucho* v. *Common Cause*, 139 S. Ct. 2484 (2019).

10. Adam Feldman, "Final Stat Pack for October Term 2019 (updated)," *SCOTUSblog*, July 10, 2020, https://www.scotusblog.com/2020/07/final-stat-pack-for-october-term-2019.

11. Angie Gou, "As Unanimity Declines, Conservative Majority's Power Runs Deeper Than the Blockbuster Cases," *SCOTUSblog*, July 3, 2022, https://www.scotusblog.com/2022/07/as-unanimity-declines-conservative-majoritys-power-runs-deeper-than-the-blockbuster-cases.

12. Steve Vladeck (@steve_vladeck), Twitter (April 6, 2022), https://twitter.com/steve_vladeck/status/1511697286270791680.

13. *Merrill* v. *Milligan*, 142 S. Ct. 879, 882 (2022) (Roberts, C.J., dissenting); *Whole Woman's Health* v. *Jackson*, 141 S. Ct. 2494, 2496 (2021) (Roberts, C.J., dissenting); *Roman Catholic Diocese of Brooklyn* v. *Cuomo*, 141 S. Ct. 63, 75 (2020) (Roberts, C.J., dissenting).

14. *Louisiana* v. *American Rivers*, 142 S. Ct. 1347 (2022) (mem.).

15. Ibid., 1349 (Kagan, J., dissenting).

16. Stephen I. Vladeck. "Roberts Has Lost Control of the Court," *New York Times*, April 17, 2022, SR2.

17. For example, see Robert Barnes, "Roberts Joins Liberals in Criticizing 'Shadow Docket' Pollution Ruling," *Washington Post*, April 6, 2022; Ariane de Vogue, "Chief Justice Roberts Joins with Liberals to Criticize 'Shadow Docket' as Courts Reinstate Trump-Era EPA Rule," CNN, April 6, 2022; Greg Stohr, "Roberts Joins Criticism of High Court 'Shadow Docket,'" Bloomberg, April 6, 2022.

18. *Louisiana* v. *American Rivers*, 142 S. Ct. 1347; "With Divisive Supreme Court Rulings Coming, Barrett Says: 'Read the Opinion,'" Associated Press, April 5, 2022.

19. *Brown* v. *Board of Education*, 347 U.S. 483 (1954).

20. The case of the cursing cheerleader is *Mahanoy Area School District* v. *B.L. ex rel. Levy*, 141 S. Ct. 2038 (2021). The credit-reporting ruling is *TransUnion LLC* v. *Ramirez*, 141 S. Ct. 2190 (2021).

21. For the ruling, see *Worcester* v. *Georgia*, 31 U.S. (6 Pet.) 515 (1832). For Jackson's response, see Edwin A. Miles, "After John Marshall's Decision: *Worcester* v. *Georgia* and the Nullification Crisis," *Journal of Southern History* 39 (Nov. 1973): 519–44.

# INDEX

Brian Birzer / University of Texas School of Law

**Stephen Vladeck** holds the Charles Alan Wright Chair in Federal Courts at the University of Texas School of Law. He is an elected member of the American Law Institute and has argued more than a dozen cases before the US Supreme Court, the Texas Supreme Court, and other state and federal tribunals. Vladeck's work has been published in the *Yale Law Journal*, the *Harvard Law Review*, and the *Columbia Law Review*, as well as the *New York Times*, the *Los Angeles Times*, and Slate. Since 2013, he has served as the Supreme Court analyst for CNN. He lives in Austin, Texas.